Campaign Talk

*

Campaign Talk

WHY ELECTIONS ARE GOOD FOR US

*

RODERICK P. HART

PRINCETON UNIVERSITY PRESS

PRINCETON, NEW JERSEY

Library of Congress Catalog-in-Publication Data
Hart, Roderick P.
Campaign talk: why elections are good for us / Roderick P. Hart.
p.   cm.
Includes bibliographical references and index.
ISBN 0-691-00126-X (cloth: alk. paper)
1. Political oratory—United States. 2. Electioneering—
United States. 3. Elections—United States. I. Title.
PN4055.U53P6428   2000
324.7'0'4—dc21   99-41740

This book has been composed in Berkeley Book

http://pup.princeton.edu

Printed in the United States of America

1   3   5   7   9   10   8   6   4   2

FOR KATHLEEN

FRIEND, INSPIRATION

*

✳ *Contents* ✳

CONTENTS

* List of Figures *

✳ *List of Tables* ✳

* Preface *

O<small>NCE AGAIN</small> the millennium approaches and once again politics beckons. For the third time in their nation's history, the American people face a turn-of-the-century political campaign. The election of 1800 saw the first contest among established political parties, and the election of 1900 marked the dawn of the modern era. During the last hundred years the people of the United States have fought four major wars (and several minor ones), changed from a manufacturing economy to one based on information, and seen scientific advances on every front, from biochemistry to space travel and from computerization to fertility drugs. Things have changed on the domestic scene as well. In 1800 a woman was called by her husband's name and in 1900 she still could not vote. When embarking on its fifty-fourth presidential election, the United States will have a female secretary of state, several viable presidential and vice presidential female candidates, hundreds of female diplomats and agency chiefs, three female governors, nine U.S. senators, almost fifty women in the House of Representatives, and a growing number of women heading major U.S. corporations. While in 1800 African Americans worked on the nation's plantations and in 1900 labored in its sweat shops, by the year 2000 they will have established a large middle class, risen to the heights in corporate, educational, and military circles, and made dramatic inroads in state and national politics as well. While progress remains to be made on all such fronts, progress is no longer the alien term it was.

If past is prologue, the election of 2000 will produce a magnificent president. Thomas Jefferson won the election of 1800, and the campaign of 1900 made Teddy Roosevelt president (after his running mate, William McKinley, was assassinated). Today, every major poll of historians places Jefferson and Roosevelt at the top rung of U.S. chief executives.[1] There is surely room for another. But even speculating about such a possibility seems hyperbole. What citizen today expects to find a Jefferson or a Roosevelt in their midst? Who can suppose that a political process so burdened by improper financing

xiii

schemes and cynical media coverage will discover a saint in a nation of sinners? How could a great leader emerge from the backroom caucuses and tiresome primaries and endless talk shows? And if some such person were found, how could he or she aspire to greatness in an Oval Office once visited by Richard Nixon's plumbers and Bill Clinton's girlfriends? A new Jefferson or Roosevelt cannot be found today because they can no longer be imagined.

Rather than lament such conditions, *Campaign Talk* offers a contrary set of facts. It examines the political language used in presidential elections between 1948 and 1996 and finds ample reason for reconsidering, perhaps even celebrating, political campaigns. The book's premise is that a campaign is a conversation among three dominant voices—the press, the people, and the nation's leaders—and its argument is that that conversation has generally served the nation well. After a detailed examination of what has been said during the past thirteen presidential elections, the book recommends that we relax a bit and come to understand that even a boisterous and ill-tempered discussion cannot fail as long as it never ends. The book finds a number of intriguing changes in campaigns over the years but finds an important durability as well. The book also looks at speeches, debates, ads, and news coverage to discover who says what, how often, and why during the campaign. Finally, the book examines what the American people themselves have said in the popular, but little-understood, letters they write to their local newspapers. The result of these labors is a complex portrait of campaigns. I argue that this complexity has made American democracy vital since its beginnings.

Campaign Talk does not present a detailed history of elections but it does offer enough data to call into question people's negative impressions of the campaign process. The assumption on which this analysis rests is that politics has always been political. For example, the campaign of 1800 featured John Adams and Thomas Jefferson, two luminaries who were described thusly at the time: *Jefferson*: "a modern french Philosopher, overturner of government," "an atheist in Religion and a Fanatic in politics;" *Adams*: "there are great intrinsic defects in his character," [he has] "a vanity without bounds, and a jealousy capable of discoloring every object."[2] But the campaign of

1800 was attacked on more than characterological grounds. Adams, the incumbent, was accused of taking a circuitous route ("fifty miles out of the strait course") when traveling from Philadelphia to Washington, D.C., in order to barnstorm for votes. Internecine strife in the newborn political parties was also decried, as were the "direct mail circulars" Jefferson sent to the "opinion leaders" of his day. That election also saw the emergence of the first "electoral tacticians" (Alexander Hamilton for the Federalists, Aaron Burr for the Republicans) and that seemed a corruption as well. Finally, the election of 1800 saw a number of familiar squabbles: between national government and states rights, between religion and science, between commerce and taxation, and between national security and freedom of the press. Only someone living today could see the election of 1800 as a hallmark of democracy.

The election of 1900 was no different, although it was more frenetic: William Jennings Bryan traveled over eighteen thousand miles trying to get elected, giving some six hundred speeches to five million Americans (like Bill Clinton, he lost his voice at the end of the campaign). For his part, Mr. McKinley mailed one million postcards to individual voters and sent administration-friendly advisories to some five thousand newspapers to get their endorsements.[3] Vice presidential candidate Roosevelt helped establish a partisan tone, warning that "the incoming of Mr. Bryan would mean terrible, widespread disaster," but Mr. Roosevelt also came under attack from those in his own party.[4] Reflecting on the new vice president, one of McKinley's supporters told the president: "Your duty to the country is to live for four years from next March."[5] Not only does this sort of smarminess sound familiar but so too do the issues: cheap imported goods versus domestic manufacturing; Big Business versus labor disputes versus federal intervention; the introduction of religion into a purely political debate (by the Democrats, interestingly enough). One summary of the campaign's rhetoric has a particularly contemporary ring: "Bryan preached—Roosevelt shouted. The Nebraskan quoted scripture—the Rough Rider waved the flag. The great Democratic leader was an artist with words—his Republican rival was a better tub-thumper."[6]

The election of 2000 will be a child born of this heritage. It will have its own issues and its own personalities but it will still be politics. Throughout the year, the campaign will be criticized for being beneath the American people. Its snide news coverage will be denounced, as will the candidates' evasions and pomposities. Its advertisements will surely be savaged, even if they are comparatively benign. Ultimately, a great cry will be raised: "Can't we do better than this?" This book suggests we cannot do better and that we need not do better. The election of 2000 will have its infirmities but it will traverse a course blazed by its forebears and in so doing it will advance the democracy. To some this will seem a preposterous claim. Revisionists, for example, will look to the past for a comparatively happier contest but I suspect they will not find one. Idealists will sketch out a perfect campaign to document the inadequacies of the current one. But they, too, will produce distortions unless they learn everything there is to learn about campaigns. Toward that end, this book asks two questions not asked before: Why do campaigns sound the way they do? Is that good or bad? The book reports much that is heartening about politics for those who still have a heart for it. For those who have lost their heart, it offers a way to find it once again.

This book has benefited considerably from the work of others. I acknowledge, first, the codirector of the Campaign Mapping Project, Professor Kathleen Hall Jamieson of the University of Pennsylvania. Two thousand miles of separation made collaboration difficult at times, and so phone conversations, faxes, e-mail notes, and plane trips became a way of life for us. All writers pray that others will like their work. But Kathleen is my first audience, in some ways my only audience. If this book does not please her, she will tell me.

The Campaign Mapping Project was generously funded by the Ford Foundation and the Carnegie Corporation of New York. Special thanks are extended to Marsha Smith and June Zeitlin of Ford, and Gerri Manion of Carnegie. These individuals are not responsible for whatever deficiencies the book may have. Similarly, the viewpoints expressed here are my own, not those of my patrons.

Several individuals kindly read and responded to my work, notably Professor Richard Anderson of UCLA, Professor David Paletz of Duke University, Professor Joseph Atkinson of the University of Auckland, and Professors Bruce Buchanan and Bartholomew Sparrow of the

University of Texas. They did their best to keep me from saying silly things. The reader will best judge their efficacy.

I want to give special thanks to Dean Ellen Wartella and Dr. Patricia Witherspoon of the University of Texas who generously supplemented the grant and who jointly stand as evidence that wisdom and humanity lie at the core of all really good administrators. I hasten to add my gratitude to Margaret Surratt who made grant money last longer than it should have lasted and who printed new money when necessary to keep the project solvent.

I am blessed with many fine colleagues on campus who have shown special interest in this project, including Dean Burnham, Richard Cherwitz, John Daly, James Fishkin, Mark Knapp, Robert Luskin, Maxwell McCombs, Jamie Pennebaker, H. W. Perry, Steven Reese, Elspeth Rostow, Daron Shaw, Anita Vangelisti, and Charles Whitney. It is good to have such friends; it is a special bonus that they are all so gifted.

The English language does not have enough positive adjectives to describe my colleague Sharon Jarvis but here are three: smart, kind, indefatigable. The Campaign Mapping Project would have foundered without her and I shall forever be in her debt. I also thank the dozens of Texas graduate students who labored long and hard on the Project, some of whom are acknowledged in the following chapters and all of whom are remembered with fondness. In addition, I am indebted to Michael Stanton, Laurence Brevard, Tom Cox, and Maureen McKeon for their programming skills and for their many personal kindnesses.

I want to thank my son, Chris, for being a completely exquisite son and a knowing and imaginative interlocutor as well. The very thought of my daughter, Katy, makes my heart glad and, from what I can tell, her talents are limitless. Finally, I want to thank my wife, Peggy, for knowing nothing of poetry or politics. Her solidity keeps me sane. Her love makes me whole.

RPH
Austin, Texas

Campaign Talk

*

* CHAPTER 1 *

Campaign Questions

THE 1996 presidential campaign was hardly galvanizing. The incumbent, William Jefferson Clinton, never really relinquished the double-digit lead he held from early September through election day. The challenger, Bob Dole, ran a campaign as plain as his name and the small Kansas town from which he hailed. Even Ross Perot failed to provide the excitement he had provided in 1992: his running mate was even less distinguished than the one he had picked four years earlier; his advertising was more traditional, as was his campaign financing (to legitimate the Reform Party he accepted matching public funds); and he lobbed fewer salvos at the press for their several impertinences. For their part, the American people spent the summer of 1996 watching Olympic runners try to outpace the Dow. Few of them voted that fall and those who did vote voted overwhelmingly (perhaps even superstitiously) to keep things as they were—Republicans in the Congress and a Democrat at 1600 Pennsylvania Avenue. The outcome of the election was determined by the fates of people's 401(k) plans.

Uninspiring though it was, the campaign was not without its curiosities. Even though the Republican Party had been unusually successful in fund-raising, by April of 1996 President Clinton had $20 million left to spend, fourteen times more than his opponent, largely because Senator Dole had spent so much so quickly trying to secure his party's nomination.[1] Money was also on the Democrats' minds when they were required to give back $235,000 in campaign contributions to a property development company in Korea whose potential importunings made everyone nervous (including federal investigators). All of this was a drop in the bucket for Steve Forbes, who spent $30 million to secure 900,545 votes, an expenditure of $33,133.16 per vote received.[2]

The 1996 campaign produced more facts: Bill Clinton embraced the V-chip; the American people embraced Liddy Dole at the Republican convention; and Clinton aide Dick Morris embraced a young woman he should not have embraced. The result of these embracings was that Bill Clinton became the first Democrat twice elected to office since Franklin Roosevelt, even though he did not capture even 50 percent of the popular vote. The media were bored as well: news coverage of the 1996 campaign was down 60 percent from 1992, 100 percent from 1988, even though campaign expenditures were at an all-time high.[3] Never bored themselves, the nation's pollsters scurried about the country uncovering such facts as these: a continuing gender gap, voters who did not trust their president but who wanted him in office anyway, two debates that changed few minds (and that were scarcely watched), a good number of voters who did not recognize Jack Kemp's name, and a sizeable majority who found New Gingrich annoying.[4]

Here is another fact about the 1996 campaign: Bob Dole, the self-declared "most optimistic man in America," used less verbal optimism in his campaign speeches than any Republican since Tom Dewey with one exception—Barry Goldwater in 1964. Another fact: Bill Clinton, who has been described as a man of "conspicuous compassion," used more human-interest language ("you," "us," "people," "family") than any candidate from either party between 1948 and the present, with the exception of Hubert Humphrey.[5] Compared to President Clinton, candidate Dole was conspicuously more ambivalent, more likely to talk about bureaucratic procedures and personalities than about concrete realities, more self-absorbed than even Ross Perot, and almost twice as likely to cling to patriotic images than either of his opponents. Whereas President Clinton stressed the common ties among the American people, Mr. Dole used twice as many denial words ("can't," "shouldn't," "couldn't") as his Democratic rival. Despite the genuine affection that many Americans had for Bob Dole, his speech was a disaster area.

When one reflects on the 1996 presidential campaign, these facts make sense. More curious, perhaps, is that they were unearthed by a computer program called DICTION, developed by me to assess the unconscious language choices people use when talking to one another.[6] DICTION is a humble device—it looks only at the kinds of words people use, ignoring completely how and why they are used.

Originally developed some twenty years ago for large mainframe computers, DICTION has been rewritten to work on the powerful personal computers now available. More recently, DICTION has been put to work in connection with the Campaign Mapping Project, a research endeavor codirected by me and Kathleen Hall Jamieson, funded by the Ford and Carnegie Foundations, and designed to map the contours of American politics during the last fifty years. In connection with that project, some twenty thousand textual samples have been inspected by DICTION, including campaign speeches, political ads and debates, print and broadcast news, and a sample of letters-to-the-editor (to get a sense of the people's voice). Texts collected from each of the thirteen presidential elections between 1948 and 1996 are now housed in DICTION's database, and this book is the result of those labors.

Many people are suspicious of computers, especially when used in connection with politics. Charges of mindless reductionism ring out when something as textured as a human utterance is transcribed, keyboarded, and then pigeonholed by a computer. Surely the novelist John Barth seemed right when observing that a computer could not "act on a hunch or brilliant impulse; it had no intuitions or exaltations; it could request but not yearn; indicate, but not insinuate or exhort; command but not care. It had no sense of style or grasp of the ineffable; its correlations were exact, but its metaphors wretched; it could play chess, but not poker."[7] Barth may be correct but I think he is not. I believe that computers can appreciate a sense of style and I believe that in the hands of a patient individual, programs like DICTION can grasp a bit of the ineffable, appreciate the roots of metaphor, and distinguish between yearning, exhorting, commanding, and requesting. Barth may well be right about poker.

This book reports what DICTION found when rummaging about in the nation's attic. Because a computer has been used here, and because it has been used to inspect such a large amount of data, the picture painted will be a landscape, not an etching ... better yet a billboard. Either way, it will be panoramic, which is what makes computers helpful. Because they are capacious, computers can collect the many different voices making up a political campaign—the politicians, yes, but the media and the people too. Because they are reliable, computers can ensure that the same thing is focused upon each time they are used; as a result, they cannot be distracted by the chance event, the momentary bias. Because my computer program focuses on language, it examines the one phenomenon that cuts across a political campaign. That is, DICTION may be deaf to a stump speaker's vocal intonations but it will remember that the speech was about Medicare. DICTION will be blind to an advertisement's visual bounties but it will remember that its topic was Medicare. DICTION knows nothing of Dan Rather's savoir faire but it will remember, most assuredly, that he reported on Medicare. Because a campaign moves so quickly, because it involves hundreds of thousands of political decisions and political personnel, having the assistance of a patient accountant like DICTION makes practical sense, especially if one is concerned with Medicare.

Using a computer to study campaigns also makes sense because a campaign is a torrent, no a hurricane, of words. As I will discuss in chapter 2, many people feel superior to language, as if they were its masters and not it theirs. This is a natural arrogance but it is also fatally revelatory. Bob Dole could call himself an optimist, but he could not behave like one. His words betrayed him, and the American people sensed that. But how? Did they focus on what Mr. Dole said, on what he failed to say, or on what he said failingly? When they listened to him did other, more utopian, campaigners come to mind? To the backs of their minds? In this book, I will not assume that knowing campaign language is all that must be known. But it is one thing that must be known, especially because it is so easily ignored or dismissed. Political language is like the air we breathe—innocent of utility until emphysema sets in or until the EPA calls attention to its detectable poisons. Studying a thing that is undervalued at best, trivialized at worst, brings out the contrarian in me.

Studying campaigns anew is also a contrarian's enterprise because so much has already been written about them. This has been especially true in the United States, where campaign analysis has become a cottage industry. Every four years, the National Science Foundation is besieged with grant requests from social scientists interested in studying campaigns, and this agency has been generous with its funds. Typically, these monies are funneled through the University of

Michigan's National Election Studies or the University of Chicago's National Opinion Research Center so that extensive surveys of political opinions can be run, thereby giving the nation a running total of how it feels about itself. Important work like Samuel Popkin's *The Reasoning Voter*, Sidney Verba and his colleagues' *Voice and Equality*, and Steven Rosenstone and Mark Hansen's *Mobilization, Participation, and Democracy in America* have told us much about what the American people think when thinking politically.[8]

But a political campaign is more than opinionizing. The stuff of a campaign must also be understood—that which did not exist before the campaign began but whose creation helped form campaign attitudes. Social scientists have often avoided studying these matters since textuality is complex. Knowing what a word means, or how it means, is no easy thing, a phenomenon that has kept attorneys handsomely employed since the beginning of that gentle profession. But just because a thing is hard to understand does not mean it can be ignored.

With that as its premise, this book covers campaign materials from a single vantage point—that of word choice. It seeks a fresh understanding of politics by presuming that all campaign texts intersect with one another: the candidate's morning speech becomes fodder for CNN's noonday report; the CNN reporter's supercilious attitude inspires an angry citizen to write a letter to the local paper; that letter is read by a neighbor while half-watching a political commercial; the ad inspires a counter-ad by an outraged opponent; a print reporter covers the resulting contretemps and then asks the candidate a question at the next photo opportunity. A campaign is all of these rhetorical things and more as well.

Given this complexity, citizens now consume campaigns in great gulps. They tire quickly when doing so, but that only inspires media professionals to find ever-new modes of engaging them. In 1992, for example, the candidates sat on the couch with NBC's Katie Couric and during the 1996 campaign Web-sites proliferated (with a result yet to be determined). But some researchers wonder how significant the mass media are to a political campaign since 65 percent of the electorate selects its candidate by the late-summer conventions and, hence, before the blizzard of advertisements.[9] And yet if political campaigns are run only for the remaining 35 percent, that still amounted to 34 million Americans in 1996, a not insignificant number. Besides, other researchers show that media-centric campaigns can be powerful, that George Bush may well have lost the 1992 election because his fellow citizens believed what the media told them about their economic circumstances rather than looking into their own pocketbooks.[10] And here is an even more ominous note: with so many news organizations now conducting their own polls, the press is increasingly in danger of making the news rather than reporting it.

And so this book assumes that what people say about governance is important. Mapping the language of democracy—across time and circumstance, across voice and medium, across candidate and party—provides a useful cultural reconnoitering even as it becomes an exercise in practical politics. By taking campaign texts seriously and even by taking unserious texts seriously (Jay Leno comes to mind, as does *Politically Incorrect*), we can better understand what ails the nation. "Politics," says Wilson Carey McWilliams, a preeminent student of the American experience, "is fundamentally a matter of speech, and in democracies, of public speech. But it also confronts America with a public that more and more lacks both the arts of listening and the friendship of critics and guides."[11] To develop that art, that friendship, facts are required. This book offers some.

MUST WE CAMPAIGN?

The remainder of this chapter asks three questions, the first of which is the most fundamental: why campaign at all? Surely when the images of Roger Ailes, Webster Hubbell, and Lee Atwater spring to mind and then are linked to the icons of the 1990s—faux Internet pages, endless advertising, MTV disclosures, mudslinging, and push-polls—many citizens declare a pox on the activity. Campaigns make politics unpretty, but we must also ask how tidy a democracy must be to be functional. Somehow, after all, the American people have blundered through fifty-three presidential elections and still seem robust. Indeed, it is only slightly casuistic to suggest that the torpor they now feel during campaigns serves a prosocial function: it keeps politics on their agenda, however imperfectly, even as it keeps totalitarianism at bay. Despite their deficiencies, that is, campaigns keep people talking about politics and they do so with a helpful periodicity. In Rousseau's terms, campaigns create an appetite for democracy by sanctioning acquiescence to the general will.[12] Every four years the American people are asked to eat their broccoli. A good many do.

But campaigns also serve more avowedly positive functions:

1. *Campaigns teach.* Russell Neuman and his colleagues have reported that the often maligned medium of television has considerable capacity to teach people about politics, that those effects are heightened during campaigns, and that television is an especially effective teacher for persons with modest cognitive skills.[13] Similarly, David Sears and Nicholas Valentino have investigated how preadults learn about civic affairs, and they find strong campaign effects. According to them, a campaign acts as a punctuating device that accelerates youngsters' political educations, especially their partisan predispositions.[14] Larry Bartels reports that people learn as much from campaigns today as they ever did, perhaps suggesting that television and the other new media have not had the dumbing-down effect some allege.[15] And numerous studies show that campaigns broaden citizens' agendas, making them pay attention to political matters previously irrelevant to them.[16] During the 1996 election, for example, young voters were required to think seriously about a declining social security trust fund, white voters to imagine the struggles undergone by Hispanic immigrants, and urban dwellers to imagine a federal government less responsive to their future needs. Some of this learning was painful, no doubt, but the campaign unquestionably brought important issues to the surface.

2. *Campaigns preach.* During elections, a democracy is re-performed. Through its rituals, its pacing, its daily unfoldings, a campaign makes a population a citizenry. Even the half-aware bus patron riding to work in the early hours of the morning becomes a citizen-rider as the campaign billboards whiz by. Our worker may decry the billboards but those cries are also part of the democratic process,

and the campaign gives them presence. Some scholars call this an "assignation of legitimacy" whereby the citizen claims the right to have an opinion about affairs removed from his own home but, just as quickly, cedes the resolution of those problems to a representative body.[17] During the campaign, our rider notices other ordinary people on campaign commercials and thus becomes a "spectacle for himself," changing from rider to citizen and then, in Rousseau's terms, to "a member of the city."[18] This is no mere academic transformation. Studies show that campaigns typically increase "regime support" among the electorate, tying them closer to the national purpose.[19] Even the grumbling, that is, becomes functional grumbling during campaigns.

3. *Campaigns sensitize.* Here are two curious facts: Allan Kornberg and Harold Clarke report that support for elected officials in Canada falls (sometimes precipitously) after elections but then picks up again when the next election rolls around—largely regardless of current empirical circumstances.[20] Bartels echoes that finding when observing that presidential debates often increase voters' admiration for both candidates, ostensibly because debaters take viewers' problems seriously.[21] Rather than alienating us from politics, that is, campaigns may be a relatively happy time in a nation's life. And the fact that campaigns are calendrical means that such systemic reinforcement is delivered on a regular basis. An unrelenting campaign schedule also ensures that candidates' awareness of the nation is heightened. The much-despised length of a campaign becomes functional when it asks candidates to become weary in their neighbors' behalf, surely an acid relational test:

> By the time a candidate becomes president-elect, he (eventually she) will have learned to cope with intense media scrutiny, to staff and maintain a flexible organization, to manage contending factions, to attract the votes of millions of citizens, to appear credible and persuasive as a speechmaker and television performer, to deflect the attacks of opponents, to survive high-pressure debates with other candidates, to devise and constantly refine a political strategy, to articulate a policy vision, and to recover and learn from inevitable, potentially fatal, political mistakes.[22]

4. *Campaigns activate.* Campaign effects are not only philosophical; they can also be overt. One study showed that between Labor

Day and election day in 1992, the number of individuals who identified voting as an important duty of citizenship increased from 48 percent to 55 percent.[23] An allied, although somewhat perverse, finding is that though only 55 percent of the American people went to the ballot box in 1992, a full 75 percent claimed to have done so when questioned afterwards by pollsters.[24] Not only do campaigns increase "civic lying," but they also heighten people's senses of political efficacy—the feeling that they make a difference in the political equation.[25] This is a terribly important effect that no system of self-governance can be without for long. If an election does nothing more than increase a people's sense of choice, it has served an important function. Indeed, a poststructuralist might even claim that the act of a citizen who makes an active, conscious, and loud decision to refrain from voting—the sort of posturing one hears when liquor is at hand and when the shadows lengthen—is itself a kind of civic attachment. Perhaps this is why researchers find that the more political information is broadcast into a community, the more likely its citizens are to talk about politics.[26] And so the newspaper editorials may be unkind, the broadcasts biased, the candidates poorly informed, and the advertising offensive, but a campaign never really fails unless it inspires silence.

Hosannas are rarely sung at the end of a campaign and that is a democratic shame. A good campaign teaches a culture its culture, helps it set its priorities, and sorts out the visionary from the visionless (one is reminded of Jimmy Carter at the end of the 1980 campaign, George Bush in 1992). A good campaign expands what we think about as citizens and puts us in touch with people whose problems are different from our own. In the United States, at least, political candidates eat a great deal of bad food as they move about from locale to locale, and that is an important, even necessary, kind of civic indigestion. It signals a willingness to embrace the expanse of the citizenry, to use its separate histories to find its common future. And so when voters roust themselves out of their slumber on those quadrennial November mornings, something sacred happens. Modern cynicisms aside, a democrat must learn to love those moments.

11

MUST WE CAMPAIGN SO BADLY?

Those of a more pessimistic bent can find within campaigns the dead-liest of sins: sloth (too few Americans go to the polls), gluttony (the media dominate the political agenda), envy (pollsters engage in inter-necine warfare), and greed (PACs as the handmaidens of Satan)—to name but four deadly sins. Presidential campaigns now last virtually an entire year, which means they can dominate 25 percent of the waking experience of citizens who have no other life. As political time contracts, political space expands. Despite the marvels of media technologies, candidates still dash from Atlantic to Pacific and to the intervening lakes with a regularity that has not changed in fifty years. (Ohio, as it turns out, has been their most popular port of call since 1948.)[27] Campaign financing is also dispiriting. In 1996, Democrats and Republicans raised over $880 million between them, a 50 percent increase over the 1992 race, a rate that ensures a multi-billion-dollar fund-raising effort by the year 2004.[28]

And to what effect? Very little, say some scholars. Pivoting off the classic work of *The American Voter*, some researchers find only mini-mal effects during political campaigns.[29] Long-term dispositions like party identification, they argue, are unlikely to be changed by even a year's worth of bunting and hullabaloo. Econometricians draw the same conclusion but argue somewhat differently: a combination of the GNP and national unemployment statistics best predicts how the vote will turn out regardless of who is running or how well.[30] Morris Fiorina has a more elaborate model that features voters keeping a "running tally" of what repels and attracts them, a tally not likely to be disturbed by the sudden intervention of campaign politics.[31] These "retrospective voters," Fiorina claims, have a much deeper and broader sense of political perspective; they are not mere manipulanda dancing at the end of the advertisers' strings but people who respond to real experiences they really feel.

A sophisticated set of studies done by Thomas Holbrook rethinks the entire matter of campaign effects.[32] He finds that "national condi-tions" (war, the economy, civil unrest) affect some candidates while "campaign events" affect others, and that some contests, the 1996 presidential campaign, for example, are more heavily affected by the former than the latter.[33] It is often the case that incumbents are most influenced by national conditions and challengers by campaign events though that is not always the case. But for many observers this whole question of campaign effects is a quibble. If the campaign did not matter, they reason, candidates and their backers would not part with their money in such prodigious amounts. With millions-soon-billions invested in campaigns and with hundreds of thousands of citizens ready to donate their time and energy as well, only a fool could gainsay the importance of campaigns. The real tragedy of campaigns, such observers argue, is not that they have no effect but that they epitomize our most profound afflictions as a nation.

Take opinion polls. Surveys are now so plentiful that citizens pay more attention to what their neighbors think than to their leaders' thoughts. As I have argued elsewhere, with one-third of all news reports now mentioning poll results, the American people have become fascinated by "what they feel—even, in some cases, before they feel it."[34] This self-absorption is fostered by the thousands of professional surveyors who make their livings by polling, even though, as Everett Ladd reminds us, they were considerably off base in 1996.[35] These ambiguities have resulted in a hyper-rhetoric as the various practitioners pit their numbers against one another. Through such transactions, says Susan Herbst, public opinion is manufactured rather than assessed.[36] But the greater tragedy is that by concentrating on polling, a simulation, voters ignore concrete realities—such as welfare subsidies.

Although they seem to like polls, the American people do not like campaigns. Larry Bartels reports that their faith in elections has declined steadily since 1956 when more than 80 percent of poll respondents felt that elections were relevant to their lives (versus under 60 percent in 1996).[37] Margaret Scammell says that some of this dissatisfaction may be attributable to the increasing "professionalization" of political campaigns whereby marketing experts, not the candidates themselves, make the important decisions.[38] This trend has also diminished the role of the political parties. Working one's way through the party apparatus, building coalitions among its splinter groups, cutting deals with regional constituencies, and smoking in back rooms have become quaint activities in a money-driven, electronic age. Researchers report that media-centered campaigns have resulted in split-ticketing as voters look to the media, not to the parties, for information and guidance.[39] With Independents now accounting for more than one-third of the U.S. electorate, the parties' roles are changing: they give birth to the candidates, or at least most of them, but they no longer discipline them (even Ronald Reagan avoided his party's platform in 1984). This trend is worrisome because, as Warren Miller notes, parties ensure a true dialectic during campaigns, an issue-orientation that forces candidates to take political stands.[40]

A media-centered campaign, in contrast, ensures only that episodic events (such as a failed interview on *Larry King Live*) receive special attention. It also permits episodic candidates like Steve Forbes and Ross Perot to have equal footing with "résumé candidates" like George Bush and Al Gore. A media-centered campaign turns television personalities into power brokers, as when Walter Cronkite nearly persuaded Gerry Ford during a live convention interview to take the vice presidential spot on the Republican ticket in 1980, much to the horror of Ronald Reagan and his minions.[41] When they do deal with issues, media-centered campaigns deal with issues du jour—gun registration today, the Middle East tomorrow—because the media have short attention spans and a hearty appetite for novelty. Reflecting on such trends, Carey McWilliams notes that citizens no longer get out of their houses much during a campaign as they consume the refracted, televised images created somewhere else for people in general. By emptying the public square, says McWilliams, the media produce an almost "totalitarian" effect, making politics a psychological and not a civic experience.[42]

Studying campaign products is no more encouraging. Advertising is often scurrilous,[43] political debates are "counterfeit,"[44] empty and misleading visuals play to viewers' biases,[45] and campaign speechmaking becomes bloated, building up people's expectations only to have them dashed by political reality.[46] These judgments are not simply matters of taste. Controlled studies by Stephen Ansolabehere and Shanto Iyengar show that negative advertising can actually depress the popular vote.[47] Ostensibly, voters become so satiated by the opprobrium candidates heap on one another that they quit the process entirely. A parallel effect has been discovered by Joseph Cappella and Kathleen Hall Jamieson, who examined strategy-centered versus issue-based news coverage and found that the former makes politics seem gamelike to voters, resulting in decreased likelihood of voting.[48]

Recent studies have also found a certain imperiousness in the media. Thomas Patterson shows that press coverage increasingly features the voice of the reporter rather than that of the candidate, a phenomenon demonstrated in the decreasing "sound bite" allotted the nation's leaders by the media, and in their disinclination to cover party conventions.[49] In *Seducing America*, I detail the ways in which the media now fill their reportage with intimate details of the candidates' personal lives (and with their presumed thoughts and feelings) rather than with more pressing issues of the day.[50] In the winter of 1998, for example, President Clinton's alleged dalliances with intern Monica Lewinsky drove the historic meeting of Fidel Castro and Pope John Paul II off the front pages of all but the most stodgy newspapers. These decisions are not without their consequences. Studies show that people are increasingly likely to cite media sources when explaining their political perceptions, but this does not mean that media coverage motivates action.[51] As Steven Rosenstone and Mark Hansen observe, declining voter turnout may be attributed in part to the electorate's inability to connect to the media's often surreal version of the campaign, a campaign that seems to have nothing to do with their health, safety, children, and pay stubs.[52]

Viewed in the large, then, the modern political campaign seems a botch. Who could admire a process that diminishes a nation's leaders even as it depresses its citizens? Increasingly, campaigns are run for the benefit of the well-paid professionals who make the ads and run the surveys and for the media personnel who preen noxiously for months on end. But that is only part of the story. We have also seen that campaigns broaden the nation's dialogue, inform citizens and candidates alike, and join them in an important cultural ritual that makes nationhood a continuing possibility. Campaigns are both grand and troublesome and yet also mysterious. Their mysteries inspired this book.

CHAPTER 1

What Must Be Learned about Campaigns?

Political campaigns in the United States are probably overstudied. From Theodore White's *Making of the President, 1960* to Roger Simon's *Showtime*, the election journal has become a publisher's staple.[53] Every four years, the advance checks are written in Manhattan for the definitive, behind-the-scenes explanations of why the presidential race turned out as it did. The facts reported in these narratives are sometimes hard to corroborate, but publishers have come to view the campaign as an elephant and their authors as blind men, and so there is usually truth enough for all. Indeed, for many people, the most definitive (or at least most delicious) account of the 1992 campaign was Anonymous's *Primary Colors*, proving that fact-checking and double-sourcing are not prerequisites for campaign analysis.[54]

Also weighing in on campaigns are serious journalists, some of whom decry how the press is treated by politicians (e.g., *On Bended Knee* by Mark Hertsgaard) or how the media degrade themselves (e.g., *Breaking the News* by James Fallows). Other works focus on the personalities that run campaigns (e.g., Woodward's *The Choice: How Clinton Won*), the obscene amounts of money now spent on them (e.g., Corrado's *Paying for Presidents*), or why, despite their fund-raising abilities, the parties are now in eclipse (e.g., Wattenberg's *The Decline of American Political Parties 1952–1992*). Still other authors use political campaigns to look deeper into the nation's life and times (e.g., *Running Scared: Why America's Politicians Campaign Too Much and Govern Too Little* by Anthony Stephen King and *See How They Ran* by Gil Troy). In addition, hard-nosed social scientists have developed superb mathematical techniques to ferret out polling trends. Works such as John Zaller's *The Nature and Origins of Mass Opinions* and Michael DelliCarpini and Scott Keeter's *What Americans Know about Politics and Why It Matters* have made secondary analysis of survey data artful.[55]

Is there anything left to learn? Only if we assume that what is said during a campaign matters, but that is not a common assumption. Members of the press are largely bored by the campaign speeches they hear and the handouts provided them by campaign staff. Too, reporters' hurried schedules root them in the moment, giving them

16

little time to put today's texts into historical context. Average citizens also feel superior to political discourse, assuming that they have the ability to sort out the wheat from the chaff without external guidance. Many scholars also do not know what to do with campaign texts and hence look to polling data for their truths. Numbers, they feel, are more substantial than metaphors, even though these numbers derive from survey questions arbitrarily asked of small groups of respondents nobody really knows. Polls tell us much about political responses but very little about political stimuli.

Happily, scholars have begun to correct these oversights. The work of Maxwell McCombs on media agenda-setting, Lynda Kaid on negative advertising, Doris Graber on campaign visuals, Kathleen Jamieson on political speech-making, and William Gamson on citizen dialogue has surveyed the campaign genre expertly.[56] My goals here are at once broader and narrower. I want to look at the sweep of discourse during the last fifty years, not at individual campaigns, but I want to do so from a single vantage point—word choice—and I want to do so voraciously, comprehensively. I want to put a number of hypotheses to the test and see which fail and which prove true. My hope is to offer a fresh perspective on campaigns by tracking what others have not bothered to track.

The stance I take toward campaigns is largely agnostic. I begin by assuming that nobody knows for sure what politicians say or why they say it or what makes campaigns special. I also assume that voters will never really be understood until they are listened to in their own words. I assume further that press coverage is no different today than it has ever been and that political advertising is a great and good thing—until data to the contrary are produced. For the sake of argument, I might also assume that political parties are still vibrant and that Ross Perot's success was an aberration. Or perhaps I should assume the opposite. Mostly, though, I will assume that making new assumptions about campaigns—and making no assumptions about campaigns—are equally heuristic. The great problem with campaigns is not that we know too little but that we know too much that may not be true.

If asked, for example, exactly how a political leader differs from, say, a religious prelate, how might one respond? The question seems trivial and the answer obvious—they have fundamentally different jobs, they answer to vastly different authorities, their ambits of control differ. Yes, but how do they speak? Do they ever say the same things, even though one deals with the sacred and the other the profane? Are there times when a president must become a preacher, when a preacher must act empirically? When they speak of death do they say the same thing? Perhaps, but how do they speak when they speak of human privation? Human sexuality? Human purpose? School vouchers? Are preachers and presidents more alike today than they were twenty years ago? Forty years ago? Is an archbishop more likely to be seen standing next to the president on the campaign trail or on the White House balcony? Why are we so sure of the answer to this question?

The results reported here will ask such basic questions, sometimes re-inquiring into what others have found. Some researchers report, for example, that campaigns now have a narrower agenda than before but I find no evidence of such narrowing.[57] Others argue that political rhetoric has become more abstract, more fatuous over time, but I find a certain constancy on that score.[58] One scholar alleges that political parties are no longer featured in press reports but my database shows this to be a marginal effect at best.[59] There are more hypotheses that need rechecking: Was the rhetoric of the 1988 campaign especially dispiriting? No, I find. Are political ads as simplistic as some authorities claim?[60] Not according to my evidence. Have Democrats and Republicans lost their unique perspectives? Do they now speak a common language? No and no, I find. Was the "people's debate" in Richmond, Virginia, in 1992 less partisan than traditional debates, as some have claimed?[61] Not really, but that debate did differ in interesting ways from its forebears.

Details like these have their value, but this book is after bigger game. For example, what gives political language its special sound? How do we know a politician when we hear one? What are we doing when we are "being political" with one another. These, of course, are comparative questions: to know a politics one must also know an unpolitics. Having a large data base helps in this regard. Because of its capacity, it sometimes produces the unexpected result: politicians use a less focused style than the press, constantly seeking what Richard

Weaver has called the "spaciousness" needed for political compromise.[62] The limits of politics are also seen when politicians and citizens are contrasted. While voters often declaim in colorful, castigatory ways, politicians are more encouraging but also more precise. But the inevitability of politics is best seen when politicians are compared to other public figures. They are, for example, more careful with their words than social protestors and religious leaders, navigating as they must the often tortuous routes of political compromise. The need for accommodation places a special "tax" on political language, depriving it of the pyrotechnic qualities seen in other venues. A comparison with business leaders yields another dimension: while highly optimistic, politicians are almost dour compared to corporate spokespersons. Because they perform their art under the klieg lights, and because they deal each day with matters of life and death, the nation's political leaders do far less glad-handing than popular myth would suggest. Only a comparative analysis could establish that fact.

How has political language changed in the United States? There has been a dramatic drop in institutional assurance since 1948. Political candidates today speak with far less certainty than they did in the days of Harry Truman and Tom Dewey, they lose their argumentative focus more easily, and they are less dependent on partisan cues for their rhetorical impact. Interestingly, these patterns hold true for the press as well as the citizenry, as if the entire culture were caught up in swirling ambiguities. In addition, American politicians speak less optimistically today, perhaps because they do not have ready access to the language of mutuality so resonant in the 1940s and 1950s. This is true for reporters and citizens alike, suggesting a widespread social transformation. The campaigns of the 1960s and 1970s also bore the marks of their eras, with the old language of assumed community being replaced by a new language of skepticism and denial. The most recent campaigns are different still: they display the psychological talisman of their age—self-referentiality—and a corresponding language of time, not space, marks their postmodern condition. Deprived of the old verities, they also depend on (1) active and (2) technocratic language for their suasive force. While there are exceptions to these patterns, and while politicians, press, and people are not always on the same page, the findings are powerful statistically and hence suggestive of a broad, enduring cultural story.

And so the logic of this book is comparative. To understand electoral pressures we must contrast campaigners to sitting presidents: What license comes with the presidency? Does residing in the Oval Office affect what one later says on the campaign trail? Is it better to be an incumbent or a challenger? A governor or a senator? And what of the press? Some allege that politicians and reporters now lie in the same bed, that their words are indistinguishable. I find no support for that claim. Instead, I find a persistent tension between them, with the media trying to stay "on topic" and political leaders trying to venture forth. Curiously, I also find that press reports are far more theoretical, more interpolative, than politicians' texts, perhaps a function of the narrative burden the press assumes. I also find some intriguing media traditions: as a campaign moves from the nominating convention to election day, the language of commonality in news reports slips steadily (especially in recent campaigns), as if an old political story were being written again and again, or as if only one political story could be written.

Other comparative questions are raised by the findings reported here: Why is it that when American voters speak about political matters they sound different from both politicians and the press? What gives citizens their special voice and how would campaigns change if those qualities were better understood by the nation's leaders? by the working press? Another comparative question asks, with the French author Buffon, is style the man? If so, is it worth it? Not according to my data. The more unique a politician's language, the more likely he is to lose. Compared to the eighteen other political candidates studied here, Ross Perot's language was highly distinct, as was Barry Goldwater's, but their candidacies were troubled too. Most of the winning candidates—people like Dwight Eisenhower and George Bush, for example—were "average" in every measurable way. Does this mean that the American people are born centrists, that they use campaign rhetoric as a compass of suitability and feel good only when it points to plain?

This book looks at traditional campaign forums—conventions, debates, and political advertising—and raises new questions about them. Generally, my findings show that each serves an important purpose. Are convention acceptance speeches hoary and brocaded? They are, but we must ask why? What is it about a culture that produces politics by formula and why does that quality worry so many people—especially those in the press? What is it about re-saying old truths that gives people special pleasure, even in the middle of a feisty political campaign? Do debates serve an important function? They do. They establish neutral ground on which all candidates can stand, they discipline the candidates linguistically, and they open the candidates to a kind of introspection found in no other forum. Political ads perform less heroic services but they are less nasty than is generally believed. Indeed, they act as a kind of "electoral poetry," letting candidates imagine an ideal political space. It is tempting to dismiss these pedestrian images but that seems unwise since a candidate who cannot imagine something wonderful is also unlikely to produce it once elected.

The findings reported in this book are not definitive. I paint in broad strokes here, teasing out questions lying beyond the reach of easy answers. While my database is large, my method of analysis is not without its problems. Because my database is large, getting the last word on individual political phenomena, on specific campaigns, is also not easy. But I trudge along nonetheless because political campaigns are too important to be ignored and too interesting to be studied solely in conventional ways. Language behavior is only a small part of a political campaign but it is a large part of the human condition. Political candidates are crafty about language but they are not crafty enough to record, store, analyze, and interpret a hundred thousand words in sixty seconds. The tools I have used here are able to do that, and so my trek does not seem hopeless.

Conclusion

Throughout this book, I will continue to reflect on why so many people find politics so disturbing. As the new millennium begins, few Americans hold their political leaders in high regard, fewer still can abide the press. Other institutions—education, the military, the courts, the church—are also being questioned but none so much as those that practice the political arts. It is as if the American people had suddenly became aware that negotiating power relations is a dirty business and that apportioning a society's goods and services takes not a saint but a sinner who bargains well with other sinners. In 1992, they got rid of a perfectly serviceable chief executive in deference to a young man who seemed far from perfect but both vigorous and photogenic. In 1996, they continued to prefer this young man over his rival, grousing all the while when doing so. They continued to grouse two years later when their amiable young man suddenly seemed younger (and more manly) than they had bargained for, which only goes to show that grousing, by now, had become their passion.

Campaigns also inspire passion because they are a parturition. Every four years, the American nation reconstitutes itself, thereby giving its citizens an opportunity to reflect on who they are and what they want to become. Their leaders help in that process, using the rhetorical arts to draft new plans and inspire new visions. Campaigns also involve a good deal of money laundering, ballot-box tampering, and horse-trading and that is what gives them their odor. But to reflect only on the shortcomings of campaigns seems cramped. If the American people agreed with one another on all matters and were preternaturally willing to share their bounties equally, there would be no need for politics. But they are not willing to do that and so I begin this book by offering a prayer: that when reflecting on campaigns we avoid feeling above politics or beyond politics or against politics or without politics. When it comes to politics—the science of social cooperation—the only acceptable prepositional injunction is to stand within politics, for politics stands at the center of us all.

* CHAPTER 2 *

Campaign Language

THE FINDINGS reported in this book make little sense unless these data seem important: Bill Clinton referred to *people* twenty-one times during his 1996 convention acceptance address while Bob Dole managed only nine such references. When the high-frequency words in both speeches were compared (that is, words used three or more times), Mr. Clinton's speech was also found to stress *neighborhoods, fellow, children, home,* and *parents* while Dole used in-the-beltway terms like *administration, congress, party, policy, compromise,* and *unions.* Whereas Clinton emphasized time (*days, future, tonight, young, century*), Dole stressed values: *trust, God, heart, right, honor.* These data look self-evident: Clinton was a Democrat and Dole a Republican, Clinton was young and Dole was not. But there is more: Out of Clinton's ninety-five high-frequency words, fourteen were economically based: *business, payment, tax, million, money, budget, cuts, interest, debt.* No such emphases are found in Dole's speech, although one of the few economic words he did use was, tellingly, *wealth* (versus Clinton's *jobs*). There are also curious data: Clinton used *mother* and Dole *father;* Clinton referenced *Chicago* (where he was) while Dole stressed *Kansas* (where he wasn't); Dole mentioned *war* and Clinton *peace;* Dole *small* and Clinton *new.*

These data sum up the 1996 presidential campaign, a campaign in which Bill Clinton ran as an ideological, and rhetorical, New Democrat and Dole as a near-caricature of the Old Republican. Admittedly, the data above ignore the context within which these words were deployed but, given the patterns they etch, that seems a quibble. Regardless of context, do these selections not predict the future employability of the speechwriters involved? Can any justification be offered for having Dole stress *soldier, violent,* and *forces* during a placid time, or for emphasizing *man* when his party faced a yawning gender gap? Perhaps a case could be made for having Dole lavish praise on *Reagan,* but was it also wise to stress *history* when facing a much younger opponent or *division* when his rival was emphasizing *community*? No matter how Mr. Dole's sixty-one high-frequency words are stitched together, disaster awaits.

This book's premise is that words are important. All by themselves. If we are patient enough to examine them carefully, if we are willing to look for connections among them, much can be learned. Much can be learned because people treat their words casually, as if they were no more substantial than gossamer, irrelevant to the relations they share with one another. But even a moment's reflection finds this a canard: Is it not meaningful, for example, that neither Dole nor Clinton referenced *race*, *class*, *religion*, *region*, or *gender* in their remarks, even though these forces lie at the epicenter of contemporary U.S. politics? Is it not also meaningful that the candidates referenced *America* and its variants forty-five times between them, a sign that their nation is still proud of its pride despite its cynicisms? Data like these are hardly matters of happenstance. By choosing one word a speaker decides not to use another, thereby creating a sociolinguistic map that can be read. This book offers one such reading.

The Nature of Political Language

On a slow news day, the nation's pundits can always be counted on to savage political language. Sunday is normally a slow news day and so the *New York Times Magazine* lets William Safire tear the belly out of the body politician in his weekly column "On Language." Not to be outdone is humorist P. J. O'Rourke, who once said this about the 1984 presidential campaign: "These candidates have a crying need for a good—even fair—liberal arts education. One longs to send [Gary] Hart back to college so he can get it out of his system, send Reagan to college in the first place, and lock Mondale up in a rudimentary speech class with a sock in his mouth."[1] Like George Orwell before him, Arthur Schlesinger Jr. sets a higher tone but his survey of political rhetoric is no less scorching: "Social fluidity, moral pretension, political and literary demagoguery, corporate and academic bureaucratization and a false conception of democracy are leading us into semantic chaos. We owe to Vietnam and Watergate a belated recognition of the fact that we are in linguistic as well as political crisis and that the two may be organically connected."[2] And then there is Schlesinger cum Emerson: "We infer the spirit of the nation in great measure from the language."[3]

It would take a tome to explain why political language is so reviled. One explanation is that politicians do special violence to language. But that seems wrong when we reflect on those who make their livings writing software documentation, insurance policies, logic textbooks, or direct-mail circulars. Perhaps politicians come under attack because they are called to a higher standard and hence obliged to treat language with special reverence. But the same could be said of those who preach the word of God or who serve as officers of the court, professions not always known for their ability to keep the inattentive awake. Most likely, political language comes under attack because it attempts the impossible: coordinating a polity's dreams with its realities. So, for example, political campaigners are denounced when claiming they will raise taxes (like Walter Mondale) but also when promising the opposite (like George Bush). The American people enjoy hearing their president declare them the salvation of the free world but they detest the attendant costs (in money and soldiers) when the bill comes due. Increasingly, voters are attracted to politicians who can woo them on television talk shows but these same voters decry them for being too slick, too coy, too charming, too practiced—the very arts that television demands. In many ways, to attack political language is to attack all the human instincts.

Political language is problematic because politics itself is problematic, as when it asks a selfish people to share with one another or an intemperate people to be civil. Politicians are vilified for not telling the truth when the real problem is that they tell a thousand truths—that Hispanics deserve the contract because of a history of discrimination; that African Americans deserve the contract because theirs is a longer, and sorrier, history; that Anglos deserve the contract because theirs is the lowest bid. And so the quintessential problem in politics is this: Which truth should I tell today? And how? Because politics so often deals with cross-cutting cleavages, because it can never articulate everything it knows at any given moment, a political truth inevitably sounds like a falsehood. That is, most political statements purport to be complete ("we are a nondiscriminatory nation") whereas the full truth is considerably more complicated ("in the United States, we take turns being discriminated against").

Truthful or not, political language must be reckoned with because it is an instrument of power. The politics of literacy tells this story, as in Quebec province where the vernacular has become a centrifuge of strife.[4] In many parts of the world, says Henry Bretton, politics is typically transacted in formal surroundings and in a citizen's second language (or, more perversely, in a citizen's nonlanguage). "Words spoken to a child in his mother's tongue," says Bretton, "evoke certain emotions, memories and thoughts. Do words spoken in a secondary language, an alien one, produce the same or even similar results?"[5] Because linguistic ability is so directly tied to the individual self, says Bretton, "fear of being deprived of communicative skills [raises] political passion to a fever pitch,"[6] a fact now seen in various parts of the United States relative to English-only legislation.

But political language is not monolithic (at least not in a democracy) and so it is used by the downtrodden as well as the powerful. "The master's tools will never dismantle the master's house," opines Audre Lorde, but she instantly dispels that myth by using language powerfully, insurgently, to carry the message of feminism.[7] Because it is an inventional art, rhetoric makes two political promises: (1) that which can be imagined can be obtained; (2) that which can be imagined powerfully can be obtained now. "The scholar may sit in his study and take care that his language is not exaggerated," once pronounced the American agitator Wendell Phillips, "but the rude mass of men . . . is caught by men whose word are half battles. From Luther down, the charge against the reformer has been that his language is too rough. Be it so. Rough instruments are used for rough work."[8]

Because language is so central to democratic politics, it is deeply implicated in all power relations. Mike Emmison reports, for example, that political use of a simple phrase like *the economy* makes it seem as if economic forces lie beyond the control of the state, that it is "on no one's side." As a result, says Emmison, "unpopular political decisions and policies can be taken and justified whilst avoiding the charge of class- or self-interest," thereby allowing the nation's economy to become more important than the nation's citizens.[9] Also, because political language is so powerfully barometric, it often signals important political phenomena. So, for example, Philip Tetlock has shown that political ideology often leaves clear linguistic traces, with conservatives using more reductionistic language than liberals.[10] In a different vein, Vanessa Beasley has explored the rhetorical difficulties assumed by Anita Hill's supporters when they testified before the Senate Judiciary Committee. "How could a genuine victim continue to associate freely with her oppressor?" the senators asked. A logic of victimhood easily explains such anomalies, Beasley replies, forcing decisions on victims that make little sense within a logic of power (the logic guiding the senators themselves).[11]

Some of the most interesting research has shown how evolving political structures are accompanied by subtle linguistic changes. Richard Merritt reports, for example, that colonial newspapers in New England imperceptibly (perhaps even unconsciously) changed the use of national self-references during the early 1700s, thereby turning *His Majesty's colonies* into *the American colonies* prior to actual political separation.[12] More recently, Richard Anderson has shown how the language of the streets quickly infiltrated the discourse of post–Soviet Russians, thereby signaling a rhetorical revolution as well as a political one.[13] Mark Moore notes a different kind of shift in the United States when observing that irony has become a rhetorical staple for media personnel as well as for politicians. Something odd is afoot, says Moore, when a politician's most reliable resource requires deconstructing the political apparatus for which he or she is campaigning.[14]

When viewed rhetorically, then, politics becomes repositioned. It no longer involves just a set of power vectors but also a relational grammar. So, for example, Lyndon Johnson used an equal assortment of masculine and feminine metaphors in his private telephone calls when simultaneously cajoling and intimidating his interlocutors, thereby reproducing the give-and-take of politics generally.[15] Paying attention to such semantic details often produces surprises. It has, for example, allowed scholars to note important statutory differences between prime ministers and presidents, differential use of obfuscation by supporters and opponents of legislation (opponents use more, it turns out), and how even a pressing issue like poverty can be "privatized" through language, making it seem a personal problem rather than a civic emergency.[16]

But the kind of work pursued in this book is different still. It features the lexicon of democracy, its unconscious word habits. Such an inquiry sheds light on fundamental presuppositions, on what people understand without knowing why. For example, Nancy Fraser and Linda Gordon have asked why *dependency* has come to be judged a political crime in the United States, especially since it was formerly associated with the hallowed traditions of church and family.[17] One might also ask, as has Raymond Williams, why a *consumer* is now given so much political respect when he or she was formerly thought overindulgent, a social pariah.[18] Also, how do people learn to distinguish easily between *communities* and *special interests*, asks Daniel Rodgers, and how does the former become sanctified and the latter vilified?[19] How can *equality* be used nonchalantly by both affirmative action proponents and opponents, ask Celeste Condit and John Lucaites, especially when the two groups operate from such different philosophical premises?[20] And why have Republicans consistently ignored such hallowed terms as *compassion*, asks Frank Luntz, thereby making love sectarian, the exclusive property of the Democrats?[21]

Tracking the kinds of words a polity uses can be especially revealing. Raymond Gozzi reports, for example, that over 45 percent of the new words introduced into the American lexicon between 1961 and 1986 were technological words, a fact that has clear implications for political affairs. Words produce "memories" in us, says Gozzi, and these memories affect how we process each day's events.[22] So, for example, when political demands are made that *charity* become *efficient* (viz., welfare reform), does the nation's technological heritage suddenly trump its Judeo-Christian roots? Because words are powerful in these ways, it becomes an open question whether people use language or are used by it, whether Americans signed the Declaration of Independence or became Americans via their signatures.[23] What is known for sure is that language makes a people a people, a fact that Harold Lasswell and Nathan Leites reported some fifty years ago:

> The dominant political symbols of an epoch provide part of the common experience of millions of men. There is some fascination in the

thought of how many human beings are bound together by a thread no more substantial than the resonance of a name or the clang of a slogan. In war, men suffer pain, hunger, sorrow; the specific source of pain, the specific sensation of one's specific object of sorrow, may be very private. In contrast, the key symbol enters directly into the focus of all men and provides an element of common experience.[24]

As this book argues, the power of language is magnified during elections. Campaigns sometimes turn on a candidate's decision to say too much (Ross Perot's constant problem) or to be reduced to inexpressibility (the fate of Mr. Perot's running mate, Admiral Stockwell). Some candidates speak too passionately (a constant problem for Hubert Humphrey) while others are wooden when they should be enraged (witness Michael Dukakis's cerebral response to a reporter's question about the hypothetical rape of his wife during a 1988 debate). Because of the temporal pressures they face, the mass media now reward the bite-sized phrase, requiring campaigners to craft their words with special care (few are better at it than Bill Clinton, few more cavalier than Bob Dole). Choosing language carefully has always been the diplomat's job, but creating "rhetorical space" is now the candidate's challenge as well, as reporters try to broaden agendas the candidate would rather leave narrow.

The relative distance between a candidate and his or her words is also important, something Teddy Kennedy showed in 1980 when he proved unable to give personal reasons for wanting to become president. In the modern campaign, choreographing language has become especially important. Because campaigners now travel with so many hangers-on, and because the mass media make instant celebrities out of anyone associated with the candidate, having the right people say the right thing at the right time becomes a constant challenge, a lesson proved painfully from time to time by such famous relatives as Billy Carter, Patti (Reagan) Davis, Martha Mitchell, Susan Ford, and Roger Clinton. The mass media present still other choices to candidates: the spontaneous word versus the practiced word; the precise fact versus the optimistic prediction; the clever retort versus the humble admission; the policy analysis versus the campaign analysis.

Speaking politically has never been easy, but in an age of inexpensive videotape it has become truly daunting.

Because of the mass media, the half-life of political words is no longer calculable. Onetime presidential candidate George Romney later wished he had never been *brainwashed*; Jimmy Carter regretted he had once *lusted* in his heart and on TV; Gerald Ford wished he had not *freed Poland* prior to its actual political liberation; and George Bush would not have referred to his (partly Hispanic) grandchild as *the little brown one* if he had thought a bit harder about it. Words used to come and words used to go but now they only come and stay. That is why this book pays attention to them. Modern people, media people, live their lives drenched in pictures but they are also waist-deep in words. Because words are so plentiful it is tempting to ignore them, but trying to understand them seems the better option.

The Campaign Mapping Project

In an otherwise good piece of research, T. N. Walters and his colleagues analyzed the press releases of the Democratic Party in 1992 and concluded that Bill Clinton had an unusually technocratic style.[25] What the researchers could not know was that this was not really a Clinton phenomenon but a bipartisan trend that had taken hold some years earlier. I am able to make that statement on the basis of the Campaign Mapping Project (CMP), a multiyear attempt (1) to assemble campaign materials produced during presidential elections between 1948 and 1996 and (2) to use them to develop a broad understanding of where American politics is going and why. Codirected by me and Professor Kathleen Hall Jamieson of the University of Pennsylvania, the Project began in June of 1995 and continues to the present. Through the good offices of the Ford Foundation and the Carnegie Corporation of New York, we were able to collect a good many of the speeches, advertisements, debates, broadcast news stories, newspaper accounts, and letters-to-the-editor generated during fifty years worth of "general election seasons" (late August through election day).

Once the campaign materials were collected, the Project proceeded in two different directions. While I studied language patterns, Jamieson looked at the arguments put forth during campaigns. Among her results were the following: (1) when "free time" was offered to candidates in 1996, they were much more likely to offer positive proposals than to attack their opponents; (2) campaign news coverage of debates typically focused more on the strategies used by the candidates than on the arguments they put forth; (3) when stump speeches and news reports of those speeches were compared, the press was found to overreport their negativity; (4) political advertising appeared considerably less vicious than contemporary wisdom suggests; (5) in 1996, at least, the media were more willing to present the evidence the candidates used in their remarks than the media had been in prior years. On the downside, the press provided less overall campaign coverage in 1996 than it did four years earlier.[26]

The great challenge, of course, is to weave individual findings like these into a larger tapestry. The CMP's assumption has been that past research has too often lunged from campaign to campaign, with few consistent questions being asked and with few broad findings emerging as a result. To gain greater perspective, the Project had four goals: (1) *to develop a comprehensive view of campaigns*; by bringing together the many different voices of politics—the people, the candidates, the press—the Project sought a broad understanding of the nation's quadrennial dialogue; (2) *to develop an objective view of campaigns*; because so much previous campaign commentary has been based on hunch and invective, quantitative analysis has been used here to add rigor to an area of study needing it; (3) *to develop a normative view of campaigns*; no campaign can be understood in isolation; by reaching across thirteen elections for its insights, the CMP sought out genuinely cultural understandings of American politics; (4) *to develop a communicative view of campaigns*; although much previous campaign research has prized attitudinal and economic data, the CMP took this position: if democracy is a dialogue, someone must speak, someone must listen, and someone must evaluate what was said; with political communications now accounting for 60 percent of all campaign expenditures, and with more and more persons now being joined together via the "old" and "new" media, there has never been a greater need to discover who said what to whom and how; the Campaign Mapping Project helps meet that need.

In short, the CMP's goal was to apply a consistent set of measures to a large collection of texts to assess the nation's political trajectory. It included both output data (candidate communications) and uptake data (e.g., media coverage) to get a sense of the energy, and synergy, defining a campaign. Because voters become so bombarded with discourse, it is hard to track when they first hear what they hear. The political scene now permits snippets from a campaign speech to be subsequently shown on network newscasts and later recontextualized in an opponent's political advertising. Tracking these "informational crossovers" therefore becomes important. It is also necessary to think in more complicated ways about sequence effects in campaigns. Sometimes a speech will be made so that an ad can be taped, or a news story will be written in order to stimulate controversy among the candidates. And yet, from a voter's standpoint, all such discourse swirls about madly, simultaneously, making it necessary for scholars to learn how campaign stimuli multiply one another. Finally, because previous campaigns affect voters' reactions to current campaigns, a sense of yesterday is needed to get a sense of today.

And so the first two years of the Campaign Mapping Project were devoted to gathering a wealth of political discourse. Speeches were obtained from presidential libraries when possible, but also from state and regional archives and, in some cases, from groups and individuals. Newspaper coverage was easier to obtain (since it existed on microfilm) but digitizing the news stories took a great amount of time. Political advertising is typically fugitive stuff but the Project benefited considerably from the fact that Kathleen Jamieson had been collecting these materials for more than twenty years. Broadcast news coverage was also hard to obtain prior to 1968 (when Vanderbilt University's archives first opened) but hardest of all were the letters-to-the-editor serving as the People's Voice in the Project. Written by ordinary people and printed in small newspapers, the letters existed in city libraries and newspaper morgues in twelve small cities scattered throughout the United States. Happily, presidential debates were more easily obtained (from Internet sources).

The Project's database is not exhaustive but it does contain a fairly representative sampling of campaign discourse.[27] Because the DICTION program breaks a text into smaller segments when analyzing it, the Texas version of the CMP database consists of a series of 500-word segments distributed as follows: (1) speeches (n = 2,357): formal remarks given by the major candidates between late July and early November of the campaign year, including nationally televised addresses as well as local stump speeches; (2) debates (n = 652): all presidential debates between 1960 and the present, with each debate being segmented by speaker prior to analysis; (3) advertising (n = 553): a sampling of major party and independent party ads broadcast over television; years include 1960 and 1976–96; (4) print coverage (n = 7,309): feature and nonfeature stories from the *New York Times*, *Washington Post*, *Christian Science Monitor*, *Atlanta Constitution*, *Chicago Tribune*, *Los Angeles Times*, as well as AP and UPI syndicate stories; (5) broadcast coverage (n = 1,219): a sample of nightly newscasts produced during the 1980, 1988, 1992, and 1996 campaigns by the news bureaus of ABC, CBS, NBC, CNN, and PBS; (6) letters-to-the-editor (n = 6,126): letters written to the editors of twelve small-city newspapers between 1948 and 1996. The cities represented (all of which have populations of approximately 100,000 persons) include a cross section of political attitudes and demographic characteristics; the papers are regionally distributed throughout the United States.[28]

All of these materials were keyboarded, introduced into a computerized database, and then analyzed with the DICTION program. The Project employed some twenty graduate assistants at the two institutions and also depended on the goodwill of colleagues and archivists throughout the United States. One unusual aspect of the CMP was that the sponsoring foundations wanted some of the results made available during the 1996 campaign itself. Accordingly, the Project was introduced at a news conference at the National Press Club in Washington, D.C., in July 1996, largely focusing on historical trends in American campaigning during the last fifty years. During the campaign itself, weekly or biweekly research updates were broadcast-faxed to some 275 reporters at forty-five news organizations in the United States and Canada, and the reports were also made available on the Annenberg Public Policy Center's homepage. In addition, the

Project directors conducted hundreds of media interviews during the fall of 1996, the point of which was to introduce factual information into the nation's campaign commentary.

The Campaign Mapping Project began with the assumption that some campaigns fail and some succeed. Campaigns fail when they do not properly forecast for the people what the successful candidate will do once in office, and campaigns fail when they do not give the winner a real national mandate, an emotionally committed citizenry. Some campaigns do succeed. The 1980 campaign succeeded when Ronald Reagan and Jimmy Carter gave the people clear, sharp choices, and the 1964 campaign succeeded when Lyndon Johnson and Barry Goldwater did the same thing. But other campaigns fail. In 1976, Jimmy Carter focused on issues of personal morality during his run for office only to have the cold facts of inflation, unemployment, and energy shortages doom his presidency four years later. And even the election of 1992 was problematic, with only 43 percent of the American people backing Mr. Clinton, in part because of Ross Perot's candidacy but also because "talk show democracy" obviated the sharp exchange with the working press that a polity needs to understand the issues and, then, to build consensus.

So history teaches us that some campaigns serve the nation and some do not. Which is which and why? Obviously, no campaign can predict the future completely. Each president will be confronted by the unexpected from his first day in office but that is not to say that campaigns cannot be improved. To do so requires evidence. Providing some of that evidence has been the job of the Campaign Mapping Project.

THE DICTION PROGRAM

All of the data reported in *Campaign Voices* are derived from a computer program called DICTION that passes over a verbal text looking for particular word groupings.[29] Using a computer for such purposes may seem surprising since, for many people, word choice is unimportant, the least consequential of the complex decisions people make when communicating with one another. But trying to understand why some words are preferred over others (*economical* versus *cheap*), why certain words are never used (*cuncator*), why other words are considered nonpareil (such as *nonpareil*)—this has always been enough work for me. I have chosen to study words because words are so often underestimated. This book tries to estimate these underestimations.

My reasoning has been thus: (1) people have scant ability to monitor their individual language decisions; (2) people have no ability to monitor their patterns of language choice; (3) people think that they have considerable control over such matters; and, therefore, (4) they invite the enterprising researcher to study that which they deem unworthy of study. In the world of politics these propositions hold with special force. Speechwriters, advertising executives, campaign consultants, and politicians alike see themselves as experts in the ways of words. They pour over the details of a press release on a touchy subject, relying heavily on lay theories of language ("*litigate* sounds better than *sue*") even though they could not provide full-bodied explanations of their assumptions if asked to do so. Politics is indeed a world of words but it is also a world of poorly understood words, poorly remembered words, and poorly theorized words.

That is where computers enter the picture. Computers remember, ostensibly forever. Computers detect consistencies and inconsistencies. If properly coached, computers can track associations across semantic space, note situational changes (and changes within those changes), distinguish the characteristic word choices of one person from those of another. Computers can also detect stabilities in language behavior, things that rarely change. Words, that is, are not important in and of themselves. They are important because they point—to people and to the situations in which they find themselves.

Words especially point back to cultural experience. For example, in most countries *progress* is enough, but indomitable Americans demand a stronger form—*good progress*. Words also point to the epistemological assumptions people make. Poets resist fixities (things *waft* for them) while engineers trust only nominalizations; for them, there is no noun that can't be verbed (once *photos* could be *copied*, that is, *photocopies* came into view and, after that, *photocopying a memo* became an inevitability). As Edward Sapir and Benjamin Whorf have argued, the use of fine-grained semantic distinctions reveals a people's special capabilities (automotive experts distinguish between *torque* and *thrust*, for example) and also their unique anxieties.[30] So, for example, young Americans now choose between being *slackers* and *droids* but none question the appropriateness of using production habits to measure their worth. Surely the gods must smile on such antics.

The God in my particular machine, DICTION, is a dictionary-based package that examines a text for its verbal tone. It deploys some ten thousand search words drawn from thirty-three word lists. None of the search terms is duplicated in these lists, allowing the user to get an unusually rich understanding of a text. Lying at the heart of the program are five master variables created by combining (after mathematical standardization) the individual word lists. The master variables have been chosen intentionally, the assumption being that if only five questions could be asked of a given passage, these five would provide the most robust understanding. As it turns out, there are virtually no statistical relationships among these five master variables, which means that each sheds unique light on the passage examined.[31]

Figure 2.1 provides DICTION's complete variable structure. Although these particular operationalizations are the author's own, each master variable was stimulated by the work of others. Certainty, for example, comes from the general semanticists, particularly Wendell Johnson, who studied how language becomes rigid and what happens as a result.[32] Definitionally, Certainty indicates resoluteness, inflexibility, and completeness, a tendency to speak ex cathedra. Leveling terms (*all, everyone*), Collectives (*bureau, organization*), and Tenacious terms (*will, shall*) make for assured statements, while Ambivalent terms (*almost, might*), Specificity (i.e., numerical citations), and Self-References (*I, me*) detract from Certainty scores. Two calculated scores, Insistence (a measure of how tightly focused a text becomes) and Variety (an index of how many different words are used) also contribute—oppositely—to the Certainty score.[33] Because politics is such an ideological business, Certainty is particularly useful for tracking those waxings and wanings.[34]

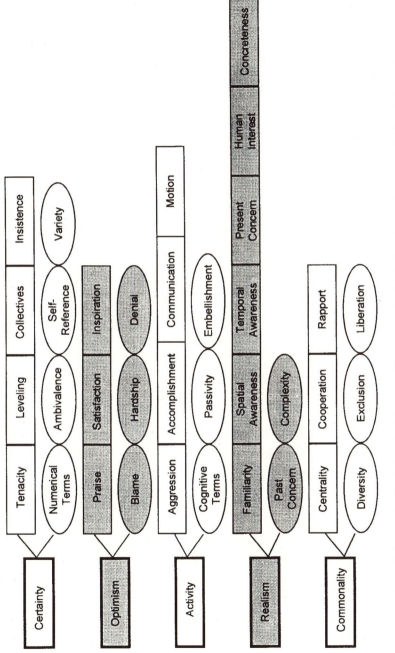

Figure 2.1. DICTION's Variable Structure. *Note: After individualized scores are standardized, "oval" variables are substracted from "rectangular" variables to construct master variables.*

Optimism, language endorsing some person, group, concept, or event, or highlighting their positive entailments, was inspired by James David Barber's work in *The Presidential Character*.[35] Optimism, for Barber, was a key dimension for understanding political personality, although Barber himself tended to use the construct anecdotally rather than empirically. Words of Praise (*good, loyal*), Satisfaction (*exciting, cheerful*), or Inspiration (*courage, trust*) contribute to the Optimism score, while Denial terms (*won't, cannot*) and terms of Hardship (*conflict, despair*) or Blame (*annoying, guilty*) lower it.

Barber was also concerned with Activity, although DICTION's development on this dimension is more indebted to the work of Charles Osgood and his colleagues who did pioneering work in the psychology of language during the 1950s and 1960s.[36] Active language features movement, change, the implementation of ideas and the avoidance of inertia and is particularly useful for distinguishing reflective from nonreflective texts. Its subcategories include Aggressiveness (*fight, attack*), Accomplishment (*march, push*), Motion (*launch, leap*), and Communication (*insist, encourage*), while passives (*quiet, hesitant*), intellectualism (*decide, believe*), and Embellishment (a measure of heavy modification) lower a passage's Activity score.[37]

A fourth dimension is Realism, language describing tangible, immediate, recognizable matters that affect people's everyday lives. This is my attempt to tap the pragmatism John Dewey found endemic to Western experience, particularly U.S. experience.[38] Realism seems an especially appropriate variable when dealing with governance although, as we will see, this variable produces a number of political surprises as well. Factors contributing to Realism include Concreteness (*building, airplane*), present-tense verbs (*going, purchase*), and Human Interest terms (*child, people*) as well as Temporal and Spatial references (*now, early, day, city*). Realism scores decrease as past-tense verbs and Complexity (polysyllabic words) increase.[39]

Finally, Commonality, language highlighting the agreed-upon values of a group and rejecting idiosyncratic modes of engagement, is a rough approximation of the communitarian instincts embodied in the work of Amatai Etzioni and Robert Bellah, although neither scholar is concerned with verbal behavior per se.[40] Factors contributing positively to this variable include terms of Centrality (*orthodox, conformity*), Cooperation (*exchange, teamwork*), and Rapport (*congenial, camaraderie*). Detracting from Commonality are words of Diversity (*nonconformist, factional*), Exclusion (*repudiate, loneliness*), and Liberation (*radical, emancipation*).

These five main scores (and their individual subscores) are produced each time the program is run. In addition, users can create their own word lists and DICTION will search for them as well. For the Campaign Mapping Project, six custom dictionaries were used to capture the unique concerns of politics. These word lists included Patriotic language (*homeland, justice*), partisan references (all variations on *Democrat* or *Republican*), voter references (*electorate, majority*), and religious (*doctrine, parishioner*) and irreligious terms (*godless, witchcraft*). In addition, an especially useful list of Leader References was constructed to capture the unique sociology of campaign discourse. Included in this list were the surnames of all presidents and vice presidents (*Adams, Lincoln*), members of the Supreme Court since 1948 (*Brandeis, Burger*), prominent members of the U.S. Senate since 1948 (*Lugar, Humphrey*), leaders of the House of Representatives since 1948 (*Rayburn, Boggs*), and all major-party and third-party presidential candidates since 1948 (*Dewey, Perot*).

Guided by search tools like these, DICTION plows through batches of texts quickly and, naturally, with unerring precision, producing verbal output for the user and a special file to make later statistical analysis possible. As can be seen in Figure 2.2, DICTION has been adapted to desktop use: It has an intuitive, graphical user interface, extensive on-line help, and is further supported through phone and e-mail.[41] Ultimately, though, DICTION does what all such programs do: it turns words into numbers. In my opinion it does so with special power and facility, and because its dictionaries have been carefully constructed, it does so with considerable scope as well. But, like any research tool, a computer program is no better than the assumptions it makes. For some, DICTION's assumptions will be unsettling.

For example, one of its key premises is the *assumption of transformativity*—that quantifying language makes sense. But sense for whom? As Robert Wachal observes, many feel that the "computer-using literary researcher is a poacher in the scholarly game preserve.

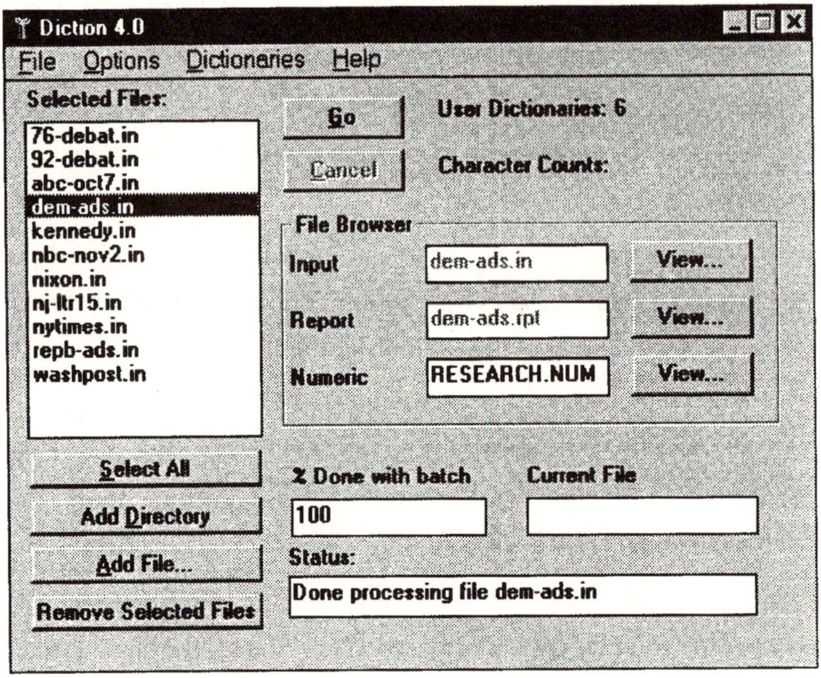

Figure 2.2. DICTION's Main Screen.

The benevolent view is that his traps mangle what they hope to capture, or that they are set for deer and only catch gnats. A more pessimistic view is that his traps have no springs in them."[42] Perhaps, but here is a contrary assumption: each day, people make judgments based on the mathematics of language. A person who "gushes," for example, is a person whose needless dilations are deemed obnoxious. Similarly, when we judge one person voluble and another taciturn we are making arithmetic judgments. Everyday social decorum demands that we talk longer to a friend we have not seen for some time, that we not monopolize the conversation during a job interview, that we refrain from thinking aloud while waiting for a bon mot to pop to mind. Professional wordsmiths also rely on such mathematical intuitions: the "arcane expression" is one with too much type for its token; the "common touch" derives from words lying at the center of the normal distribution; "political dexterity" is exhibited by those able to make successful adaptations to social situations. Rather than being alien, then, programs like DICTION depend on very human understandings of proportionality.

A related but equally troubling postulate is *the assumption of additivity*—that quantity is related to quality, that ten uses of a term like *death* are precisely twice as worrisome as five uses. There is a straightforward linearity to this assumption, even though everyday experience sometimes shows that infrequent appearance of a word or phrase can be especially meaningful. If, for example, the mayor of an American city cursed but once during his monthly remarks to the city council, that fact would be headlined in the local tabloid, even though the mayor might also have invoked the deity twenty-seven times that evening. Because it is inherently more attracted to central tendencies than to outliers, DICTION would therefore miss some of the news in the mayor's speech. But it would not miss all the news. It might note, for example, that sin still captures the imaginations of American Puritans even as the millenium approaches, that the depravities of the human spirit still excite them. It would figure such excitement at the precise ratio of 27:1.[43]

DICTION makes an even more troubling assumption—*the assumption of semantic independence*—that words are meaningful outside of context. That is, DICTION breaks a text into its individual words, counts them (especially some of them), concatenates them, associates them with a databank foreign to that text, and then invites the user to comment on the entirety of the text-as-received. Such presumptuousness is beyond the pale for many. For them, any program that confuses a sentence like *the dog bit the man* with *the man bit the dog* cannot be taken seriously—even though the sentences are lexically identical. A computer program has done sorry work indeed, they would argue, if it cannot decide whether a mental health worker or an officer from the dog pound should be called to the scene.

But what if we looked at these sentences differently? Instead of being concerned with who sank their dentures into whom, what if we concentrated on the co-occurrence of people and animals in the two sentences? By concentrating on textual similarities a DICTION-user might note these things: that people more often take their dogs to the park than their microwave ovens; that if dogs are bitten in the year 2001 they are more likely to be bitten by people than, say, by

41

mountain lions (as they might have been in 1701 in the United States); that man and dog are equally capable of biting, a token of their common mammalian status and, hence, of their natural reasons for affiliating; that biting, not singing and dancing, is being done, which may explain why people also need people as well as their pets. By attending to these matters and not to the forensic aspects of the man-dog encounter, DICTION could therefore shed light on domestic ecology or interspecies collaboration or human compensatory behavior. There are enough civil servants to explore the remaining matters.

And so DICTION provides different data, not better or worse data. By focusing intently on lexical choice, it flags our attention to matters normally ignored. But the different-not-better argument is hardly its sole defense. One must also consider these matters:

1. *Context is evanescent.* Anyone who has found something new to appreciate when rewatching *It's a Wonderful Life* at Christmastime knows that one's changing level of maturity makes for a different viewer and a different movie from year to year. Unless one posits a Manichaean world, context at Time #1 is never the same as context at Time #2.

2. *Context is deconstructive*, vanishing the moment it comes into existence. During a campaign, that is, voters become "gist processors," taking what they need from an election event and leaving the rest behind. They become victims of "spreading activation," inundated by associations suddenly triggered off in their minds. They are assaulted by "lexical leakage" as they link half-remembered, half-imagined feelings to new campaign experiences.[44] In other words, verbal context may be far less important to an in-the-moment voter than to an after-the-fact analyst.

3. *Context is not determinative.* Everyday experience suggests that we often listen not for an entire text but for enough "lexical weight," for a certain amount of assurance, sensitivity, or vitriol in the remarks of another. For example, do not certain word families (slang, for example) sometimes have an almost autonomous power over us? Given enough patriotic, religious, or financial language, can our hearts not be won over no matter how the constituent elements of those word-

families are arranged? As Mikhail Bahktin has argued, "even when syntactically isolated, the word is pervaded by previous contexts, previous usages and social conflicts."[45] While context is undeniably important, so too are the lexical histories to which all words are heir.

And so the case being made here is this: there is an art to political discourse but also a science—a geometry, a dimensionality. Is it so heretical to be reminded that the Notre Dame Cathedral is made of stone or that Picasso painted with paint? To know how much paint Picasso used, on which occasions, in what colors, and with what proportions, is not to deny his art but to study it from the ground up. Asking after such matters cannot tell us everything but it cannot tell us nothing. Double negatives sometimes produce insight, particularly in an arena like politics, where things are so often murky.

DICTION's case can be made more positively as well. It is, for example, transparent, fully operationalizing the constructs it uses. DICTION will always find what it searches for, nothing more and nothing less, and that makes it an unusually dependable search tool. It is also capacious, able to inspect large bodies of text and to notice continuities and discontinuities that might not be seen (or even imagined) with more conventional procedures. Sometimes, but not always, DICTION can be subtle, helping explain phenomena that are powerful but elliptical—things like "tone" for example or, potentially, "public mood."[46] DICTION can also be heuristic when it frustrates the "demand characteristics" of discourse, its ability to seduce the analyst as well as the audience. Who, in the new millennium, for example, could inspect the remarks of Louis Farrakhan without having his or her blood stirred (out of attraction or repulsion)? Any good rhetoric can turn an observer into a confederate in these ways, but DICTION interrupts this transference by pushing its questions to the fore, insisting that its verbal categories receive exclusive consideration. And so if DICTION found fewer religious references in Farrakhan's remarks than, say, in the speeches of Martin Luther King Jr., it might well open up discussion of how the American civil religion has changed during the last thirty years.

There are two major research traditions in textual analysis: (a) case studies and (b) global studies. DICTION research clearly falls in the latter domain, focusing as it does on gross phenomena, on cumulative perceptions. By assuming that voters' reactions are always affected by their experiences with previous political texts, DICTION depends heavily on normative data—on things in general. In doing so, it may well simulate the behavior of the average voter. When a contemporary American listens to Bill Clinton, that is, he or she may be simultaneously relistening to Ronald Reagan and Jimmy Carter. In other words, people use all they have to use when decoding, applying their histories of consumption to each new text. As a result, DICTION becomes more useful the more often it is run. "Deviance," "singularity," and "representativeness" are, after all, comparative concepts and hence statistical concepts. As Nils Enkvist has said, "comparison is . . . the essence of all study of style" and so, to know one thing, a researcher must inevitably learn two things.[47] That is the very logic of the Campaign Mapping Project.

Most people who study politics do so at the grassroots level. They focus on individual politicians, on specific pieces of legislation, on some unique economic trend. Those who study political discourse do the same thing. They examine the new political documentary, the great inaugural address, the inept press conference, the peculiar media interview. Studies like these stay close to their texts; they are awash in details. This book, in contrast, hovers farther out, surveying its scene from an aerial perspective. But there can be advantage in doing so because hovering lets us see things in-the-large, trajectories suggested but not yet fully developed. Viewing politics from such a distance can be frustrating when it calls attention to the regularized and the recurrent, and away from the odd-but-fascinating. So be it. DICTION's limitations are also its strengths, and in that sense, it seems almost human.

CONCLUSION

Assembling a large database is both a blessing and a curse. Modern computers make it comparatively easy to run statistical tests on twenty thousand cases but that hardly ensures insight. Indeed, a large database can even be misleading since it encourages what statisticians call Type 1 error—the tendency to find spurious differences simply because so many cases are available for examination. I have guarded against that possibility as much as possible, but the ultimate value of this book lies in its questions, not in its answers. The statistical tests of difference applied here are largely descriptive and even then they are consigned to footnotes, freeing the reader to attend to the book's narrative. Eventually, perhaps, more elaborate mathematical models of political language can be built, but the emphasis here will be on basic questions: What makes a politician a politician? Have the media changed their behavior? In what ways are voters distinctive? What, if anything, has changed in the political arena over time? In short, while the modest statistical procedures used in *Campaign Voices* prohibit it from being the last word on these matters, my hope is that it will be a useful first word.

Quantifying political language requires tightrope walking since it is so easy to forget that the numbers stand as mute proxies for that most rich and subtle of stuff—human communication. The ability to fashion ideas into symbols and, later, into public policy is a miraculous process. Accordingly, throughout this book I will take pains to ground the statistical trends in the texts from which they derived and, with these examples, to say no more than good sense permits. The twenty-one individuals who have run for the presidency since 1948 deserve to have their words understood in all their complexity. No computer should be allowed to frustrate that mission and I shall try to see that that does not happen here.

CHAPTER 3

Campaign Evolution

Nₐₜᵢₒₙₐₗ politics in the United States reconstitutes itself every four years. Sometimes dramatically. The Cold War debates between John Kennedy and Richard Nixon now seem, at the dawn of Al Gore's millennium, positively quaint. With George Bush having been so successful in prosecuting the Gulf War, it is now hard to understand how Jimmy Carter could have lost his job to a mere ayatollah in 1980. Were Lyndon Johnson still among us, he might be surprised that a man from his own party could run for office in 1996 on a platform of entitlement cuts and reduced government spending. Dwight Eisenhower would be similarly perplexed that a creature from the House of Representatives would be chosen to fill in for Richard Nixon when the latter's exit was suddenly required. And it is almost impossible to imagine a conversation between Harry Truman and Ross Perot, although it is surely tantalizing to do so.

Time passes slowly, but politics itself is a swirling tempest. American politics seems especially prone to sudden shifts in attitude and demeanor and so a good case can be made that painting a large mosaic of the last fifty years is a fool's errand. Many would argue that each four-year cycle in presidential politics tells its own story and that gathering them together in a single narrative violates their essential autonomy. Surely that is the view of the psychobiographers who look within the individual leader, not within the culture, to determine what happens in politics and why.

I make a different assumption here. While I do not doubt the uniqueness of each presidency, I do assume that time shapes our horizons, our politics, our imaginations, our memories, our language. We each live in our own moment, yes, but we also live in a common moment, a cultural moment, and these moments shape how we expe-

---

With William Earnest

rience the time allotted us. We are, all of us, like Molière's bourgeois gentleman who suddenly became aware he had been speaking prose all his life. Had our gentleman made a more studied reflection of the matter he would have discovered that the prose he spoke came from his own imagination but also from the language habits of his contemporaries, the philosophical worldview of his times, and the geopolitical history to which his nation was heir. It was determined further by the small-scale exigencies of his job, his family, his schooling, and by grosser phenomena like region, class, economic structure, and a small army of political hegemonies.

And so this chapter will examine American politics broadly, looking back over the last fifty years for both the time-transcendent and the sudden reversal. What has changed in American political discourse? What has stayed the same? Why, and when? I seek out no grand periodizations here, since fifty years is too short a time to discover them and because individual differences among campaigns often cancel one another out. These preliminaries aside, I shall argue nonetheless that political times have changed in the United States and that these changes, while subtle, are both insistent and important. Further, I shall argue that these linguistic variations point to a number of political uncertainties vexing us as a nation, a fact that makes campaigns productive in their own right but also diagnostic of our political condition. That, at least, is the claim I shall make here.

POLITICAL CONSISTENCIES

Language is both a watch and a compass. It tells us what time it is and where we live. Politicians of yesteryear spoke of *halcyon* days; now, our days are *challenging*, as if life must be fought rather than lived. *Dudes*, on the other hand, is a word used by a most curious pair—western frontiersmen in the early 1800s and California surfers in the 1990s. This is to say that we speak our cultures unknowingly but almost always revealingly, as time and language become tied together in complicated ways. On some occasions, for example, language "lags" culture, as when elderly prefeminists call adolescent females *girls*. At other times language "paces" culture, as when hip-hop postfeminists call adult women *girls*. The paradigms of an age become impregnated in a society's language, says J. G. A. Pocock, leaving behind traces of assumed understandings and taken-for-granted social relations. Political language, according to Pocock,

> invokes values; it summarizes information; it suppresses the inconvenient; it makes certain kinds of statements and does so by means of formulations which can often convey several kinds of statement at once, while simultaneously diverting attention from others. . . . A political society contains a great variety of authority-structures, variously indicated and prescribed, and [so] the purpose of political activity—including political speech—is to appeal to numbers of these simultaneously, by means which can neither politically nor linguistically be identical.[1]

When studying political language, then, one is wise to adopt a subtle, yet dauntingly empirical, attitude. For example, even though scholars have found a steady drop in "denominational voting" in the United States from 1950 to the present, as well as a corresponding decline in people being "integrated into religious networks and exposed to the religious cues that can guide the vote,"[2] I found no meaningful difference in the use of Religious References between 1948 and 1996. This was true for politicians, media personnel, and letter-writers as well. Religious images, scriptural citations, and invocations of the deity are deployed roughly as often today as they were in the post–World War II period, and no political campaign has failed to use such language. Naturally, peaks and valleys to this usage can be found, with the 1960, 1976, and 1984 elections making heavy reference to God and the 1956, 1968, and 1992 campaigns cutting back on same (in each case, the three political voices—people, politicians, and press—followed each other's lead).

Stabilities like these are significant. As I have argued elsewhere, one of the defining features of the American experience has been how it has dealt with its civic-religious tensions.[3] Generally, it has done so rhetorically, institutionalizing a complex array of quasi-religious rules that have grown up around this rhetoric: It must be heartfelt but not confessional, frequent but not cloying; pointed but never sectarian. In the United States, at least, political rhetoric must avoid being overly religious, and religious rhetoric overly political. Those who violate these strictures (Billy James Hargis in the 1960s, Pat Robertson today) are marginalized, heard but not listened to. The data assembled here shows that this contract continues. While other studies find that religious allusions have sharply declined in general newspaper coverage, that is not true when votes are being solicited.[4] Campaigns return the nation to its basics.

Another essential: neither Patriotic (*freedom, citizenship, democracy*) nor Inspirational language (*authority, confidence, dedication, fortitude*) has varied dramatically over time. Such language found special favor in the Goldwater-Johnson contest of 1964 and then again when George Bush and Michael Dukakis adjudicated liberalism in 1988, but these are two lonely peaks in an otherwise flat trajectory. That is, despite the predictions one could make on the basis of 1950s folklore (the Communist Scare, and the like) or the later Red-baiting of the Reagan era, *God* and *country* have been mutually sustaining throughout recent presidential history. Stump speeches have averaged a dozen or so patriotic refrains during that time, and the average newspaper story has averaged slightly less than half that number; letters-to-the-editor lie somewhere in between. But it is the consistency of such usages that is most telling. As numerous scholars have argued, the American people have always been politically self-conscious, at times jingoistic, and campaigns often bring those feelings to the surface.[5] Why this is true is less clear: the relative youth of the nation? its physical isolation from much of the world? its lack of a common ethnicity? its political self-will? Whatever the reason, American political language has focused squarely on Americana.

A third stability: Human Interest language (*you, us, people, neighbors*) has not substantially changed over the years, nor has the language of Cooperation (*ally, brotherhood, coalition, communities*). As Carroll Arnold has argued, American politics has always been a curious blend of the Transcendental and the Pragmatic, but even more frequently has found its greatest resources in the mutuality of its people.[6] To be sure, with soaring crime rates and constant neighborhood dislocations, the American sense of community has been as much myth as reality, but that of course is the point: political campaigns become what Kenneth Burke calls "secular prayers," rhetorical attempts to make manifest that which is not yet manifestly true.[7] And so the following passage trots out a timeless text. Only pure guesswork could establish it as the property of Tom Dewey in 1948:

> In this campaign . . . I have talked with many people about many problems. Wherever I have gone I have repeated my belief—my unshakable belief—that for America no job is too big when we are a united people. I can report to you tonight that this is also the confident belief of our people. As a nation we are not looking backward; we are looking forward. We are looking ahead prayerfully and hopefully to a peaceful world. We are determined to make that peace secure by the strength that comes only from competent leadership expressing the will of a united people.[8]

There are bromides here but that, too, is the point. The image of neighbors pulling together has become entrenched, since the stark facts of life in the United States have often been unkind to genuine interdependence: the nation's material standard of value makes axiological coalescence difficult; its geographical breadth conspires against common identifications; its demographic variety makes strangers out of all Americans. Politics exists to contravene these facts. Political rhetoric exists to make those contraventions artful.

God, country, community. These are quintessential American consistencies, quintessential American prayers, and they point up the nation's strengths as well as its fault lines. They also show the political power of time itself, how precedents—even rhetorical precedents—can buoy a people up. These incantations are important not because they are true but because their performance is so consistent, so popularly sanctioned. Their regular pursuit makes a people a people and gives them political identity. On the American plan, at least, presidential elections are cyclical and these cycles build and rebuild a taste for a particular set of political values. The campaign rituals surrounding them champion the irreversibility of time, universal cultural meanings, and the significance of human agency. "Any of these ideas is contestable on ethnographic grounds," says Carol Greenhouse, "but that is beside the immediate point."[9] In the United States, it has been consistently beside the point.

Politics and time are bound up in complex ways. As Greenhouse also notes, "late medieval concepts of kingship in Europe divided the king into two 'bodies,' his natural body and the body politic. The natural body lived and dies, but the body politic was constant, 'by the grace of God.' "[10] Thus, says Greenhouse, European monarchs became identified with "history" (their natural life course) but only indirectly with "time" (transcendence itself). Chinese emperors, in contrast, were regarded with awe; they were creatures of time, not history. Given the United States' youth as a nation as well as its extraordinary size and complexity, neither time nor history has been in sufficient supply to give it an organic sense of community. Accordingly, commonweal had to be manufactured, and political campaigns have been part of that process. And so it is not surprising that optimism in the United States rises at four-year intervals coincident with presidential campaigns.[11] During these special moments of choosing, the American people have been united by their anticipations.

DECLINING ASSURANCE

In his magisterial work, *The Fifties*, David Halberstam surveys the United States of that decade, keying on the stability its people felt. The American people "lived in God's country," says Halberstam, "a land far from oceans and far from foreigners, and they were all-powerful in their own small towns." A landed people, Halberstam claims, has a republican bent, but according to him this bent is more sociological than ideological. Says Halberstam:

> Many had gone to college and returned home to succeed their fathers in family businesses. They had always controlled their political and economic destinies locally, and they presumed that by acting in concert with others like themselves in other small towns, they could control their national destiny. Earlier in the century they had regarded Taft, Hading, Coolidge, and Hoover as the guardians of their values in Washington; they had considered the nation's capital an extension of their own small towns.[12]

Such a people knew what they knew, did not give into whims, and were obdurate because the land on which they stood informed them. People who live in space, not time, have anchor points all about them and so they develop a distinctive political psychology: Trust the enduring, not the ephemeral; above all, know your location.

When he wrote his letter-to-the-editor of the *Salinas Californian* in 1964, R. W. knew his location. For him, the state of California was a civic entity and also a political topography. Each road, each hamlet, was suffused with political meaning and he used these meanings to order his world:

> From Santa Barbara on, Goldwater enthusiasm reaches a furor. It is a strange feeling for a Northern Californian to see Johnson supporters in the minority. As you drive southward Republican headquarters become beehives of activity. You see children of elementary school age; business men; housewives; senior citizens; teenagers; all these people crowding into Goldwater headquarters, and all working. Each person is sure that California will determine the next president. Each person is further convinced that his own precinct will determine California. Indeed these people are conducting more than a campaign, they are conducting a crusade. The sole purpose of that crusade is to elect Barry Goldwater president of these United States.[13]

For R. W., California politics was reduced to locality—Democrats in the Bay Area, Republicans nearer Los Angeles. These local understandings related to larger geopolitical truths of who lived where in the world and what those locations meant—allies in Europe, Communists to their east, trouble in Mexico, greater trouble farther south. A person with a map in 1964 could make political sense of the world.

Thirty years later, another letter was written to the *Californian*, but J. M. used psychology, not geography, to get his bearings:

> Colin Powell disgusts me. He is a Democrat who just wants to be in the Republican party. All of General Powell's social ideals fall in place on the Democrat side of the political spectrum. During his speech at the GOP convention I would not have been surprised if he denounced the Republican party and threw his support toward Bill Clinton. But he remained true to his former bosses, Ronald Reagan and George Bush,

not true to his ideals. In the military he is a leader, in politics he is a follower. . . . If Colin Powell hopes to effect change from within the Republican party, then he will have to live to be 200 years old. That's how long it may take for the conservatives who are firmly cemented to the GOP to agree with his positions on affirmative action, gun control, abortion, welfare, immigration, education, etc.[14]

J. M.'s letter has a contemporary ring when it reaches directly into Colin Powell's motival universe to discover his essential character. There is a certain cynicism here too, and that is also contemporary. The stabilities J. M. features—loyalty, leadership, integrity—are stabilities of the heart and the soul, not of the land. J. M.'s world is a modern world where satellites beam messages across vast spaces and where Sri Lankans and Nevadans become neighbors via the Internet. Television has allowed him to transcend vast spaces, and its intimacies have opened up the essential Colin Powell to him in ways that would have been unimaginable in 1964. J. M.'s is an interior rhetoric and he is comfortable with it.

In writing as they do, R. W. and J. M. tell the story of their particular moments in history. As figure 3.1 shows, the language of space declined consistently between 1948 and the present. The old charm of specific localities with their unique political traditions has given way to more cerebral matters. These localities still exist, of course, but they are now more backdrop than foreground, no longer featured in political commentary or in political case-making. CNN, housed in Atlanta, reports on the New Hampshire primary in a manner similar to that of CBS, housed in New York. And the New Hampshire primary is no longer itself, as candidates superimpose national agendas (abortion rights, the Bosnia peace accords) on the stalwart Yankees whose votes they solicit. "National television has no organic relationship to our lives," says Carey McWilliams, and so we are no longer afforded the indigenous "cue-giving" that once helped us know where we lived and what it meant to live there.[15] Instead, we are asked to pay attention to campaign strategy and depth psychology, as CBS's Bill Lagattuta demonstrated when reporting on the campaign scene in 1992:

I think the attacks will continue, Dan, most definitely. It's no secret that Ross Perot does not like George Bush; last night he really let him have

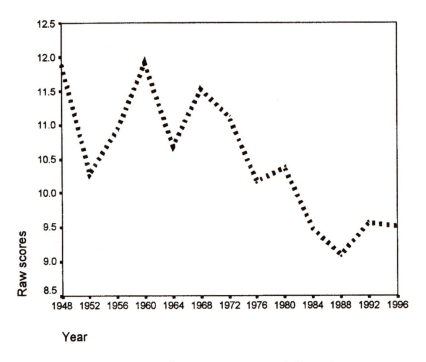

Figure 3.1. Spatial Terms across Time (All texts).

it. And tonight the campaign is preparing to unleash a brand-new round of Bush-bashing. What we're seeing is Ross Perot in the role of power broker. His intent last night at the joint appearance was unmistakable. Vote for me, Perot was saying, but if not me, then at least not George Bush.[16]

A metaphysics of place can be confining since nobody wishes to be thought provincial. But it can also keep abstractions grounded and help one get one's footing. Perhaps that is why a New Primitivism has made inroads recently, with urbanites seeking out places in the country they might have previously repudiated. According to Ralph Reed, modern Americans are looking for something else as well: "If [politicians] want to lead America into the 21st century, they need to quit talking like accountants and . . . start talking like moral leaders because that's what the American people are hungry for."[17]

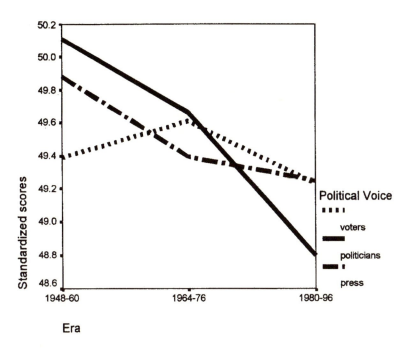

Figure 3.2. Certainty Scores across Time (Voices contrasted).

If such a hunger exists, it is a hunger fed by nostalgia, for figure 3.2 shows that the language of Certainty has declined sharply in the last fifty years, and that drop has been especially precipitous for political candidates. The "traditional warrants of leadership" have changed in the United States, says Stephen Skowronek, and they have not yet been replaced by a satisfactory alternative. Skowronek is quick to add—contra Reed—that the nation's leaders ought not suddenly become reactive by reaching back to "the classic claims of leadership authority that have endured despite their growing irrelevance."[18] Professor Skowronek need not worry, for the assurances that sustained the American people during the Second World War and the Korean conflict have given way to a self-referential, often confessional, style that trades authority for comradeship. Speaking of his wartime injuries during the 1996 campaign, Bob Dole exemplified that style:

It was a very difficult time in my life. I couldn't walk. I couldn't feed myself. I couldn't do anything. Well, I could have fed myself early, but we had some very attractive nurses, and it took me a long time to learn. So I'll confess I did drag it on a bit, but at any rate—I learned then about the generosity of the people of Michigan. They would come to visit us. They'd take us out for rides. They'd take us out for dinner. And I even got into the car business. I lined up a [car] with an Oldsmobile dealer in Battle Creek. And you could only have a car if you were a disabled veteran. Of course, I had a captive market in the hospital, and I was selling cars like mad, and I got 6 percent. But then the government said I couldn't do it anymore. I have always believed in free enterprise, just like you do.[19]

As is his wont, Senator Dole takes a serpentine route here, but he still manages to draw the voter in, displaying a few innocent warts (a certain flirtatiousness, a modicum of expediency) when making the following case: "I am no different from you; therefore I should lead you." This was the sound of leadership in 1996. Missing was a sense of distance between the candidate and the voter. In its place was a kinship based on the most ordinary of human foibles. Two other matters were completely unmentioned: (1) the extraordinary bravery that landed Mr. Dole in the hospital in the first place and (2) the connection between his hospitalization and his current political platform. That is, there is disclosure here but no argument. Mr. Dole charms his audience but persuades them to do nothing in particular.

Perhaps because we have become accustomed to such intimate language it is now hard to imagine an alternative to it. But even a moment's reflection will show what is missing in Dole's remarks: conceptual relevance; a clear plan of action; a sense of closure. Mr. Dole's language is attractive at first but it ultimately leaves one hungry.

Dwight Eisenhower, in contrast, was brought up in a different era, and his language signals that fact. He was rarely eloquent and almost never opened up in public. But on those few occasions when he did, he did so to forward an argument. Whereas Mr. Dole sold cars to his fellow patients, General Eisenhower advanced their cause more substantively:

Well, as you know, there came World War II and then finally Normandy. And out of all that—and of course you know I have been given different types of honors by all of the allied governments that were associated in that war—I think the greatest thing that I brought back from the war was the knowledge of friendship with thousands—literally hundreds of thousands—of GIs. I know of no single GI in all the A.E.F. who didn't believe that I was his friend, that I would try to do whatever I could for him as long as he lived; whether he stayed in the army or was a civilian, but especially if he were a disabled veteran. I promised also to those men to help care for the orphan and the widow whose father or whose husband never came home. I promised them I would always do my best for them. That promise still holds, and it doesn't make any difference where I am. I can be in civil life, a contented President of my university, or on a farm, or in a position of highest responsibility, but I shall never forget America's obligation to those veterans of all services.[20]

It is easy to ignore the differences between Dole and Eisenhower, but the decline in Certainty is too widespread and too pronounced to be dismissed easily. The differences in degree reported in figure 3.2 have become differences in kind, as the American people thrash about looking for candidates who sound like leaders rather than politicians. Most likely, they do not have a clear idea of what they are looking for (or what they find wanting in the current batch of candidates), but their occasional dalliances with Colin Powell, Pat Robertson, Jesse Jackson, and Ross Perot suggest they still have an ear for the language of traditional leadership, even in these most postmodern of times.

The absence of such a language may have consequences, since Norman Luttbeg and Michael Gant report a stark decline in political trust among the American people during the last fifty years. While no direct causal link can be established, the overlapping trend lines are suggestive. Luttbeg and Gant dismiss the usual explanations for the decline in trust—Watergate and Vietnam—and suggest that a more pervasive cultural shift is underway. They further report that political efficacy has also dropped off, that voters no longer feel they have influence over their government. They also note the following: "Such changes in political trust are particularly engaging when one considers that distrust of government was unheard of in the 1950s."[21]

Perhaps the American people at the turn of the century miss what they only faintly remember but, if that is true, they are being downright inconsistent since, as Ronald Inglehart reports, their overall regard for hierarchical, authority-based systems is in decline, both in the United States and in Western countries generally.[22] Does this mean that American voters want something they will not permit themselves to have? Are they nostalgic for ideas that stand still but unwilling to accept the political consequences of traditional authority? Perhaps a certain part of them thinks back fondly on a fellow like Harry Truman, who once wrote to his daughter, Margaret: "We are faced with exactly the same situation with which Britain and France were faced in 1938–39 with Hitler. Things look black. A decision will have to be made. I am going to make it."[23] Here is Certainty aplenty, but are the American people really willing to embrace the policies proceeding from the language Harry Truman spoke?

A final feature of declining assurance is the sharp drop in partisan allusions during the last fifty years. Political candidates are now three times less likely to make party-based references than they were in the 1950s. No such drop can be found among the letter-writers, who still use partisan markers regularly. The press lies somewhere in between, but generally follows the lead of the nation's political leaders. What are we to make of such findings? Should we rejoice at this rhetorical de-alignment and be pleased that "the business of the people" has finally transcended "petty partisan differences?" Or, more ominously, should we be concerned that a new kind of stealth politics has emerged and that the old stabilities of party and ideology no longer provide the political discipline the parties traditionally provided for the nation?

Ronald Lee takes up this latter possibility, observing that a New Politics has emerged in which "the answer is not an ideological program, nor a set of policies, but a state of emotional being. The president's capacity to radiate the moral fervor of 'The People' assures a virtuous state."[24] This is an attractive model and coincides with the phenomenological strengths of television, a medium especially well suited to building bridges between its performers and its at-home viewers. Television's ability to strip candidates bare flatters its viewers' abilities to read human personalities from a distance. For them, political parties are overweening and antiquated in contrast.

Psychological forces like these dramatically change the rhetorical dynamics of the modern presidential campaign. Even political ads are now devoid of partisan markers, focusing instead on characterological issues. Indeed, even though partisans could argue that the ACLU-coddling, Mexico-protective Democratic Party has been more permissive than the Republicans when it comes to recreational drugs, Republican ads in 1996 focused on the personal indiscretions of Bill Clinton, not on party ideology:

Announcer: Bill Clinton never took the drug crisis seriously.

Question: "If you had it to do it over again, would you inhale?"

Clinton: "Sure, if I could. I tried before."

Announcer: You know the result. Under Clinton's liberal policies, teen drug use has doubled. But now Clinton admits he was wrong.

Clinton: "I wish I'd never done any of that . . . uh . . . although I did such a little bit, but it was wrong."

Announcer: For the thousands of young Americans who became hooked on drugs under Clinton, his apology is too little, too late. America deserves better.[25]

What is one to make of a politics that is neither (1) grounded nor (2) firm nor (3) partisan? Many will be tempted to decry it as a politics unwilling or unable to stand up to the challenges that confront it. But that is too easy a gloss. The political rhetoric fashioned by the American people during the last fifty years has been fashioned out of both their inadequacies and their possibilities. American technologies have helped them transcend the spaces that once separated them, and so if their politics now has a virtual cast to it, that is largely because their lives are increasingly virtual as well. Yes, the rhetoric of the Cold War had its attractions, but are the American people willing to reestablish world Communism just to preserve a bracing discourse? Political parties add stability to politics but stabilities can quickly turn into fossils, and so there is a price to be paid there as well. As Stephen Skowronek has argued, "we are [now] witness to the waning of political time, to the practical disintegration of the medium through which presidents have claimed authority," and that is enough to make us instinctively reactionary. But we are ill advised, says Skowronek, to opt for some "dismal politics-as-usual" but must choose instead a politics "that is less familiar and more open-ended."[26] The data I have assembled here suggests that such a politics has now been found. But, one must ask, has that been fully pleasing to the American people?

INCREASING PERSONALIZATION

There are two key aspects of certainty: universality and institutionalism. Highly certain language is designed for all times and places, all conditions, and so it is not surprising that it found such favor during the Cold War when international politics was a binary affair and when the eternal debates between right and wrong seemed settled. Back then, institutions like the church, the family, the corporation, political parties, and government itself were rarely questioned (at least by today's standards) and politicians spoke easily, solemnly, about the Unquestionable. Their rhetoric was built out of confident distinctions folded into short, clipped sentences. Hubert Humphrey illustrates:

> Ten million people have come out of poverty in the last five years in America under this Administration and Mr. Nixon says he is not sure whether he is for these poverty programs. I know about it. He doesn't need to try to kid me. I know he is not for them. He never voted for them. There wasn't any war on poverty when he had something to say about this country. There wasn't any Federal Aid to Education. There wasn't any medical care for our elderly. There wasn't any consumer protection. And you know it. So, when you ask, is there any difference between the Democratic nominee, is there any difference between the Democratic nominee and the Republican, the answer is, all

the difference in the world—the difference in education, in health, in jobs, in the economy.[27]

If political assurance has declined, what has replaced it? The language of the self. As Bob Dole illustrated above, even a hard-bitten ironist can be reduced to gut-spilling by the pressures of modern campaigning. During the last twenty years we have seen those personal disclosures accumulate: in 1984 Mario Cuomo lionized his father's sinewy hands at the Democratic National Convention; four years later Ann Richards spoke of her Baptist upbringing and the sound of dominoes clacking on Sunday afternoons; in 1992 Bill Clinton reflected on his undershorts; and in 1996 Liddy Dole electrified the Republican convention by declaring that she loved her husband. Even a stiff patrician like George Bush was made to see the light. When asked in 1988 if he had learned anything in particular from his Democratic opponent, Michael Dukakis, Mr. Bush responded on cue:

> Barbara and I were sitting there before the Democratic convention, and we saw the governor and his son on television the night before, and his family and his mother who was there. And I'm saying to Barbara, "You know, we've always kept family as a bit of an oasis for us." You all know me, and we've held it back a little. But we use that as a role model, the way he took understandable pride in his heritage, what his family means to him.
>
> And we've got a strong family and we watched that and we said, "Hey, we've got to unleash the Bush kids." And so you saw 10 grandchildren there jumping all over their grandfather at the, at the [Republican] convention.[28]

Harry Truman would have been positively mystified by Bush's comments, as well as by my findings that self-references in political discourse have increased significantly during the last twenty years. Truman's old distinctions of matter and manner have fallen away, overwhelmed by an onslaught of Jerry Springer shows and White House trysts. By now, *L'état, c'est moi* has become a universal political motto, as fulsome biographies and homey photo opportunities fill a void created by the now-absent campaign white paper. Were he confronted with Jimmy Carter's lustful heart, Ronald Reagan's colonoscopy, and the "distinguishing characteristics" allegedly found in Bill Clinton's nether regions, Harry Truman would have been unnerved. In response, he might have uttered a banality: "You see the thing you have to remember. When you get to be president, there are all those things, the honors, the twenty-one gun salutes, all those things, you have to remember it isn't for you. It's for the Presidency, and you've got to keep yourself separate from that in your mind. If you can't keep the two separate, yourself and the Presidency, you're in all kinds of trouble."[29]

Given Truman's concerns, why has American politics gone personal? A number of possibilities exist: (1) *cultural*—buoyed by the attractions of Conscsiousness III, Esalen encounter groups, and Rogerian therapy, the 1960s and 1970s created an insatiable appetite for full disclosure (often called "authenticity"); (2) *psychological*—performed as they are under the klieg lights, campaigns now create enormous emotional pressures on candidates, inviting them to respond cathartically to their circumstances; (3) *political*—because it is easier to manage a candidate's persona than construct a foreign policy, settle a labor-management dispute, or take a strong stand on such powderkeg issues as abortion or affirmative action, there is also considerable strategic advantage to going personal. *Narrative* concerns provide a fourth explanation: the mass media now dominate political campaigns, and their dramatistic appetites must be satiated. Purging the emotions televises well (it makes little difference which emotions), and even dour candidates (Lloyd Bentsen and Bob Dole come to mind) become intriguing when their hearts are opened wide. Talking about oneself is a natural obsession, and television takes advantage of it.

Thomas Patterson has found that media reportage today features the voice of the reporter, the omniscient narrator, rather than the thoughts and ideas of the nation's political leaders.[30] Other researchers find that the average "sound bite" accorded politicians has declined over time.[31] All of this may be true, but that does not mean that the politician's persona has disappeared. My data show a sharp rise in Leader References in the press, a trend beginning in 1964–1976 and then ratcheting up a notch in 1980–1996. How can these data be reconciled? How can politicians be there and not there at the same time? A thoroughly ordinary story about the 1996 presidential race shows how:

> As the polls showed the race getting closer, the president was energized, cheered on by massive crowds much the same way Michael S. Dukakis was four years ago. By the weekend, however, the mania was replaced by a sense of resignation among Bush aides: What would be would be.
>
> Bush himself insisted to [Larry] King that he has "literally not thought about losing" and compared this final campaign of his as being behind in sports but playing your best every moment. But the president knows that many Republicans, in his own camp and out, believed two weeks ago that he had given up, that his curiously passive performance in the first two debates was a clear sign he believed, even if he never told anyone so, that his presidency was lost.
>
> "I've had some criticism from our own people," Bush said Friday night to people who asked, " 'What the heck. Has this guy lost his fight?' My not being out there slugging back made people wonder, 'Does the president got the, you know, has George Bush really got the drive to do this?' "
>
> Bush said he revived himself, and the conventional wisdom that the race was already over two weeks ago apparently helped him to do it. "I don't like it, being written off, especially by the Republicans," he told King, "I don't like it one bit. . . . Having been decreed 'dead and buried,' " Bush said, "it makes me say I'm going to show they're wrong."[32]

Several things are noteworthy here. For one thing, news stories now interpolate candidates' thoughts and action, using a few quotations here and there to flesh out the larger argument intended for the story. In the case above, for example, the *Washington Post* enters directly into the presidential mind. There is no "news" here in the classic sense—actions taken, programs endorsed—but the story is interesting nonetheless. One might also note that Mr. Bush's direct quotations are themselves awash in self-references, thereby making the story introspective ("Has this guy lost his fight?"), ruminative ("I don't like it, being written off"), and precursory ("It makes me say I'm going to show they're wrong."). And so a news hole has been filled even though no news has been reported, and the president has received coverage even though he has done nothing presidential.

What might one expect when disclosive politicians are paired with a personality-obsessed press? A natural symbiosis, perhaps, but then one must confront Martin Wattenberg's data: Between 1952 and 1988 there has been a steady decline in candidate popularity in the United States, and that has been true for both losing candidates and winning candidates. So, for example, Dwight Eisenhower won his first term with 70 percent popularity but George Bush mustered only 53 percent several decades later. Their rivals for the presidency, Adlai Stevenson and Michael Dukakis, scored 60 percent and 50 percent, respectively. Even more distressing, Wattenberg finds that these drops in popularity held true for both opponents and supporters of the candidates.[33] That is, we are getting to know our candidates but are not enjoying what we are learning. As if to add insult to injury, Shanto Iyengar reports that "episodic framing"—news stories focusing on candidates' private actions and motives rather than on deep-seated social or economic conditions—draws voters' attention away from broad-based, systemic concerns and toward transitory (often irrelevant) political issues.[34] And so, despite the narrative attractions of personality politics, it may be creating a dissatisfied and undereducated electorate.

Another piece of data is relevant to this discussion: especially since 1964, the language of Satisfaction (*comfort, enjoy, excitement, nurture*) has replaced the language of Inspiration (*commitment, dedication, honor, hope*) in politicians' remarks. The result is that the old pieties have given way to more immediate, and more empirical, gratifications. So, for example, Adlai Stevenson once deployed the traditional Democratic trope of increased educational benefits when declaring, "In our hearts we know that the horizons of the New America are as endless as its promise, as staggering in its richness as the unfolding miracle of human knowledge. America renews itself with every forward thrust of the human mind."[35] There is an archness here, a stiffness, that rings oddly in the modern ear. We have become accustomed to a more human touch, one that puts people in the center of things. Also speaking of education, Bill Clinton obliges: "I have asked the American people to join with me in building a bridge to the twenty-first century, a bridge that we can all walk across together, a bridge that will be strong enough to realize our dreams for the future, to give every child a chance to live up to his or her God-given potential. And I want you to help me build that bridge. Will you do that?"[36]

A parallel trend can be found in media coverage: Over time, the press has significantly increased its use of Voter References. When that datum is combined with the media's growing fascination with political personalities, the press's essential story line becomes clear: all politics can be reduced to relationships—among political leaders, among party professionals, among the citizenry. We have now become so accustomed to this story that it is hard to imagine an alternative to it. We expect to find reportage littered with polling studies, class-based voting reports, stories of gender and racial politics. As Joseph Turow has observed in connection with mass advertising, the American experience has turned into a kaleidoscope of experiences;[37] governance too has become more sociological than ideological. Again, this makes campaigns interesting for readers, but one wonders if something is lost when political ideas are replaced by sociograms or when bloc voting, and bloc reporting, hold sway:

> The 1996 presidential election in large part is a referendum on whether Clinton has fought his way back to become the national advocate for the economic interests and cultural values of ordinary Americans. But the fits and starts of his policies—and the changing shades of his public image—leave a middle-class record laced with contradictions. Clinton, in the view of Republican challenger Robert J. Dole, wooed the middle class with a promise of a tax cut that he abandoned as soon as the votes were counted.[38]

Stephen Skowronek observes that the United States has now entered an era of plebiscitary politics, an era that allows presidents to appeal to voters over the heads of Washington's elites.[39] My argument here is that the press, particularly, has conspired with presidents in this regard. Both have their eyes on the same target—the hearts and minds of the American people (but mostly their hearts). Both have reduced politics to its most human level, and this can be seen as a sign of increased democratization: a language of the people, a government of the people. But one must also reckon with what may have been lost over the years: comfort with a set of overarching verities; willingness to embrace a politics of ideas; the courage to risk unpopularity if popularity becomes a trap. The rhetorical trajectories sketched out here are hardly definitive, and their effects may be subtle. But collectively they are robust, and cumulatively they may have impact. For these reasons alone they deserve our scrutiny.

INCREASING COMPLEXITY

Figure 3.3 tells an impressive story: For all three campaign voices, Familiarity has plummeted dramatically and consistently over time. The Familiarity dictionary consists of forty-four simple words that C. K. Ogden calculates to be the most common words in the English language.[40] Included are prepositions (*across, over, through*), demonstrative pronouns (*this, that*), interrogative pronouns (*who, what*), and a variety of particles, conjunctions, and connectives (*a, for, so*). To Ogden's way of thinking, it is almost impossible to communicate in the English language without using these pedestrian tokens. My findings here suggest that political campaigns are now attempting the impossible.

Why has Familiarity dropped so precipitously? One possibility is immediately available: the dramatic technological advances made in the United States during the last fifty years. People now carry a passel of electronic identification cards; some new technical marvel is described in the press each day; programming a VCR occurs in the living room, programming the microwave oven in the kitchen; the nonscientists at cocktail parties now talk like scientists and the nonlawyers like lawyers. Experiences like these make it easy to accept Raymond Gozzi's findings that 45 percent of all new words in the English language are technical in nature. Biological and chemical terms head Gozzi's list, but he also finds mathematical, medical, computer, electronic, pharmaceutical, military, and environmental words pouring into the nation's lexicon each day.[41] As Jacques Ellul predicted thirty years ago, Westerners have fallen madly for Technique, thereby producing "the most artificial world that ever existed"[42] and opening themselves up to a new set of modernist myths.

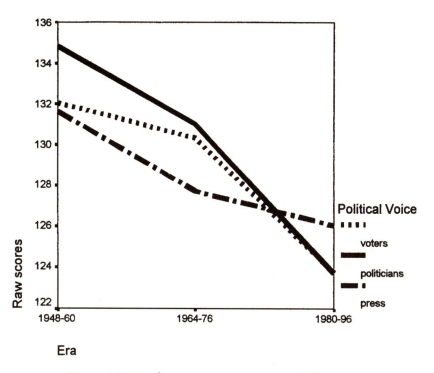

Figure 3.3. Familiarity Scores across Time (All texts).

These myths have infiltrated politics as well. When Bill Clinton spoke of building a bridge to the twenty-first century his metaphor reflected the zeitgeist of his age. Mr. Clinton also imagined putting computers in every grade school classroom and insisted that every American youngster go at least as far as community college. In doing so, Clinton became but the most recent avatar of Technique. For him, it was now possible to think oneself out of all political problems, either by deploying high-tech weapons in the Persian Gulf or by Ethernetting the entire inner city. Not surprisingly, then, Numerical Terms have increased dramatically for politicians and Cognition terms for the press during the last fifty years. The result? A confident, precise vocabulary that reduces all axiological matters to technical considerations: "The question is not whether we should move forward but how much it will cost"; "our will is beyond question; we just need the means to secure our bounties"; "we can reach the stars if we can but measure the distance."

67

More than anyone else on the political scene, Ross Perot epitomized the new politics of technique. He made his millions with computerization and systematization and by delivering goods and services to an increasingly complex network of state and federal bureaucracies. Unlike the independent candidates before him, Perot did not appeal to ideologues, as did George Wallace, nor did he appeal to the thinking crowd, the social do-gooders, as did John Anderson. Instead, Perot's constituency was made up of fairly well-educated suburbanites, ex-military personnel, and voters disheartened by the antediluvian commitments of the two major parties. Modernists that they were, Perot supporters were convinced that a better mousetrap could be built if a professional maker of mousetraps were given the job.[43] In that sense Perot's supporters were revolutionaries. Incrementalism held no appeal for them; only massive structural changes would do (modernism has always been about structures). And so when he spoke to his followers, Mr. Perot spoke a language that was essentially apolitical:

> OK, now, since this is just imploding our job base and our tax base, which would give us the ability to balance our budget and pay our debt, why did both parties—and I mean they were bound at the hip on this one—pass these stupid trade bills? I'm for fair, free trade. I'm against stupid trade. This is stupid trade.
>
> Well, you know the answer, and I want to make sure that all the American people know the answer—the special interests who paid for their campaigns and all that glitz you saw last week and you'll see next week. Our conventions cost about $800,000 together. They spent over $30 million on theirs. I think ours are better than theirs.
>
> Don't you think if we had that kind of plain thinking in Washington, if we can do—keep in mind I remember last—in '92, they had spent $20 million, $30 million a piece. We had spent $1.5 million getting petitions signed. I think we've made the point that we're more cost effective than they are.[44]

A technocratic rhetoric is hardly pretty. Numbers sing no hymns, "plain thinking" is, well, plain, and words like *implosion, job base,* and *balanced budget* exhaust the poetic possibilities of physics. But language of this sort makes sense when ultimate terms—*human rights, citizenship, justice,* and *equal opportunity*—seem precarious, undecidable. During such times, says Stephen Skowronek, a rhetoric of technique can submerge "the difficult issues of substance that tend to accumulate among the commitments of long-established regimes."[45] That is, a people may not be able to agree on right and wrong, but more and less may be an easier judgment. The ability to make such judgments was part of Jimmy Carter's appeal, says Skowronek, and more recently, Al Gore had a gift for making rationality comforting. But one wonders how comforting it can be in the long run, especially when contrasted to the now-distant eloquence of Adlai Stevenson:

> In the few minutes we are together this afternoon I want to talk to you about the people who run their own farms, keep store, work for themselves. These people are an issue in this campaign. Their prosperity, possibly even their existence is being threatened. They are threatened by what a great man and a great Justice of the Supreme Court once called "the curse of bigness." They are in danger of being swallowed up by big corporations in alliance with big government in a world which has become dangerously indifferent to the fate of the little man.
>
> This threat of bigness shows itself in many forms. It shows itself in the struggle of the farmer to survive, in the fact that the family farmer in many parts of our country has his back to the wall. It shows itself in the tendency for big business to become bigger and for the small businessman to be squeezed out. This force shows itself in the tendency to build an America so massive and so impersonal that the ordinary individual feels dwarfed and powerless in the shadow of bigness. The danger is not new. Bigness has been on the verge of triumph before. But always when the danger was greatest a leader appeared who spoke for the ordinary man—the small farmer, the small businessman, the worker.[46]

Stevenson's is a homely rhetoric and it hearkens back to an era when God was in His sky and when the Democratic Party meant exactly what Mr. Stevenson said it meant—solutions for problems that would not go away. Since his time, the problems have gotten more complicated and the solutions more limited. But that does not mean that campaign discourse has become feckless. Quite the contrary. For politicians and press alike, campaign language is now much higher on Variety (use of many different words); it is increasingly preoccupied with the here-and-now; and it has become especially concerned with matters of Time (versus Space). There is something almost Sartrean about these developments: the past recedes as the existenz presses upon us; we are cut adrift, lost in a sea of time. But if this effect is Sartrean, it postdates Sartre since the sharpest rise in Variety, Temporal References, and Present Concern occurred in the 1980–96 time period. Once again, Bill Clinton—that adolescent of a president—epitomizes the temporal anxiety of his age:

> *Tuesday*, October 1st, 10 million Americans will get a pay raise *when* the minimum wage goes into effect because Senator Kennedy worked and Senator Kerry helped him and we got a minimum wage increase. It was the right thing to do.
>
> Well, we've been here a *long time* and I know you want to go home, and I don't want to take a lot of *your time*. But I want to say something especially to the *young people* here *tonight*. . I want to tell you something about being on the right side of *history*. And I want you to think about it seriously just for a *minute*.
>
> Once in a *generation* or so our people in our *long* march of democracy have been confronted with a set of decisions that are so profound that they will affect how we live and how we relate to each other and the rest of the world for a very *long time*. This is *that sort of time*. We are being asked, basically because of the differences between ourselves and our opponents, to decide two fundamental questions about what we're going to be like *when we go* roaring into the *21st century*. No matter what happens, those of us that are well-prepared, especially our *young* people, will have more chances to live out our dreams than any *generation* of Americans has ever had.[47]

Let us take a moment to recapitulate the existential drift of this chapter: a decrease in assurance; an obsession with the Self; an on-rush of technocracy; temporal anxiety, a crowded agenda. Has modernism not indeed collapsed upon us? Let us also recapitulate how this conclusion has been arrived at: A computer has been told to look, rather randomly, for certain groups of words in press coverage, party documents, and letters-to-the-editor. The texts were not searched for profound philosophical insights nor were they asked to be self-interpreting. The computer simply reported that some words have been used more often than others during the last fifty years. The results suggest that a new kind of political discourse has grown up among us, a less confident, less rooted discourse. And here is an intriguing adjunct: the language of Motion (*accelerate, embark, haste, launch*) has risen even as the language of Space has declined. That is, in politics today we are moving constantly but going nowhere in particular.

The result of these changes is subtle. It is subtle because people grow up in a particular culture at a particular time and unconsciously pick up its folkways. Because this learning is so incremental it results in taken-for-granted knowledge: a given discourse may, by objective standards, be presentistic, varied, and the like, but if it is truly a product of its age it will appear unremarkable. One such unremarkable text is the following:

> *PBS*: Vice President George Bush had kind words today for the Dukakis acceptance speech in Atlanta last night. At a news conference in Milwaukee, he said it was a good speech, but he had this to say about the differences between Dukakis and his running mate.

> *Bush*: Now the interesting debate is going to be the debate between Lloyd Bentsen and Gov. Dukakis. Now if he's suggesting that Bentsen can change his views on gun control, that's good. That would be an effective use for Lloyd Bentsen. If he's suggesting that he can convince Gov. Dukakis never to have a furlough program that will furlough a man like Willie Horton again, never again, that would be good. That would show that Bentsen was doing what Gov. Dukakis said last night. If he can convince Gov. Dukakis that, you know, the values that he has are not in accord with being "a card carrying member of the ACLU," then maybe that's a good role for Sen. Bentsen, and on and on it goes, Jerry. The differences are enormous.

> *PBS*: Bush also said he didn't mind that polls showed him trailing Dukakis, saying he had never thought it would be a cakewalk. He added, "I do better when I come from behind fighting back."[48]

At first inspection, the above passage seems thematic. But a closer look finds a bouillabaisse of issues: George Bush, Michael Dukakis, the Democratic convention, a Milwaukee news conference, Lloyd Bentsen, gun control, Willie Horton, the ACLU, ideological differences, campaign polling, pugnacity, and someone named Jerry. But despite the seams in this highly fractured text, we take it in whole. It has a kind of energy that moves us along without boring us. And yet it also seems fair to ask how one could learn anything from this report other than the essential campaign dialectic: Bush versus Dukakis yesterday, Bush versus Dukakis today. That is, there is really no news here. Instead, the broadcast's producers have assumed that (1) viewers have short attention spans; (2) they like to be entertained, and, failing that, they at least want to be kept busy; (3) they are bored by anything longer than a day old; and (4) they like conflict.

Frenzy, in other words, has become central to modern politics. It is also central to modern television. Situation comedies, cartoon shows, sporting events—as well as the news—are hyperkinetic texts featuring something different each moment. Judging by television's popularity, the formula works. Accordingly, campaigners, too, have committed the formula to memory. As George Bush shows above, a good sound bite packs as much information and attitude into whatever time is available. If necessary, information can be sacrificed to attitude.

When Bill Clinton sermonized about the twenty-first century during the 1996 campaign, he was responding to more than a need for sloganeering. Time urgency was part of his cultural circumstance. Reinhart Koselleck traces this anxiety to the Enlightenment's concern for the New, the Scientific,[49] while Joseph McGrath and Janice Kelly sees it as a psychological, not an intellectual, matter. They define "temponomic" personalities as persons for whom time is money, "who see time as passing more quickly than it actually does" and who become highly anxious as a result.[50] Uri Merry views industrialization, with its fast "rates of transformational crises and chaos," as the primary contributor to our sense of urgency.[51]

Whatever the reason, political discourse has been transformed during the last fifty years and these changes now seem both natural and unremarkable to us. Because we have internalized them so thoroughly, it is hard to read the following passage at one sitting. It contains none of the lexical features described in this section. It is thematic from beginning to end; it is neither abbreviated nor filled with random motion; it contains no sudden transitions or false leads; its direct quotations are a meal, not a bite. Without question, it is a news report from another age:

A strong and consistent foreign policy based upon the premises that peace cannot be achieved by appeasing Russian aggression and that the United States, for its own security, must help strengthen free governments in all parts of the world was promised tonight by Gov. Thomas E. Dewey of New York.

The Republican candidate for President spoke at a campaign rally in Mormon Tabernacle on the tenth anniversary of the signing of the Munich pact surrendering the Sudetenland of Czechoslovakia to Germany. He said that the lesson of Munich, as to the futility of attempting to appease an aggressor, must never be forgotten.

"There must not be another Munich," he declared solemnly.

Mr. Dewey asserted that the best way to get along with Russia was to deal with Soviet leaders as "strong equals" and by doing so to "restore their respect for us."

"It is not too late," he added, "to develop and pursue a consistent and effective foreign policy and to make the Soviet understand that, just as we intend to deal fairly and honestly with others, so we insist that others must deal fairly and honestly with us."

Mr. Dewey promised that his administration, if he is elected, would wage peace with all the vigor, imagination, skill and energy with which the war was waged.[52]

CONCLUSION

This chapter has moved across a grand sweep of time and ignored the details of individual elections. Its approach has been more cultural than historical, an attempt to tease out gross changes in campaign politics. As we have seen, there have been stabilities too: God, country, and community are stressed as often today as they were in

1948. But the differences are more profound and more intriguing. The press, the people, and their leaders no longer speak as confidently; their talk is shot through with careful distinctions and qualifications. They speak for the moment, not for the ages, as if all truths now must be negotiated and then renegotiated. The clear, bright voice of Harry Truman is gone.

His voice has been replaced by a lively intimacy. We now get to know civic leaders and news personalities well, although such knowledge has not led to liking: public opinion polls show that politicians and the press now battle one another for the lowest ranks of public regard. The reason for that opprobrium may lie with the individuals themselves but it may also lie with the era: things move quickly today, and community is a fleeting thing. Campaign language reflects both qualities. Homespun is out, technocratic in; the pressures of time goad us constantly; politics is not about one or two things but about many things. It is too strong to say that the United States is now rootless, but its discourse no longer features the specific places that once helped orient us. We live somewhere, but where?

The story of modern politics has more to it than this. The transformations sketched out here have been rendered in bold strokes; more can be learned by attending to the details. It is noteworthy, for example, that many of the changes outlined here were not true of the letter-writers. The voice of the people seems to have a greater constancy to it and the implications of that fact will be explored in chapter 8. Too, we need to know how the various campaign forums (conventions, debates, stump speeches, and ads) differ from one another and how broadcast and print news open up the world of politics differently. Historical time is important, but so too are incumbency, party, and pedigree, factors to be explored in greater depth as well. The political changes noted in this chapter have helped make politics what it is today but other forces are also at work. To those forces we now turn.

* CHAPTER 4 *

Campaign Functions

E<small>LECTIONS</small> elect people but what do campaigns do? This question
is not completely simpleminded. A presidential campaign is a long,
drawn-out affair beginning in the snows of New Hampshire and ending in autumnal splendor. In between, it subjects the American people to smiling candidates and ill-tempered reporters, gaggles of pundits and prognostication, marching bands and fifteen-second spots,
an array of twinkling flashbulbs. Even though presidential campaigns
are eagerly anticipated for four years at a time, by early November
few Americans wish for more politicking. Campaigns come and campaigns go but they never go quickly enough. Yet what do they do?

Assessing the overall purpose of campaigning is not easy for several
reasons: (1) each campaign seems unique—different candidates, different times—making generalizations about them risky; (2) life itself
refuses to stop during campaigns, thereby making it hard to sort out
campaign effects from, say, the effects of the Vietnam War (in 1968)
or the effects of the Iran hostage crisis (in 1976); (3) distinguishing
stimulus and effect can also be difficult: Did television come to the
aid of John Kennedy in 1960 or did Mr. Kennedy teach television
how to cover a political campaign? Did the 1972 Democratic primary
make George McGovern a radical or did the general campaign make
him a centrist? Was George Bush or Ronald Reagan responsible for
getting George Bush elected in 1988? Did a good economy reelect
Bill Clinton in 1996 or did his campaign heighten the importance of
economic matters in the minds of the American people?

There are, of course, many ways to describe campaign processes.
Political anthropologists tell us that any civic ritual can build bonds
of community, of mutuality, and there is some evidence that campaigns do just that.[1] Political psychologists tell us that campaigns

---

With Erika Allen and Mark Peterson

"prime" us to become concerned about some issues and not others, thereby affecting our position-taking.[2] Political philosophers, particularly those of a Leftist stripe, argue that campaigns spread false consciousness, making voters feel empowered when they are, in fact, mere factotums in a Grand Spectacle.[3] More conservative scholars argue that campaigns, when run correctly, foster rationality, thereby building the political legitimacy and battle-tested ideas a regime must have to survive.[4] And communication scholars have shown how campaigns help a society adjust to its future as it passes new information and habits from person to person to person.[5]

My business here is a different business. I shall approach the matter of campaign functions inductively, looking at particular language effects to see what larger tale they might tell. A primitive campaign function might be revealed, for example, when a sitting president hits the campaign trail. Do the demands of electioneering change how he behaves, or does he simply superimpose his Oval Office habits atop the campaign? Similarly, do incumbents and challengers behave differently? If so, do their differences reflect how innovative, or how traditional, a campaign must be? Similarly, do winners and losers speak distinct languages or do they differ only on the basis of how much money they raise or how hard their staffs work to get them elected? Alternatively, if victory can be linked to a certain set of language habits, what does that say about the electorate's expectations for how campaigns ought to be run? And what of pedigree and ideology? Does a candidate's personal background and prior experience change his or her campaign style? Finally, one can ask these questions: How far from the norm can a candidate stray during the campaign? Do the American people know what they want to hear even before they hear it or are they genuinely open to something new every four years?

The answers to these questions suggest that campaigns serve four distinct functions. Because my evidence is language based, the functions I identify differ from traditional understandings. But that is the value of rhetorical data. Because language is so easily underestimated, it can shed new light on old pathways. To say that "elections elect" seems clear enough, but to say that "campaigns campaign" is to say too little. I offer four more precise statements here.

The Immediacy Function

Judged by contemporary standards, Dwight Eisenhower was not an easy man to listen to. Columnist Merriam Smith described his style as "formal and wooden," his sentence structure "complicated and hard to follow."[6] Author John Steinbeck complained that Ike had no "ability to take any kind of stand on any subject," a man whose mind would instinctively "crumble into uncertainty, retire into generalities."[7] Ostensibly, Mr. Eisenhower's rhetorical liabilities were known even to himself. When confronting a particularly difficult press conference one day, Eisenhower calmed his staffers by saying he "would just confuse the reporters."[8] As if to give evidence to such charges, here is President Eisenhower on defense planning:

> Let me tell you how we approached this analysis. We did not set any fixed sum of money to which our defense plans had to be fitted. We first estimated what is truly vital to our security. We next planned ways to eliminate every useless expenditure and duplication. And we finally decided upon the amount of money needed to meet this program. Such an analysis rejects the extreme arguments of enthusiasts and of all groups of special pleaders both in and out of the military services. But I assure you what has been done so carefully evolved as a sound program. It contemplates in each of the armed forces calculated risks which have been prudently reasoned. And it represents, in our combined judgment, what is best for our nation's permanent security. There is, I believe, only one honest, workable formula. It is not magical, but it is the best that competent men can define. It is this: a defense strong enough both to discourage aggression and beyond this to protect the nation— in the event of any aggression—as it moves swiftly to full mobilization.[9]

These remarks were delivered by President Eisenhower from the Oval Office and they show him to be made of right angles. Eisenhower is here the macrotactician that he was during the war—the spare, efficient chooser of words. His self-interruptions, dependent clauses, passive voice, and subjunctive moods conspire to make his statements entirely rational, eminently sensible, but they do not produce an Eisenhower Moment. And if that is Dwight Eisenhower, who is this?

Well, first of all, let me say this: I belong to a family of boys who were raised in meager circumstances in central Kansas, and every one of us earned our way as we went along, and it never occurred to us that we were poor, but we were. My workweek the last year before I went to West Point was 84 hours, 7 nights a week, 12 hours a night, and I thought I had a good job. Now, when I see what unions have done for the working man of America as compared to that record, you can well imagine that I don't have to have any doubt in my mind as to what they have done for America as a whole. . . . So I believe that if the laboring man today—and that really should include all Americans when you come down to it, we all ought to be laboring for our living and most of us do—if they will look at the record, I think they will find nothing here that they can say this administration is their enemy; on the contrary, they are good friends.[10]

There is run-on syntax and circumlocution here, but there is also a charming transparency, a humanity one does not find in his earlier remarks. Eisenhower becomes Ike here, at least for a time, and in so doing traces out the effect for presidents generally. When the remarks of sitting presidents were compared to their campaign addresses, dramatic increases were found in Self-Reference, Present Concern, Motion, Activity, and Realism. That is, their stump remarks took on an unmistakable energy and immediacy, as if the campaign had reached out to them—and into them—commanding their direct involvement with the people they govern. The abstractions on which working presidents depend—balance of powers, executive privilege, inflation and recession, states' rights—are modulated too, replaced by an unmistakable directness. But high Realism scores do not preclude poetic flourishes. Powerful imagery is often manufactured out of concrete referents. Dwight Eisenhower, that Spartan of a poet, illustrates:

Ladies and gentlemen, when Abraham Lincoln was nominated in 1860, and a committee brought the news to him at his home in Springfield, Illinois, his reply was two sentences long. Then, while his friends and neighbors waited in the street, and while bonfires lit up the May evening, he said simply, "And now I will not longer defer the pleasure of

78

taking you, and each of you, by the hand." I wish I could do the same—speak two sentences, and then take each one of you by the hand, all of you who are in sound of my voice. If I could do so, I would first thank you individually for your confidence and your trust. Then, as I am sure Lincoln did as he moved among his friends in the light of the bonfires, we could pause and talk a while about the questions that are uppermost in your mind.[11]

When remarks like these are contrasted to the deadly stuff sometimes delivered from the Oval Office, one almost wishes that campaigns would never end. Rhetorically, at least, elections function just as the Founders envisioned (particularly the Hamiltonians among them): they inspire a gentle regicide, stripping the president of his grandeur (by increasing his Self-References), forcing him to lay out his plans in easily understood ways (via Realism), denying him the refuge of grand theory and bureaucratic distinctions. It is easy to become cynical when watching presidents "return to the people" in these ways. But if this be cynicism, it is a democratic cynicism, one born of the need for leader and follower to periodically renew their compact. George Bush was rarely accused of being overly clear when serving as president, for example, but the 1992 campaign changed that, driving down his Complexity scores (as campaigns do for all sitting presidents), and extracting from him a clarity and directness not seen in the White House. Declared Mr. Bush in his 1992 acceptance speech: "Governor Clinton and Congress want to put through the largest tax increase in history, but I won't let it happen. Governor Clinton and Congress don't want kids to have the option of praying in school, but I do. Clinton and Congress don't want to close legal loopholes and keep criminals behind bars, but I will."[12]

As we see here with George Bush, campaigns make politicians' thoughts crisper and more pungent. Some observers complain that campaigns also produce bromides and elisions, but that makes sense too—bromides for the things that ail a democratic people, elisions because something is always left unsaid in a large and diverse society. The alternative to campaign language is Government Speak, a language rife with abstractions and nominalizations. There is little doubt that George Bush performs important governmental work in the following passage, for example, but there is also little doubt that his remarks were not delivered on the stump:

> Limited *manufacture* or *importation* for *purposes of export* or for sale to Government agencies would be authorized, but such *large-capacity devices*, like a firearm today, would be subject to identification by requiring serial numbers. While *an ammunition feeding device*, like a firearm itself, is not inherently evil, the *enhanced potential for danger* to law-abiding citizens posed by the unlawful use of weapons equipped with such devices in criminal hands makes it necessary to impose these restrictions in the interest of *public safety.*
>
> Fourth, my proposal would establish a nationwide program of mandatory drug testing for defendants on *post-conviction revised release*. It is estimated that upwards of 81,000 individuals will be on some form of *Federal supervised release* in 1990. The *known association* between criminal behavior and drug abuse is such that drug testing as a *condition of release* for convicted persons is an *essential precaution* to help enhance the public safety, while also promoting *rehabilitative goals.*[13]

Another major difference between governance and campaigning can be seen in the general uplift elections inspire. Sitting presidents raise their Optimism levels significantly during campaigns and dramatically increase their Human Interest words (*you, me, us, neighbors*). For most sitting presidents, especially for presidents like Ronald Reagan and Bill Clinton, campaigns therefore become a kind of political recreation, and pressing the flesh a moral obligation. In a way, says scholar Rachel Holloway, rhetoric of this sort asks "citizens to vote for themselves."[14] But for the puritans writing in the nation's newspapers, a happy rhetoric like this is an abomination. Hence the constant struggle: politicians looking for common ground, championing a new set of possibilities; journalists exposing it as a graven image costing the nation its soul. Nobody likes negative advertising, it seems, except journalists.

The data gathered here across nine presidencies (John Kennedy excepted) show that campaigns reengage the chief executive by licensing a new, more vibrant discourse. When Bill Clinton campaigned he spoke that language like a Democrat:

I want all of us to be able to say, we don't need to look down on anybody else to feel good about ourselves and our families and our future. And I want all of us to say we believe that we have an obligation to serve as citizens to help our children to read; to deal with the other problems in our community; to save the generation of our young people who are in trouble still today because they're more vulnerable to gangs and guns and drugs, and other problems that threaten their future. We're going to help them and we're going to do it together.[15]

When Dwight Eisenhower campaigned he used a Republican dialect of that same language:

My friends, I believe that these facts plainly mark the path of our nation's progress. If you also believe this, if you want to keep on this way, then each of you must do your part to the full in making your decision clear and emphatic. Whatever you believe, my fellow citizens, you know what your personal role in this coming decision must be: To register, to get all your friends to register to vote—to get all your friends to vote—so that on November 6th your voices—the voices of all of you—will be heard. Your decision can then assure and direct our progress in the years ahead—progress in our farm life, and in our whole national life, progress toward our great goal: The prosperity of our people, strong and free, in a world of peace.[16]

Another interesting difference between governance and campaigning lies in the strength of the language used. When presidents speak from the Oval Office they use more Certainty than when campaigning and more Centrality as well, words stressing institutional regularity and core values (*established, customary, legitimate, standard*). That is, sitting presidents typically use the perquisites of office—authority, conventionality—to warrant their arguments. The American people expect such language from their presidents and perhaps even demand it. As Lawrence Rosenfield has observed, citizens often listen for style rather than content, attending primarily to the level of command implicit in the president's remarks. When they hear the hoped-for resonance, says Rosenfield, political language becomes "like the ocean's roar," reassuring them "that things are normal and [that] the public institutions remain healthy."[17]

Such strains can be heard in the remarks of Jerry Ford: "The countries of Asia should be free to develop in a world where there is mutual *respect* for the *sovereignty* and territorial *integrity* of all states; where people are free from the threat of foreign aggression; where there is *noninterference* in the internal affairs of others; and where the *principles* of *equality*, mutual benefit, and *coexistence* shape the *development* of *peaceful* international *order*."[18] Note Rosenfield's principle in action here: Ford says nothing new, but the lilt of his lexicon, the steady, rhythmic deployment of key ideas, lulls us. It is the co-presence of these terms, not their syntactic force, that functions most powerfully. Words like these convince us that the president is presiding and that we are free to return to the sports page.

The campaign of 1976 brought out a less magisterial Jerry Ford. In his radio address on election eve, for example, the president turned supplicant. Gone are grand expostulations and in their place one finds democratic interdependencies:

- I believe I offer experienced leadership; you will have to decide whether my opponent can make the same claim.
- I think my approach could properly be called steady and dependable; it is my opinion, that even as I speak to you, his claims are unclear and untested.
- To stay on our steady and dependable course I need your help; I need your vote.
- For these past 2 years, I have been careful never to promise what I could not deliver . . . and in these past 2 years, I think America has come a long way back.
- Perhaps only one who has served as your President without your mandate can desire as strongly as I do to serve as your President with your mandate.[19]

Admittedly, there is some amount of ritual here, some predictable inveigling at the eleventh hour. But that is to be expected: campaigns remind presidents they are inveiglers.

Do campaigns frustrate the development of an imperial presidency? In some ways they do. As we have seen here, campaigns create an immediacy in presidential discourse not always seen on state occasions. These language cues are subtle, but they are also steady and common. Presidents seem to respond instinctively to such demands, and the best politicians among them (which is to say, most of them) make the transition from Oval Office to campaign trail easily. But are these organic, deeply felt changes or mere manipulation? From the standpoint of democratic theory that is an irrelevant question. Democracies fare best when their leaders behave as if they were the servants of the people. Affect and attitude are important but, in politics, behavior counts most.

THE DIALECTICAL FUNCTION

Campaigns reengage a sitting president, insisting that he earn his right once again to lead the nation. Most presidents in American history who have sought a second term have met that challenge, although some have been turned out of office. Of the presidents studied here, Gerald Ford, Jimmy Carter, and George Bush lost their option on the White House, while Harry Truman, Dwight Eisenhower, Lyndon Johnson, Richard Nixon, Ronald Reagan, and Bill Clinton held onto their jobs. As various scholars note, incumbents normally have a significant advantage, being able to use strategic appointments, foreign policy credentials, the trappings of the office, and the timing of policy decisions to put their best foot forward during an election.[20] Do incumbents have a distinctive style? In part, they do. Challengers do as well. The result of these differences is the clash that gives politics its energy and the American people their electoral options.

Given the different political personalities of the incumbents studied here—two war heroes, several longtime Washington operatives, three former governors—one might not expect to find systematic differences related to incumbency. But differences there were: incumbents were generally more convivial than their opponents, producing higher Commonality scores and far higher Optimism scores. At first glance these differences appear unremarkable: incumbents defend and challengers attack. But these differences ought not be underestimated, since a democracy that cannot sustain a dialectic cannot sustain itself. A nation that can only produce hagiography will soon lose its self-respect; one that can only imagine a world gone dark will soon create such a world. Dialectic strengthens and dialectic cleanses, and, out of such processes, political choices emerge.

Phrased this baldly, the democratic creed sounds simplistic. But it does respond to the charges leveled against campaigns: "Give us a real choice," the people cry. "The parties are failing us," the media complain. But my data show that campaigns do present clear alternatives between incumbents and challengers. Consider the Clinton references made by Bob Dole, the classic challenger, during the 1996 race:

- *President Clinton* says the era of big government is over. Yet, for nearly four years now he has been doing everything in his power to make sure the government stays big and gets bigger.[21]
- *Bill Clinton's* nationalized health care plan would have resulted in $1.5 trillion in new federal spending and imposed a total of 17 new taxes on American workers to pay for it. . . . How is he going to pay for all this? Since he's never offered a list of specific spending cuts, that leads to only one conclusion: Bill Clinton will have to raise taxes again on the American people.[22]
- You know, the *Clinton-Gore* team have given the California Gold Rush new meaning. They're now holding fund raisers in Buddhist temples where you take a vow of poverty before you can get in.[23]
- We ought to stop some of these frivolous lawsuits. They're putting small businessmen and small businesswomen out of business. There ought to be some limit on punitive damages. I know the trial lawyers give *President Clinton* millions and millions and millions of dollars a year, along with the labor bosses and the Hollywood elite.[24]

Rhetorically, the job of the challenger is to make distinctions—between the haves and have-nots, between right and wrong, between the sensible and the impractical. Senator Dole does just that, sacrificing high Commonality and Optimism scores to the case he must make. The burden of proof, as they say in debating circles, always resides with the antagonist, and even the likable Mr. Dole played that role in 1996. His often feisty opponent, on the other hand, was made to act presidential. Consider some of President Clinton's comments about Mr. Dole:

- I thank *Senator Dole* for being a part of this debate, and I felt after it was over that both of us were able to demonstrate that we can disagree strongly and firmly without letting our political dialogue disintegrate into a rude shouting match. We can be civil and decent to one another and build this country together, and that is a good thing. That is a good thing.[25]
- I believe that *Bob Dole* and Jack Kemp and Ross Perot love our country, and they have worked hard to serve it. It is legitimate, even necessary, to compare our record with theirs, our proposals for the future with theirs, and I expect them to make a vigorous effort to do the same.[26]
- And, you know, as I've said repeatedly, I had a good personal relationship with *Senator Dole* when he was the Senate Majority leader. I had a good personal relationship when I vetoed the budget he passed. It wasn't personal. I realized that he thought it was a good thing to cut education by $30 billion and get rid of the national service program and undermine our environmental protection programs. He thought it was good because he thinks the government is a disembodied, bad force in our lives. And I honestly disagreed.[27]

Given his youth, Clinton's courtliness is noteworthy. Given his age, Dole's frostiness also draws attention. This is not to imply an insincerity on either man's part but it is to highlight the role constraints they faced. Of the nine incumbents who ran for reelection in the present sample, only Harry Truman failed to be more optimistic than his opponent; in terms of Commonality, only George Bush was outscored by his challenger in 1992. Otherwise, the formula held. Another component of the formula is this: challengers tend to be more ideological than incumbents, using more Patriotic language and generating lower Realism scores (thereby making their remarks sound more axiological). This pairing seems reasonable since incumbents have an empirical record on which they can run, while challengers can only hypothesize an alternative. The result is an almost Platonic dialectic: the challenger's Imagined Ideal counterposed to the incumbent's Proven Actuality. In a sense, then, political campaigns are the stuff of dreams—that which might be versus that which is. Given this choice, it is not surprising that incumbents almost always have the advantage in a nation of pragmatists.

85

One cannot be naive about these matters: rhetoric is part of the campaign story but incumbents also win because they find it easier to raise money, to leverage power in Congress, and to command the nation's airwaves. With armaments like these, incumbents can stick to the record, leaving challengers with largely hortatory alternatives. During his brief but brilliant debating career, Bill Clinton epitomized both options:

1992: Clinton the Challenger

Ross gave a good answer, but I've got to respond directly to Mr. Bush. You have questioned my patriotism. You even brought some right-wing Congressmen into the White House to plot how to attack me for going to Russia in 1969–1970 when over 50,000 other Americans did. Now I honor your service in World War II. I honor Mr. Perot's service in uniform and the service of every man and woman who ever served, including Admiral Crowe who was your Chairman of the Joint Chiefs and who is supporting me. But when Joe McCarthy went around this country attacking people's patriotism, he was wrong. He was wrong. And a Senator from Connecticut stood up to him named Prescott Bush. Your father was right to stand up to Joe McCarthy. You were wrong to attack my patriotism. I was opposed to the war but I love my country and we need a President who will bring this country together, not divide it. We've got enough division. I want to lead a unified country.[28]

1996: Clinton the Incumbent

I have a simple philosophy that I've tried to follow for the last four years: Do what creates opportunity for all, what reinforces responsibility from all of us; and what will help us build a community where everybody's got a role to play and a place at the table. Compared to four years ago, we're clearly better off. We've got 10.5 million more jobs. The deficit's been reduced by 60 percent. Incomes are rising for the first time in a decade. The crime rates, the welfare rolls are falling. We're putting 100,000 more police on the street. Sixty thousand felons, fugitives and stalkers have been denied handguns. I think what really matters is what we can do to help build strong families. . . . Strong families need a strong economy. To me that means we have to go on and balance this budget while we protect Medicare and Medicaid and education and the environment.[29]

Between 1792 and 1996, presidents have run for reelection twenty-five times and lost on only five occasions.[30] Given their statistical advantage, how can incumbents lose at all? Even more curious, why have three of the last five incumbents lost their reelection bids? Political scientists agonize about such matters, drawing up elaborate regression models that factor in international tensions, the state of the economy, voter turnout, regional demography, and so forth.[31] Should rhetoric be factored into the equation? Perhaps it should. Three variables in particular distinguish incumbents who lose from those who win: losers have lower Activity scores, focus heavily on just a small number of issues (high Insistence scores), and, as we see in figure 4.1, become caught up in the political fray (i.e., high Leader and Party References).

Ostensibly, these are three different pieces of the same puzzle. The first piece seems obvious: an incumbent who cannot generate a sense of momentum hardly seems a good bet for another four years in office. This was surely George Bush's problem in 1992. Another of Bush's problems was his inability to broaden the national dialogue, to use his record to advantage—his success in the Gulf War, a low inflation record, domestic accord, increasing educational standards, and so on. Typically, incumbents cover the waterfront of issues while challengers fight a small-bore war, as did Bill Clinton in 1992 with his highly Insistent campaign—"it's the economy, stupid." Oddly, though, George Bush responded in kind to Clinton, sacrificing broad appeal to score a point or two. His remarks in the third debate of 1992 illustrate:

> I think everybody's paying too much taxes. He refers to one tax increase. Let me remind you it was a Democratic tax increase and I didn't want to do it and I went along with it. And I said I make a mistake— if I make a mistake, I admit it. That's quite different than some. But I think that's the American way. I think everyone's paying too much. But I think this idea that you can go out and—he, then he hits me for vetoing a tax bill. Yes, I did. And the American taxpayer ought to be glad they have a President to stand up to a spending Congress. We

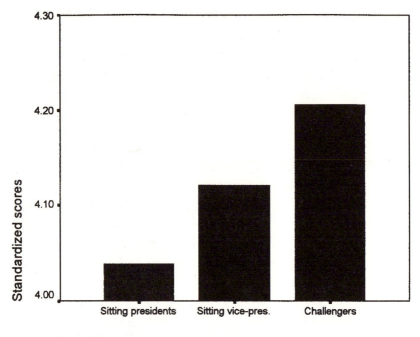

Figure 4.1. Use of "Beltway" Language and Incumbency
(Leader references + party references).

remember what it was like when we had a spending President and a spending Congress and interest rates—who, who remembers that? They were at 21.5 percent under Jimmy Carter. And inflation was 15. We don't want to go back to that. And so yes, everybody's taxed too much and we want to get the taxes down. But not by signing a tax bill that's going to raise taxes on people.[32]

Mr. Bush shows no transcendence here, no ability to place his tax increase in a larger perspective. He focuses on the micropolitics of Washington, D.C., and thus seems like a petty bureaucrat rather than the leader of the free world. There is also a listlessness in his remarks, a wallowing in mistakes past, an inability to move the discussion to higher terrain. Mr. Bush becomes Gulliver, a giant tied down by the tax-and-spenders running the nation's capital. This makes him just another citizen, hardly a role we expect for a sitting president.

Successful challengers (who included Jimmy Carter, Ronald Reagan, and Bill Clinton) managing to replace a current chief executive differed from unsuccessful challengers in several ways. Intellectually, they focused on just one or two issues (thereby producing high Insistence scores). For Jimmy Carter is was ethics in government; for Ronald Reagan, an international embarrassment; for Bill Clinton it was a poor economy. In addition, they were able to tell these tales in ways ordinary people could understand (high Familiarity scores). Most important, they fashioned a clear, alternative vision, promising significant bounties (somewhat higher Optimism) to a broad sector of society (exceptionally high use of Collective terms—*community, humanity, nation, public*). These seem like obvious rhetorical choices but, by and large, they have not been the strategies used by the typical challenger during the last fifty years. And given the polling data reported by Martin Wattenberg, such an oversight seems odd. He finds that "American voters cast their ballots with a focus more on the positive than the negative."[33]

Jimmy Carter proved the truth of that assertion even though popular memory resists. Today, Carter is remembered as the malaise-fearing president who hectored the American people to death. In fact, Carter's Optimism scores in 1976 were actually higher than Ronald Reagan's in 1980 or Bill Clinton's in 1992, although all three challengers ran bracing campaigns that sent a new sense of possibility throughout the land. While Jerry Ford was himself fairly upbeat, Carter equaled him with his Baptist sense of mission:

> We've lost the spirit of our nation. A spirit of youth, vigor, a spirit of confidence, self-reliance, a spirit of work and not of welfare, a spirit of caring for one another, a spirit of unity between the President and the Congress, between federal, state and local levels of government. Between government itself and our great private enterprise system. Labor, management, agriculture, science, education, industry. This has been lost, and that's not part of the consciousness or character of the American people. . . . It's not an easy thing for an outsider like me to defeat an incumbent President. We need a standard of ethics, a standard of excellence, and to make us proud once again. And demonstrate to our own people, and to the rest of the world, that you and I still live in the greatest nation on earth.[34]

In a number of ways, then, political campaigns present clear choices to the American voter. Incumbents and challengers play distinct roles, the former casting a broad net, refusing to become caught up in particulars, and the latter asking if the nation cannot do better. This yin and yang of politics has been fairly consistent across the years. Oddly enough, challengers only win when they talk like incumbents, when they forcibly change the national conversation. And here is an interesting footnote to these results: When electoral races are close (0–9 percent polling spread), the eventual winners change what they are doing. They cut back sharply on populism (shown by decreases in Optimism, Human Interest, and Familiarity) and speak more forcefully about basic values (evidenced by drops in Realism). From the standpoint of democratic theory, such changes are important. They show that campaigns matter, that politicians do react to the (perceived) will of the people, in this case by substituting a more fundamental kind of political discussion for retail politics. In short, while many in the press complain that campaigns are now stultified, I find considerable dialectical life left them.

The Renewal Function

Between 1948 and 1996, twenty-one individuals have received one of the two major party's nominations for the presidency of the United States or campaigned as significant third-party candidates. Of this group, seven have had gubernatorial experience—Thomas Dewey, Adlai Stevenson, George Wallace, Jimmy Carter, Ronald Reagan, Michael Dukakis, and Bill Clinton. A mixed bag. But one of the strongest and most surprising sets of findings in this study is that governors campaign for the presidency in remarkably different ways than those with federal experience (or, in the cases of Dwight Eisenhower and Ross Perot, those with military or corporate experience). I did not anticipate these findings but I also could not dismiss them.

Writing in 1972, Joseph Schlesinger noted that governors tend to be nominated for president when their party is out of power.[35] Since that time, the pattern has continued, with the sole exception of Walter Mondale's selection by the Democrats in 1984. Ostensibly, parties look for a "new voice" when their political fortunes are low, somehow sensing that choosing a governor for their party's nomination will shift the national dialogue. As pollster Louis Harris says, "a governor can duck most of the controversial national issues" or, more positively, can offer up a new agenda. That was Tom Dewey's attempt in 1948 when trying to dismantle Rooseveltian hegemony and it was Bill Clinton's in 1992 when campaigning against the Reaganites. On the negative side, however, Harris notes that "governors do not have a natural forum to become nationally known and to campaign on a round-the-clock, four-year basis for the Presidency." Also, says Harris, "in a cosmic, atomic, mass-media age, Governors have shrunk to being thought of all too often as local figures."[36]

Lou Harris made these observations in 1959. The mass-media age he then envisioned has come and gone and a new one has replaced it, thereby making "locality" a postmodern reality and, hence, no reality at all. Today, governors with enough money can flood the nation's airwaves with torrents of political advertising and any local Internet provider can be assigned to handle their Web-pages. Also, with federal officials now dominating the political scene for three years at a time, governors offer a welcome respite during that fourth, and crucial, year of national politics. If nothing else, governors bring novelty to the campaign, especially when contrasted to members of Congress. "Senators," says Harris, have "tended to conjure up an image of stentorian windbags whose clubbishness was born of a capacity to compromise any and all issues away, including more often than not principle itself."[37]

What makes governors special? Generally speaking, they are more Realistic than their federal counterparts (thereby offsetting the latter's "stentorian" qualities) and they are considerably more Optimistic as well. They are humbler, less inclined to refer to themselves, and also less prone to making patriotic allusions. Intriguingly, their Variety scores are also higher, indicating that governors tend not to repeat the same tired phrases commonplace in national politics. In other words, theirs is a somewhat adolescent style: energetic, buoyant, comparatively unpretentious. Patrick Anderson, speechwriter for Jimmy Carter during the 1976 campaign, evidences this naïveté when quoting the private Jimmy Carter: "I don't want to attack Ford. People are sick of hearing one politician attack another. I want to be positive. Let's talk about creating a sense of unity between the president and the Congress, and between the government and the people. I want to say that my campaign started with nothing, and formed an alliance with the people."[38]

And so he did: governors had significantly higher Commonality scores, more Voter References, and more Collective Terms than their federal counterparts. Although virtually any governor who has run for office during the last fifty years could be chosen to exemplify these trends, Carter will certainly do. In a speech delivered in Dallas, Texas, in September 1976, for example, Carter demonstrated the gubernatorial style from beginning to end:

Governors are experiential

Think about a father proud like you are, competent like you are, self-reliant like you are. The head of a household—like many of you or a mother, eager to work—can't find a job. They come home at night, face the children with the authority and the responsibility and the respect that should go to the breadwinner stripped away. Put yourself in that position. Think of going down and drawing your first welfare check. When you've worked all your life. It tears a family apart. It destroys their self-respect, it eliminates basic human dignity. And in this last 2 years, 2 1/2 million more Americans have had to accept that circumstance. Let's look at inflation. When it was announced that the inflation rate was only 6 percent. . .

Governors are communal

We ought to be sure that we have cooperation with one another. And at the same time respect the differences among us. There ought to be some inclination between the President and the Congress to cooperate for a change, between a mayor and a governor and a President [to] recognize that they represent exactly the same people. There ought to be some way for our free enterprise system—agriculture, manufacturing, and labor—to work with the government, with mutual respect, achieving common goals, but still independent. Competition ought to be ensured, tough competition, to protect the small businessman and not be a favor to the big businessman.

Governors are idealistic

I don't believe any other human being in this country has traveled more than I have in the last years. I've been to more places, talked to more people, listened to more questions, answered more questions. I see our country's economic strength solid, our system of government is the best on earth, Richard Nixon hasn't hurt it, Watergate hasn't hurt it, the Vietnam and Cambodian Wars didn't hurt it, the CIA revelations didn't hurt our system of government. It's still as clean and decent, a basic foundation on which we can predicate an answer to complicated questions, correct our mistakes, bind ourselves together and approach the future with confidence.[39]

It is tempting to dismiss such remarks as traditional rhetoric with a populist spin. Perhaps it is just that. But why? For one thing, governors are closer to the people they govern and thus easily able to pick up their modes of expression and issues of concern. Governors travel out among the people constantly and the state legislators with whom they deal are themselves only an election away from the local school board or the country courthouse. Governors deal each day with highly practical realities and also witness those realities: hurricanes and tornados; dissident citizens militias; corporate relocations; the bruised egos of the lawyerly class. Federal legislators are hardly immune to such pressures but their staffs insulate them a bit as does the theoretical nature of their congressional debates. Because they are less well protected, governors have different instincts.

Is this to say that governors are provincial? It is indeed. And therein lies their appeal. People in the provinces have no choice but to cooperate with one another and to deal with gritty realities in a gritty manner. And the charm of the provincial style is not dictated by the province from which the politician hails. Rather, use of any provincial token shows that its user retains the core identifications of his youth and that he will not gainsay them in his maturity. Bill Clinton demonstrates:

You know, I feel good about Michigan tomorrow for a reason that nobody's talked about. I read, when I began to campaign in Illinois, that Illinois had more Poles, Chicago had more Poles than any city outside

Warsaw. Michigan has more people from *Arkansas* than any state out-side *Arkansas.*[40]

Let me tell you something, folks: you can tell by my accent that I'm not from South Philadelphia. I grew up in *South Arkansas.*[41]

I see a lot of signs out here from the Hispanic-Americans in the crowd that say "Adelante con Clinton!" I thank you. Muchas gracias for that. I also can't help noting that we're just about six blocks from the *Arkansas River,* so I feel right at home.[42]

The problem with the law is, as Georgia knows, it's never been fully implemented, and it didn't go far enough. But *Arkansas* wanted to be in the forefront of that law, and so, as Governor Miller said, we started Project Success, to give child care, health care and education and train-ing, and then move people off welfare.[43]

Some may guess that the gubernatorial style is borrowed for the campaign and then forsaken but my data show that not to be true. When governors-turned-presidents run for reelection, their Realism, Commonality, and Optimism scores go even higher. In addition, they decrease their Leader and Party References, suggesting that even though they now live in Washington, D.C., they still hear the echoes of home. In contrast, when Dwight Eisenhower, Richard Nixon, and George Bush ran for reelection, their "beltway" language increased.

Immediately after the 1976 election, columnist James Reston wrote that Jimmy Carter "had not delivered a single memorable speech dur-ing the campaign."[44] Mr. Reston may well have been correct, but it is also necessary to remember the Olympian perspective from which the *New York Times* often judges such matters. For most of the *Times* writers, Jimmy Carter was a rustic, as was Bill Clinton and George Wallace. Tom Dewey and Michael Dukakis were not rustics but that is only because they were locals. For the East Coast establishment, Ronald Reagan was a pure exotic. So it is not surprising that that establishment typically judges the gubernatorial style bumptious, too filled with enthusiasms, and that it prefers the thrust-and-parry per-fected in the District of Columbia.

But voters seem to like the gubernatorial style, so one can only hope that governors continue to seek the presidency, for it helps narrow the gap between national and local politics.[45] As these observations are being written, for example, pundits are still baffled by how Bill Clinton's national repute remained near the 70 percent level even as he was being impeached by the Congress of the United States. To the extent that Clinton's rhetoric is part of his charm, so too is his pedigree. Like the Teflon chief executive who preceded his predecessor, Mr. Clinton never lost the ability to make a phrase like *embracing the people* sound plausible to most even though it seemed a double entendre to some. Despite his Oxford education, that is, Bill Clinton never forgot that politics is about possibility. He learned that lesson while serving as governor.

THE CENTRIPETAL FUNCTION

The traditional understanding of presidential campaigns is this: a gaggle of candidates begins the race in New Hampshire, is winnowed by a series of grueling primaries in the other states, and then a magnificent, lone candidate emerges to hold his party's standard aloft in the general election. The folklore surrounding campaign politics is therefore appositional—the great leader has qualities possessed by no other person; he is distinctive in mind and manner. Ipso facto, the great leader produces the great text. Says scholar Edwin Black of the Gettysburg Address:

> Its career has recapitulated that of many another exalted work of art, a career that begins, invisibly, as an amorphy of inchoate ideas within the mind of the author. Those mental fragments, combined and recombined under the impulse of aspiration, are subjected to an impenetrable process of discrimination and refinement by the author, who finally forms them into an autonomous creation. That product somehow takes hold, it endures; it survives controversy and the vicissitudes of fashion; in time it achieves . . . an iconic status.[46]

Of the 2,500 speech texts housed in the Campaign Mapping Project's database, not a single Gettysburg Address can be found. For that matter, no Lincoln can be spotted among the two dozen or so candidates seeking the presidency during the last fifty years. What is found instead, says Stephen Hess, are men consumed by ambition, not exceptional talent, persons who are bright, aggressive, responsive, imaginative and good with people.[47] According to Hess this is not a new observation. Lord Bryce inquired into the same matters at the turn of the century when asking why great men are not chosen president. Bryce found this to be a peculiarly American phenomenon and attributed it to several forces: (1) business pays better than government, thereby allowing more opportunities for "personal distinction"; (2) eminent men "make more enemies" than do lesser mortals; (3) generally speaking, the American voter does "not object to mediocrity"; and (4) the party system in the United States ensures that the most loyal individuals, not the most talented, are ultimately rewarded.[48]

While political leadership surely involves more than campaign style, my data largely reinforce Bryce's conclusion. Candidates who spoke common parlance were most successful in their election bids; those with the most distinctive styles were rejected by the American voter. This conclusion was arrived at by comparing how often (i.e., on how many variables) the various candidates differed from one another on each of DICTION's dimensions. Figure 4.2 presents the results, showing, for example, that while Ross Perot differed from his cohorts on twenty different stylistic markers, Ronald Reagan clung steadfastly to the mean except on four variables. For the present analysis, which factors separated the candidates was deemed unimportant; only how often the candidates differed from the mean was calculated.

Clearly, the three designations offered in figure 4.2—Centrists, Episodics, and Outliers—are arbitrary. But they do highlight the overall effect produced: normalcy seems best in American politics. This is a hard notion to accept since so many models of leadership lionize the extraordinary individual. From Horace, who sang a person's praises only "if one has gifts inborn, if one has a soul divine and tongue of noble utterance"[49] to Wordsworth, who assumed that "the poet is chiefly distinguished from other men [by having] a more comprehensive soul,"[50] an exceptionalist model has been used to measure rhetorical worth. More contemporary scholars find that great style clusters "around the concept of genius,"[51] stands against "the general mass of

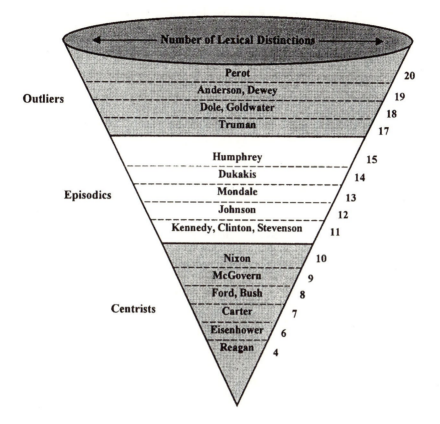

Figure 4.2. The Impact of Normalcy on Campaign Outcomes.

linguistic features common to English,"[52] or lies in "the domain of the verbal anomaly."[53] But it is also the case that these scholars were largely concerned with literary creations and not with the quotidian arts of governance.

Substituting normalcy for distinctiveness makes more sense when we consider DICTION's five main variables. Americans like their presidents to be assured, for example, but too much Certainty produces dogmatism and too little fecklessness. Similarly, too much Optimism becomes utopian and too little leads to despair; too much Realism borders on expediency, too little on metaphysics. We like our leaders Active, but we do not like them either reckless or sedentary. We want them to have a sense for the general welfare, but too much Commonality produces socialism and too little a dangerous individualism. Phrased in these ways, a centrist style makes sense, especially in a nation balanced on so many edges of so many knives. The American landscape is awash with both starry-eyed idealists and cadres of extremists, and both have their followers. Too, corporate life and popular culture are filled with the pyrotechnic, and people find that compelling as well. At the same time, citizens seem to feel that political life should be somehow safer and more dignified than life in general. In a nation whose contradictions have bedeviled it from the beginning, normal therefore becomes oddly acceptable in politics.

Nobody better exemplifies that than Ronald Wilson Reagan, the most centrist of the speakers studied here. Although it is true that President Reagan was enormously popular and although commentators have praised his panache on television, nobody has accused him of being a stylist. With the exception of the ceremonial speeches Peggy Noonan wrote for him, the Reagan oeuvre is plain stuff. That was especially true when he first ran for the presidency. As Jeff Greenfield has reported, "television and the media made almost no difference in the outcome of the 1980 Presidential campaign. The victory of Ronald Reagan was a political victory, a party victory, a victory of more coherent . . . ideas, better expressed, more connected with the reality of their lives, as Americans saw it."[54] Even when one looks at Mr. Reagan's most sumptuous address, his convention acceptance speech, one finds . . .

- *resolute triteness*: "More than anything else, I want my candidacy to unify our country; to renew the American spirit and sense of purpose."
- *consistent vagueness*: "Never before in our history have Americans been called upon to face three grave threats to our very existence, any one of which could destroy us."
- *calculated understatement*: "I will not stand by and watch this great country destroy itself under mediocre leadership that drifts from one crisis to the next, eroding our national will and purpose."
- *artless borrowing*: "Four score and seven years later, Abraham Lin-

coln called upon the people of all America to renew their dedication and their commitment to a government of, for and by the people."

- *uninspired questions*: "Isn't it once again time to renew our compact of freedom; to pledge to each other all that is best in our lives; all that gives meaning to them—for the sake of this, our beloved and blessed land?"
- *recycled jargon*: "The Republican program for solving economic problems is based on growth and productivity."
- *tired parallelisms*: "Adversaries large and small test our will and seek to confound our resolve, but we are given weakness when we need strength, vacillation when the times demand firmness."
- *hackneyed imagery*: "Let us pledge to restore . . . a spirit that flows like a deep and mighty river through the history of our nation."
- *and more hackneyed imagery*: "You know, there may be a sailor at the helm of the ship of state, but the ship has no rudder."[55]

Reagan's address could easily be mistaken for a high school declamation at the VFW. That, of course, is the point. Ronald Reagan had an ear for sophomores and spoke directly to them—in sentences they could immediately diagram on the blackboard. It is notable that the only real flourish in Reagan's acceptance speech also came from his proletarian instincts: "It is impossible to capture in words the splendor of this vast continent which God has granted as our portion of His creation. There are no words to express the extraordinary strength and character of this breed of people we call Americans."[56]

By definition, it is hard to describe a centrist style because it is a style that does not distract. To listen to Ronald Reagan was to be unaware that one was listening. That was also true of the other centrists: Ford, Bush, Nixon, Eisenhower, Carter, McGovern.[57] The Episodics are a bit more distinctive and, except for Michael Dukakis, more memorable. But the campaigners that cannot be forgotten are the Outliers, particularly Perot, Dole, Goldwater, and Truman. All belted out their prose: Truman with his partisan sniping, Goldwater with his colorful overstatements, Perot with his tear-stained issuances. Indeed, Ross Perot's style was almost completely oxymoronic: he combined long-winded historical reflections with numbing lists of facts and figures and delivered it all in rapid-fire fashion. A staccato effect resulted: quick, short sentences appended to one another by a shallow breath or two. Perot's greatest strength was his rhetorical energy, the ability to pack so much into a sentence that one felt dared to pay attention:

> We must make adequate television time available in equal amounts to competing candidates. We must eliminate the need to raise millions for campaigns. This corrupts our process. As a matter of principle, we must get rid of all the freebies in Congress and the White House such as free hair cuts, free gymnasiums, free prescription drugs, free ambulance service, and the list goes on forever. These people are our servants. We don't have those things, why should they? We've got to give the voters the exclusive right to grant Congress, federal employees and the President a pay raise. That'll keep their heads clear on who they work for. Congress has given itself a retirement plan that is worth two to three times more what you and I get. We need to bring it back in line with ours. Makes no sense for the people who work for you to have a better retirement plan than you have. You wouldn't let that happen in your business.[58]

Bob Dole was equally interesting. He detested reading from a manuscript and so he often extemporized. Like Perot, Dole had a way of letting audiences think he was saying something for the first time (he often was). But Dole also exemplifies the danger of the Outlier's style. One of his most distinctive features, for example, was his overuse of "beltway language" (Leader and Party references). During the 1996 campaign, Dole made four times as many references to political personalities in Washington, D.C., as did Bill Clinton, ten times as many party references. In part, Dole was playing the challenger here, decrying "politics as usual" and pointing a finger at the specific causes. But he did so excessively and that sent a metamessage to the American people: Dole was trapped in the routines of Congress; Salinas and Port Arthur did not exist for him. These are unfair accusations but Mr. Dole made them more plausible each time he mentioned Teddy Kennedy or Al Gore by name.

Scholar Craig Smith has observed that Dole's loss in 1996 may "have had more to do with voters' divergence from the Gingrich Republicans than with their convergence around Clinton and his policies."[59] The data I have gathered here suggest that this kind of negative logic may now be a political universal in the United States. Political scientist Arthur Miller and his colleagues note, for example, that voters use certain "cognitive schemas" to reduce the political information they must sort through, evaluating "candidates by comparing each one individually with some abstract ideal or exemplary president."[60] My suggestion here is that voters may also listen for rhetorical distinctiveness. When they find too much of it, they turn away. Michael Burgoon's theory of language expectancy suggests just that—people come to expect (centrist) language and become discomfited when their expectations are not met.[61]

Thus, voters may become "reactive" during political campaigns, directing their attention to what seems odd rather than to what seems right. John Herstein has some data to suggest that this sort of negative thinking may well affect voters, although he does not focus on language per se.[62] Susan Fiske arrives at much the same conclusion when observing that "negative or extreme information plausibly might be easier to understand than other information" because it is rarer.[63] But why would the American people be so concerned with political distinctiveness? According to Anthony King, it is because they have adopted an "agency democracy" that keeps their leaders tightly tethered to the frequent elections they must face. This makes it hard for American politicians to make tough decisions, says King, or "to court unpopularity, to ask for sacrifices, to impose losses, to fly in the face of conventional wisdom"[64] or, as we have seen here, to venture too far from the stylistic norm. If American politics is an art, that is, it is bas-relief: voters listen for formulations that stand out and, finding same, become suspicious.

This is either a cup half full or half empty. For many it will be depressing to learn that true individuality is abhorred, that Americans must content themselves with colorless, dry campaigns. "How will the bold new idea, the riveting metaphor, take hold in a society loath to trust its imagination?" some will ask. A fair question, but U.S. voters have other issues on their minds. Political campaigns function centripetally because the American people realize that the pluralism they so cherish is also the pluralism they most fear. That makes them centrists by default, which is perhaps how centrists have always been created.

Conclusion

There has always been a strong tendency in the United States to denigrate political campaigns. Campaigns last too long, cost too much, only fitfully get out the vote, and put a good many citizens in a foul mood come November. But the findings reported here tell a happier story. Campaigns are hardly perfect but they make politicians and their constituents more interdependent, more immediately engaged, and also foster genuine give-and-take or, at least, they apportion roles differently among incumbents and challengers. I have also found that campaigns reinvigorate the political process, bringing regional perspectives to bear on national matters (in the person of the nation's governors). Finally, campaigns continually help the American people find their center point. With only a few exceptions, candidates with distinctive profiles have not found favor among the American people, while those who seem most ordinary, least distinctive, have become president.

Naturally, one must offer a thousand qualifications to all of this. My determinations have been based on that most fragile of vehicles— human language—and I have not even looked at all campaign words, just some of them. But while the qualifications are being ticked off, the larger point can be lost and I think that unwise. There is much that is wrong with campaigns, and those sins have been amply documented elsewhere. But far more sinful would be to overlook the great good done every four years when the American people are confronted with their political leaders and asked to choose among them. Sometimes their leaders are not worthy of them, and the reverse is true from time to time as well. From a God's-eye perspective there is probably something terribly wrong with an immediate, dialectical, innovative, and centrist political discourse. Not having access to that perspective, I opt for the discourse that is.

* CHAPTER 5 *

Campaign Forums

Every book has a premise and this book is no exception. Its premise is this: A political campaign is an extended conversation. A campaign is other things as well—a mobilization of the electorate, a transfer of political power, an extraordinary expenditure of money—but mostly it helps leaders get to know their constituents and become known by them as well. These re-introductions are necessary because most political leaders live their lives apart from the people they govern. Most of the time, they work as bureaucrats. They answer constituent mail, draft legislation, oversee staff meetings, consult with colleagues, and dine with their financial backers. Only rarely do they reflect on what the price of soybeans in Illinois or the transit problems in Boston feel like to people in those areas. As a result, voters can easily become abstractions to their leaders or, more precisely, a series of abstractions: farmers, union workers, the Religious Right, student loan applicants, Cuban Americans.

Things change during an election year. When a U.S. senator runs for the presidency, for example, he or she must travel to areas of the country not seriously contemplated since high school geography class. When a sitting governor runs for national office, he or she must invent a more exalted, less parochial, discourse that appeals to all the people in all the places that are not back home. Campaigning can be especially hard for vice presidents since life in Washington, D.C., often insulates them from the concerns of everyday people. A campaign pries leaders away from their comfortable work routines and favorite restaurants and introduces them to the ill-mannered louts who pay their salaries. That makes campaigning a humbling experience.

To imagine a campaign as an extended conversation brings up questions of both form and content. Content-wise, a presidential

With Hannah Gourgey, Sharon Jarvis, and Bryant Hill

103

campaign often introduces new issues to the national agenda. The New World Order was first debated in earnest by John Kennedy and Richard Nixon in 1960. Four years later, the indelicate topic of race was discussed, however delicately, by Lyndon Johnson and Barry Goldwater. Less delicate was the national conversation about American hegemony held in 1968 and 1972 by Democrats and Republicans. In 1976, the campaign between Jimmy Carter and Gerald Ford pivoted on the concept of public morality. These campaigns did not invent such discussions but they did highlight ideas adrift at the time. Months, sometimes years, later the topics were still being discussed but these campaigns changed how the American people talked about these issues and, hence, how they thought about them.

This chapter focuses on form, not content. It addresses three modes of political interaction—party conventions, political debates, and campaign advertising—and inquires into the purpose of each. Its argument is that these forums help the campaign do what it must do—engage the electorate. Because political engagement comes hard these days, conventions try to inspire political imagination, to get the party faithful to envision a broader, brighter, grander set of possibilities. Debates promote engagement by offering new types of political information, by insuring that fresh ideas freshly tested remain central to enlightened decision-making. Even the much reviled political advertisement becomes an agent of engagement when it inspires political emotion. No society can thrive, after all, when its people do not care enough to vote and do not care that they do not care. If it takes party hats, clever one-liners, and colorful graphics to turn taxpayers into voters, a nation must follow that course. Modern campaign forums, I argue in this chapter, are adjuncts to democracy even when they are profoundly imperfect.

POLITICAL CONVENTIONS

On 2 July 1932, Franklin Roosevelt, then governor of New York, broke tradition by arriving at the Democratic convention in Chicago to personally accept his party's nomination for the presidency of the United States. Mr. Roosevelt not only altered convention routine but headlined the meeting as well, presenting a long and passionate address that ended with the promise of "a new deal for the American people." Roosevelt took delight in his transgression, attacking "the absurd tradition that the candidate should remain in professed ignorance of what has happened [at the convention] for weeks, until he is formally notified." "You have nominated me and I know it," Mr. Roosevelt declared, "and I am here to thank you for the honor."[1]

Thus began a ritual that has remained unbroken to this day despite the legion changes political conventions have seen during the past seventy years. The brokered conventions that allowed party bosses to dictate political outcomes are now distant memories, thanks to the McGovern Reforms effected after another famous Chicago convention in 1968. Gone as a result is the discontinuity (and excitement) of political decisions being made in-process; gone also is the mayhem (and fisticuffs) resulting when radio and television reporters elbowed their ways across convention floors. Thanks to Teddy Kennedy in 1980 and Pat Buchanan in 1992, gone as well are the "rump speeches" delivered by beloved also-rans. Now, podium time is jealously guarded, seconding speeches are effectively written by those being seconded, and lavish campaign videos dominate the scene. By the 1980s even spontaneous protests at the national conventions had become planned, with pressure groups accorded just so much footage in remote parking lots.

Despite these changes, and despite the convention's transition from a "forum of decision" to a "ceremony of ratification," party conventions persist.[2] They persist because an unratified politics cannot be a functional politics and because only a ratified politics can command authority. They persist, in Bruce Gronbeck's language, because they connect candidates' dramas to voters' fantasies, thereby providing reasons to think in particular ways about political life.[3] They persist, also, because conventions provide a rather predictable "bump" to political campaigns, although the magnitude of those "bumps" varies considerably from year to year.[4] Through conventions, says Sean Wilnetz, "Democrats will be reminded that they are Democrats; Republicans will be reminded that they are Republicans. . . . At a time when elected officials and the media have eviscerated trust in politics, the

105

public needs these reminders. In this respect, the conventions are as remarkable and necessary today as they have ever been."[5]

Conventions have been sharply criticized, then, and yet remain. As a result, Mr. Roosevelt's revolution of 1932 has also become a staple. The acceptance address now constitutes the only passably climactic moment in an otherwise predictable affair. But since these speeches are often dreary intellectually, dull televisually, and predictable politically, why bother with them? I argue here that the modern acceptance address is a political homunculus, a miniature version of the stresses and strains now besetting mainstream American politics. Given media demands, the acceptance address cannot do everything that should be done; nor can politics. Given intraparty feuds, the acceptance address cannot give vent to unrestrained passion; nor can politics. Given voter cynicism, the acceptance address cannot trade on unquestioned principles and premises; nor can politics. Today's acceptance speech is as important for what it expresses as for what it represses, for the emotions it indulges and eschews. There are few political principles the acceptance address cannot teach, or so goes my argument here.[6]

In many ways, American political oratory is an odd art form. In one of its moods it soars to the very heights on the backs of Truth and Justice and, in another of its moods, plummets to earth in search of tax breaks and nuclear waste sites. In that sense, American oratory carries within it what Kathleen Hall Jamieson calls the "chromosomal imprints" of the kingly/churchly island from which the nation sprang and, at the same time, the rugged pragmatism nourished in the souls of its colonists by the Enlightenment.[7] The convention acceptance speech knows such tensions too.

As can be seen in table 5.1, the acceptance is one part ceremony and the other part stump speech. It is a rhetorical hybrid, strangely suspended between the pontifications of inaugural oratory and the quotidian promises of the campaign trail.[8] The acceptance speech is equal parts flag-waving and accountancy, so it is not surprising that a New Ager like Bill Clinton would find it easy to tack back and forth between both qualities in his second acceptance. By directing a narrow agenda (high Insistence) toward tangible goals (Concreteness, Numericals) and by using clear-cut verbs (Tenacity), he managed to speak, at times, like the head of General Motors:

TABLE 5.1
Hybridized Nature of Acceptance Addresses

Rhetorical Features	Variables	Rhetorical Genre		
		Presidential Inaugurals	Acceptances Addresses	Stump Speeches
Functional				
	Concreteness	Low	Medium	High
	Insistence	Low	Medium	High
	Numerical Terms	Low	Medium	High
	Tenacity	Low	Medium	High
Ceremonial				
	Patriotic Terms	High	Medium	Low
	Religious References	High	Medium	Low
	Liberation	High	Medium	Low
	Inspiration	High	Medium	Low
	Embellishment	High	Medium	Low
Dialectical				
	Hardship	High	Medium	Low
	Cooperation	High	Medium	Low
	Rapport	High	Medium	Low

Look at what's happened. We have the lowest combined rates of unemployment, inflation and home mortgages in 28 years. Look at what happened: 10 million new jobs, over half of them high-wage jobs. Ten million workers getting the raise they deserve with the minimum wage law. Twenty-five million people now having protection in their health insurance because the Kennedy-Kassebaum bill says you can't lose your insurance anymore when you change jobs, even if somebody in your family has been sick. Forty million Americans with more pension security. A tax cut for 15 million of our hardest-working, hardest-pressed Americans and all small businesses. Twelve million Americans, 12 million of them, taking advantage of the Family and Medical Leave law so they can be good parents and good workers. Ten million students have saved money on their college loans. We are making our democracy work.[9]

Then, by reaching into the nation's sacred lexicon (Patriotic and Religious terms) and touching on its sacred truths (Liberation, Inspiration), Mr. Clinton suddenly became an archdeacon in the Anglican church:

> Tonight, my fellow Americans, I ask all of your fellow citizens to join me and to join you in building that bridge to the 21st century, four years from now. Just four years from now. Think of it. We begin a new century, full of enormous possibilities. We have to give the American people the tools they need to make the most of their God-given potential. We must make the basic bargain of opportunity and responsibility available to all Americans, not just a few. That is the promise of the Democratic Party. That is the promise of America. I want to build a bridge to the 21st century in which we expand opportunity through education, where computers are as much a part of the classroom as blackboards, where highly trained teachers demand peak performance from our students, where every eight-year-old can point to a book and say, "I can read it myself."

The Clinton acceptance shows how an American politician is constantly trapped between the Scylla of Old World certitude and the Charybdis of New World functionality. The convention orator cannot "preside" (even if he is a sitting president) as he can during an inaugural, for party truths are sectarian truths and thus need a delicate touch. So it is not surprising that acceptances contain significantly more Ambivalence than inaugurals, but significantly less than stump speeches. In other words, conventions can insulate a political speaker better than the give-and-take of the campaign trail, but not as well as the inaugural. So, for example, in his 1996 acceptance Mr. Clinton (1) took pride in the nation's security but warned against becoming the world's policeman, (2) endorsed the cutting of taxes but not at the expense of Medicaid and Medicare, (3) took pride in the dropping crime rate but declared it still too high. This push-pull rhetoric seems unique to the acceptance address, with the inaugural address having more push, the stump speech more pull.

The acceptance affords other luxuries. Table 5.1 tells us that the acceptance speaker embraces a much broader agenda than is possible on the campaign trail, where higher Insistence scores are more regularly produced. During the acceptance—and perhaps because of widespread television coverage—a speaker is more likely to roam across a broader set of topics, maximizing the political space available on such occasions. Mr. Clinton's favorite terms included *children*, *jobs*, *cuts*, *welfare*, *peace*, and, of course, *bridge*. Such a mélange of symbols opens up the candidate to charges of becoming all things to all people, a charge to which Mr. Clinton, for one, could easily plead guilty:

> So look around here, look around here. Old or young, healthy as a horse or a person with a disability that hasn't kept you down, man or woman, Native American, native-born, immigrant, straight or gay—whatever—the test ought to be: I believe in the Constitution, the Bill of Rights and the Declaration of Independence. I believe in religious liberty, I believe in freedom of speech, and I believe in working hard and playing by the rules. I'm showing up for work tomorrow. I'm building that bridge to the 21st century.

But it is not just Democrats who must work to create political space—to broaden the agenda—during the political convention. Bob Dole also called the roll (his favorite terms included *history*, *right*, *trade*, *war*, *criminals*, and *government*). He did so a bit less pointedly than Clinton but clearly with an eye toward expanding what is typically thought of as the (constricted) Republican agenda:

> A family from Mexico who arrived this morning, legally, has as much right to the American dream as the direct descendants of the founding fathers. The Republican Party is broad and inclusive. It represents many streams of opinion and many points of view. But if there is anyone who has mistakenly attached himself to our party in the belief that we are not open to citizens of every race and religion, then let me remind you: Tonight this hall belongs to the party of Lincoln, and the exits, which are clearly marked, are for you to walk out of as I stand here and hold this ground—without compromise. Though I can only look up, and at a very steep angle, to Washington and Lincoln, let me remind you of their concern for the sometimes delicate unity of the people. The notion that we are and should be one people rather than the "peoples" of the United States seems so self-evident and obvious that it is hard for me to imagine that I must defend it.[10]

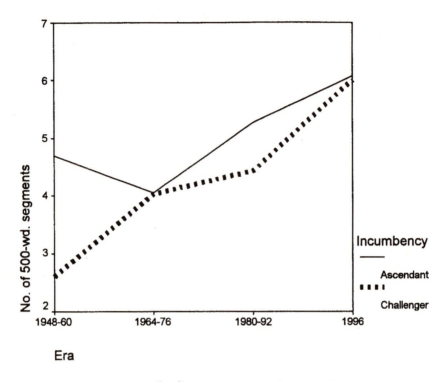

Figure 5.1. Length of Acceptance Speeches over Time.

"Breadth" of this sort is typically the sort of thing expected on a near-ceremonial occasion, but, as we have seen, the acceptance speech is also filled with practical political business. One consequence of this "middling" approach is that acceptances are more heavily Embellished than the standard stump speech but less so than the inaugural. Because they must do so many contrary things, acceptance speeches have gotten longer over the years (see figure 5.1). This effect has been true both for ascendants (sitting presidents and sitting vice presidents) and for challengers. But how is it possible, one might ask, to be both concrete and abstract, theological and time-bound, at the same time? One need only ask Bill Clinton:

Well, for four years now, to realize our vision, we have pursued a simple but profound strategy: opportunity for all, responsibility from all, a strong, united American community. Four days ago, as you were

110

making your way here, I began a train ride to make my way to Chicago through America's heartland. I wanted to see the faces; I wanted to hear the voices of the people for whom I have worked and fought these last four years. And did I ever see them.

I met an ingenious businesswoman who was once on welfare in West Virginia; a brave police officer, shot and paralyzed, now a civic leader in Kentucky; an auto worker in Ohio, once unemployed, now proud to be working in the oldest auto plant in America, to help make America No. 1 in auto production again for the first time in 20 years. I met a grandmother fighting for her grandson's environment in Michigan, and I stood with two wonderful little children proudly reading from their favorite book, *The Little Engine That Could*.

In so many ways, Mr. Clinton's acceptance shows the peculiar waltz between the Pragmatic and Transcendent so characteristic of U.S. political culture in general. For a modernist like Bill Clinton, a child's book about trains is eminently suitable for making a point about morality. Similarly, Opportunity and Responsibility can also be made to stride the political stage, tied as they are to practical matters such as crime, welfare, and deficit spending. Mr. Clinton's speech is thus a salad of observations, all vaguely tied to an experience that only a loosely bounded culture could see as a single experience.[11]

There is also a dark side to the convention address, as there must be to any political ritual. Kenneth Burke tells us that all discourse must "perfect" itself by playing off the forces of Darkness against the forces of Light.[12] My findings show that maintaining this balance is harder on the campaign trail since crowd responses are less predictable and since members of the press take such delight in skewering the bloated image. Thus, as we see in table 5.1, stump speeches do not as readily reach out to the dialectical possibilities of oratory. But in a raucous convention hall, dragons can be slain with panache. Bob Dole found a clutch of them to slay in San Diego:

> After decades of assault upon what made America great, upon sup-
> posedly obsolete values, what have we reaped, what have we created,
> what do we have? What we have, in the opinion of millions of Ameri-
> cans, is crime, drugs, illegitimacy, abortion, the abdication of duty, and
> the abandonment of children.

And after the virtual devastation of the American family, the rock upon which this country was founded, we are told that it takes a village—that is, the collective, and thus, the state—to raise a child. The state is now more involved than it has ever been in the raising of children, and children are now more neglected, abused, and mistreated than they have been in our time. This is not a coincidence, and, with all due respect, I am here to tell you: it does not take a village to raise a child. It takes a family.

Over time, U.S. citizens have become so familiar with the refrains of convention oratory that it is hard for them to realize how remarkable this all is—a speech that is happy and sad, concrete and abstract, assured yet tentative, specific but unfocused. Statistically speaking, some of these tendencies are stronger than others but no matter how one peruses the data the contradictions do not fall away. The convention acceptance is a dialectical text because it must appeal, simultaneously, to the faithful and to the merely curious, because it must preach and also sell. In many ways, this is the story of American politics itself.

Acceptances have gotten longer over time because they have so many different tasks to perform. In addition, television and its stringent production values have added to their length, as candidates surf the rhetorical waves looking for something for everyone. Perhaps not surprisingly, then, Activity scores have risen sharply in recent years, as candidates work themselves into a fever pitch to create the sense of energy and excitement that a visually demanding electorate has come to expect. In 1996, this led to Bill Clinton's sortie into bridge-building as he sought to do for a picture-hungry audience something that words can only fitfully do—create a sense of motion about things that are essentially motionless:

> So tonight let us resolve to build that bridge to the 21st century, to meet our challenges and protect our values. Let us build a bridge to help our parents praise their children, to help young people and adults to get the education and training they need, to make our streets safer, to help Americans succeed at home and at work, to break the cycle of poverty and dependence, to protect our environment for generations to come, and to maintain our world leadership for peace and freedom.

Tonight, my fellow Americans, I ask all of your fellow citizens to join me and to join you in building that bridge to the 21st century, four years from now. Just four years from now. Think of it. We begin a new century, full of enormous possibilities. We have to give the American people the tools they need to make the most of their God-given potential. We must make the basic bargain of opportunity and responsibility available to all Americans, not just a few. That is the promise of the Democratic Party. That is the promise of America.

Mr. Clinton is as active here as language alone can make him. But what is he active about? That has become increasingly less clear. One of the most curious findings is that something of a rhetorical dealignment has occurred in the convention address, with fewer and fewer Party References being made over time (either by ascendants or challengers) even though the addresses are being delivered in the immediate presence of the party faithful. These findings are similar to those of Martin Wattenberg who reports that news coverage no longer links candidates to their parties of origin.[13] Ostensibly, it would seem, the media generation has outgrown party labels, fully confident in its abilities to look through the television screen to the very souls of the candidates who solicit them.[14]

And what do they see within such souls? Something of a muddle, it would seem, since the crisp language of assurance spoken in the Johnson-Nixon era has become passé, with recent acceptances having dramatically lower Certainty scores than those in the 1960s. As we saw in chapter 3, this has been true for campaign discourse in general, but the fact that it is also found in the (1) highly supportive and (2) largely ceremonial confines of a political convention surely suggests that the old certitudes have become scarce. Some of this temporizing, of course, may be traced to the sixties themselves, where ideological clash and moral resolve were in fashion but also costly. Thus, we have now entered a more delicate age where one takes with the left even as one gives with the right. In 1996, Mr. Clinton demonstrated:

> We respect the individual conscience of every American on the painful issue of abortion, but believe as a matter of law that this decision should be left to a woman, her conscience, her doctor and her God. *But abortion should not only be safe and legal; it should be rare.*

113

My fellow Americans, we all owe a great debt to Sarah and Jim Brady and I'm glad they took their wrong turn and ended up in Chicago. I was glad to see them. It is to them we owe the good news that 60,000 felons, fugitives and stalkers couldn't get handguns because of the Brady bill, *but not a single hunter in Arkansas or New Hampshire or Illinois or anyplace else missed a hunting season.*

My fellow Americans, I have spent an enormous amount of time with our dear friend, the late Ron Brown, and with Secretary Kantor and others, opening markets for America around the world, and I'm proud of every one we opened. *But let us never forget the greatest untapped market for American enterprise is right here in America, in the inner cities and the rural areas who have not felt this recovery.*

Clinton's speech reads like a political road map, with each sentence identifying the pressure group likely to be offended by the idea it embraces. With Mr. Clinton's mind so filled with Right-to-Lifers, the NRA, and the Congressional Black Caucus, it is extraordinary that he managed to say anything at all in August 1996.

If the acceptance speech has become cautious even as it has become busy, what are the candidates busy doing? By and large, very practical things. Over time, acceptances have become more Concrete, more Numerical, less attracted to Inspirational language, and less likely to use Familiar words—all of which combine to produce a technocratic discourse. Again, chapter 3 reports these same general trends for campaigning in general. The fact that they are replicated in the safe and hallowed halls of the party convention suggests just how powerful such effects are. These changes have been quite linear over time, an interesting contrast to inaugurals—which scholar Lee Sigelman found to be preachier over time.[15] Acceptances, in contrast, have become increasingly didactic, as Bill Clinton's remarks in 1996 indicate:

First, we are working to rally a world coalition with zero tolerance for Terrorism. Just this month I signed a law imposing harsh sanctions on foreign companies that invest in key sectors of the Iranian and Libyan economies. As long as Iran trains, supports, and protects terrorists, as long as Libya refuses to give up the people who blew up Pan Am 103, they will pay a price from the United States. . . .

We need, in short, the laws that Congress refused to pass. And I ask them again: Please, as an American, not a partisan matter, pass these laws now. Third, we will improve airport and air travel security. I have asked the Vice President to establish a commission and report back to me on ways to do this, but now we will install the most sophisticated bomb detection equipment in all our major airports, we will search every airplane flying to or from America from another nation—every flight, every cargo hold, every cabin, every time.

The issues Mr. Clinton addresses here are undeniably important. They result in the loss of life and the tearing of the social fabric. But these are also matters of a legislative, not a ceremonial, nature. They do not cause the head to bow or the eyes to tilt skyward. In many ways, they suggest the increasing commodification of governance, with the party platform turned into retail politics and the fall campaign into a marketing exercise. Perhaps a nation at peace, a wealthy nation, can afford to let focus-group issues substitute for leadership, but one wonders what is lost when the presentistic determines everything. John F. Kennedy, for one, might have wondered about such matters:

> One hundred years ago in this city Abraham Lincoln was nominated for President of the United States. The problems which will confront our next President will be even greater than those that confronted him. The question then was freedom for the slaves and survival of the nation. The question now is freedom for all mankind and the survival of civilization and the choice you make—each of you listening to me makes this November—can affect the answer to that question. What should your choice be and what is it?[16]

The trends in acceptance addresses reviewed here are important not because the speeches themselves are so important but because they reveal so much about mainstream American politics.[17] As we have seen, the acceptances have gotten longer over the years but they have also become less assured, as the candidates search for political stabilities that are now hard to find. The political parties no longer figure prominently in these addresses, even as the speeches are delivered in the presence of party members. The speeches have gotten more Active, but since the old certitudes are no longer relied upon, this increasingly sounds like freneticism rather than propulsion. According to scholar Ray Dearin, the rhetorical complexity of the acceptance address may be attributed to the still-unsettled debate between American individualism and communitarianism that has been waged, perennially, within the U.S. polity.[18]

For a number of reasons, then, the acceptance address hangs on tenterhooks. It is, at once, part entrepreneurial and part metaphysical, a modern embodiment of the symmetries the early Puritans tried to effect. Modern Americans like these symmetries at times but seem equally frustrated by them at other times. Perhaps that is how it must be in a large and diverse nation where political problems tend to stop rather than end. And the happy-sad qualities of the acceptance tell a story too—of a nation whose citizens both do and do not get along with one another. Every four years, convention speakers retell this story and then ask the nation to do better. The American people hear this story every four years. As the convention orators might say, that is probably a great and good thing.

POLITICAL DEBATES

The importance of presidential debates has become an article of faith to most academics and to a good many citizens as well. When a sitting president (Gerald Ford) deigned to debate his challenger in 1976, the inevitability of future debates seemed assured. Eight years later, Ronald Reagan cemented that outcome when agreeing to face Walter Mondale, who trailed him badly in the polls at the time. In 1996, President Bill Clinton and Senator Bob Dole squared off in two debates, further ensuring that debates would remain a centerpiece of future campaigns.

Are debates worth the trouble? If popularity is a guide, they seem to be. In 1960, 80 percent of the American people watched at least one of the debates,[19] and, since that time, they have typically drawn between sixty and eighty million viewers.[20] According to Susan Hellweg and her colleagues, presidential debates surpass the standard audience share for all but a handful of televised events (e.g., the Olympics).[21] Even with the advent of cable television's cornucopia of programs, the 1996 debates managed to draw a crowd, with 82 million Americans watching the two debates.[22]

Rather than celebrate these spasms of civic rectitude, many scholars are discomfited by them. Some liken the banality of political debates to the average TV game show while others disparage them as "joint press conferences" or "counterfeit debates" devoid of genuine intellectual clash.[23] Many scholars trace the inadequacy of presidential debates to the gods of television. The staging, camera treatment, choice of interrogators, and debate formats demanded by television, say Robert Tiemens and his colleagues, make real dialogue all but impossible.[24] Alan Schroeder is more hopeful about televised debates but still concludes that because debates are (1) personality-centered, (2) conflictual, and (3) spontaneous, voters will never learn as much from them as they should. He goes on to observe, however, that because debates offer "one of the few common-denominator experiences left in American public life," they provide "an immediate connection to the larger national agenda."[25]

Some scholars are even more hopeful. Norman Ornstein argues that debates emphasize issues and voting records more than any other form of campaign communication,[26] while Michael Pfau and J. G. Kang have shown that debates reveal the candidates as people, a not unimportant effect since voters often search debates for characterological cues.[27] Diana Owen argues that debates are particularly helpful for informing undecided voters or those with low political interest and further reports that 50 percent of the American people surveyed in 1992 thought the presidential debates quite helpful.[28] Besides, argue Diana Carlin and her colleagues, the whole point of debate is to sharpen differences among the candidates, to produce political clash, and debates can do that despite their several infirmities.[29]

Surprisingly, though, comparatively little research has been done on the precise characteristics of presidential debates, on what political debates do that other campaign venues do not do.[30] My data suggest five unique functions:

1. *Debates add prudence to the campaign.* Traditional lore holds that contesting ideas produces not certainty but instability, that the ideal debate pits two advocates of equal skill against one another and that Truth emerges from the interaction. Even in the rough-and-tumble

117

TABLE 5.2
Comparative Features of Presidential Debates

Rhetorical Features	Variables	Rhetorical Genre		
		Debates	Ads	Speeches
Prudence				
	Certainty	Low	Low	High
	Ambivalence	High	Medium	Low
Restraint				
	Optimism	Low	High	High
	Realism	Low	Medium	High
	Embellishment	Low	High	Medium
	Patriotic Terms	Low	High	High
	Voter References	Medium	Medium	High
	Religious References	Low	Medium	High
Focus				
	Insistence	High	Low	Medium
Reflection				
	Self-References	High	Low	Medium
	Human Interest	Low	Medium	High

world of politics, this image has substance. Consider these facts: As we see in table 5.2, debates use significantly less Certainty than stump speeches and significantly more Ambivalence than political advertising, as the easy overstatements of the campaign trail are replaced by more precise, less global assertions in debates. Also, these trends have largely held up throughout the years, suggesting something of a truly generic order.

Consider, for example, Bob Dole's situation prior to the second debate in 1996. During the first debate, his handlers complained, Dole had been too courtly to President Clinton, especially with regard to the Administration's ostensible ethical lapses. They urged Dole to step up his attack during the second debate, but this is the best the senator could manage:

There's no doubt about it that many American people have lost their faith in government. They see scandals almost on a daily basis. They see ethical problems in the White House today. They see 900 F.B.I. files, private persons, being gathered up somebody in the White House. Nobody knows who hired this man. So, there's a great deal of cynicism out there.[31]

Mr. Dole is almost completely elliptical here: no specifics are provided, no names named, no charges leveled. And instead of pressing this already blunted attack further, Dole continues in an almost dreamlike state:

But, I've always tried in whatever I've done to bring people together. I said in my acceptance speech in San Diego about two months ago, the exits are clearly marked if you think the Republican Party is someplace for you to come if you're narrow-minded or bigoted or don't like certain people in America. The exits are clearly marked for you to walk out, as I stand here without compromise because this is the party of Lincoln. I think we have a real obligation. Obviously, public officials. I'm no longer a public official. I left public life on June 11 of this year. But it is very important. Young people are looking to us. They're looking to us for leadership. They are watching what we do, what we say, what we promise and what we finally deliver. And I would think, it seems to me, that there are opportunities here.

Mr. Dole's last sentence—"I would think, it seems to me, that there are opportunities here"—may well set a record for Ambivalence. The rest of his statement is no stronger since it is rife with self-interruptions ("I'm no longer a public official"), vague historical references ("the party of Lincoln"), and airy philosophizing ("they are watching what we do"). These remarks constituted, in Mr. Dole's mind, his attack on Clinton's ethics.

It is not as if Dole were incapable of being tough. Consider the stump speech he made the very next day:

Let's take a look at the White House. Let's take a look at Craig Livingstone—who is rifling through somebody's files. Let's take a look at that six month gap where they said nobody checked anything out. But then this one young lady who testified, under oath, said oh yes, they did check things out. So, this is the kind of administration we're dealing with. They'll do anything. They'll look at anything. That shouldn't happen in America. This is the United States of America. The White House should be a place of public trust, public trust not public suspicion. When Bob Dole and Jack Kemp are elected, it's going to be a place of public trust. You can count on it. You have my word.[32]

Miscreants are named here, principles invoked, promises made. Why not the day before? Is it possible that public debate raises standards of accountability, making candidates adhere to models of evidence not expected on the hustings? Does the physical presence of an opponent cause a candidate to pull his punches? Does the formality of the debate experience—the history-making—establish implicit ground rules for how it will be conducted? All of these are possibilities, and all are predicted by academic theories of debate. That these hoary truths could operate so powerfully as to affect the language patterns of an experienced politician like Bob Dole seems a rather extraordinary thing.

2. *Debates reduce campaign bombast.* In many ways, presidential debates are a way station, a place of refuge from campaign histrionics. As we see in Table 5.2, debates are considerably less Optimistic than ads or speeches, and far more idealistic as well. On the stump, candidates indulge their fantasies, promising new bounties for the nation. In some ways, this is as it should be, for a good campaign requires candidates to articulate new solutions to old problems and to set the nation on some imaginative course. Even campaign ads become a kind of political poetry in this model (witness Bill Clinton's "Born in Hope" spots from the 1992 campaign). In their own, expedient ways, these venues set forth workable solutions to workaday problems. In 1996, Bill Clinton, the nation's foremost optimist/realist, was more than ready to accept that challenge when stumping in October:

> I want to talk to you about how we can demand responsibility from all our young people by taking firm steps to stop teens from driving under the influence of alcohol and drugs. My vision is of an America where we offer opportunity to all, demand responsibility from all, and build a stronger community where everyone has a place. That's America's basic bargain. That's how we will keep our young people safe and give them

the futures they deserve. We've done a lot to expand opportunity for our young people—reducing the cost of college loans and improving the terms for repayment, expanding scholarships to college, creating millions of new jobs. We've preserved the summer jobs program and created AmeriCorps, which gives young people the opportunity to serve in their communities and earn money for college. I want to do more.[33]

Over-promises of this sort are often disparaged as an evanescent fog that undermines national purpose. Such a charge is often justified, but a good campaign needs many things; practical hopes and dreams are among them. Campaigns also need debates, however, because they must have a device for calling unwise visions into question. Notice, for example, how Mr. Clinton's plans for the nation's youth take on a less rosy glow when examined in light of his opponent's voting record:

What I'm against is Senator Dole's plan to take money away from all the children we now help with limited federal funds and help far fewer. If we're going to have a private voucher plan, that ought to be done at the local level or the state level. But Senator Dole has consistently opposed Federal help to education. He voted against student loans. He voted against my improved student loan plans. He voted against the National Service bill, against the Head Start bill. He voted against our efforts in Safe and Drug-Free Schools. He has voted against these programs. He does not believe it. That's the issue. Ninety percent of our kids are out there in those public schools, and we need to lift their standards and move them forward with the programs like those I've outlined in this campaign.[34]

In other words, those who argue that presidential debates are little more than glorified stump speeches are off the mark. Table 5.2 shows that debates cut through the political glad-handing—the rallying of the troops, the overly embellished claims, the invocation of the deities. Debates produce an almost philosophical, or idealistic, discourse by establishing a space for examining basic premises. No doubt, idealism's opposite—realism—will always be the nation's most native political vernacular given its people's modernist tendencies. Still, that voice is temporarily suspended as candidates confront the difficult questions often asked of them.

3. *Debates bring focus to the campaign.* Particularly when delivered by someone as unique as Bob Dole, a stump speech in Philadelphia can be an interesting thing. Something of a rhetorical wanderer by nature (Dole is not quite a free-associator but he is often close), Mr. Dole used his campaign stops in 1996 to get things off his chest and often did so in a serpentine way:

> Oh, these governors are going to do a great job [curtailing crime] in their states. But to coordinate it and to put it together and to make it work for you, make it work for America, make it work for your family, your neighbors, make it work for the Delassandro family, who's been waiting 23 years, and worried every month that the murderer may be paroled. So I would just say, you know, give me your help. I'm not a rocket scientist, but this is not rocket science. This is life and death, life and death. And I want you to give me your support and give me your vote, and join with me so that we can bring a new day, a better day to our nation, for ourselves and our children and the generations yet to come. It's important. It's not about Bob Dole. It's not about Jack Kemp. It's not about Bill Clinton or Al Gore. It's about America. It's not about your politics—liberal, conservative, Democratic, independent, Republican. It's about America. It's about the future, about your kids, about your schools.[35]

Stump speeches can be dizzying, then, but presidential debates are considerably more businesslike. Table 5.2 reports a distinctive feature of debates—high Insistence scores—indicating a narrow rhetorical agenda. Insistence measures how often key words are repeated in a text, with a high score indicating conceptual redundancy. No doubt, the strictures of formal debate—the time limits, the question controls, the badinage from one's opponent—keep the discussion on track. While Edward Hinck may argue that debates are often "virtual containers of political character" that permit a candidate "to enact any image of leadership they desire,"[36] that seems untrue. More than any other forum, debates force candidates to deal with one another's arguments. Standing five feet away from one's adversary, it appears, concentrates the mind.[37]

There has been some waxing and waning of Insistence over the years (although it always stayed above the level for advertisements and speeches), with the 1984 debate being especially unfocused. In these debates, Ronald Reagan averaged 32.9 on Insistence (versus a debate mean of 64.0) and the reason for his low score was memorable: At one point in the second debate he dreamily recounted—or imagined—a trip down the coast highway in California, a trip whose purpose was never clarified. As a result, the morning newspapers questioned the president's fitness for office and made a political recovery necessary. History records that Mr. Reagan made such a recovery, but history records an even more important lesson—that debates serve as cuing devices, revealing which candidate is "on point" and which is not, which is focused on the people's business and which is amiably occupied with other matters. In these ways and more, debates matter.

4. *Debates ensure self-involvement.* A presidential debate is not a bloodless encounter about ethereal matters but a personal contest between two people, each of whom wishes to become (or remain) commander in chief. That this contest is being carried out on the most public of public stages cannot be forgotten, and so debates open up a candidate for public inspection in powerful ways. As Kathleen Jamieson and David Birdsell suggest, "So skillful have candidates and their consultants become at choreographing themselves for news, that news can no longer assume the complete burden of disclosing the person who would be president." As a result, the authors argue, debates "create a climate more conducive to political learning than any other which the typical voter will seek or chance upon."[38]

Table 5.2 tells two additional tales: (1) debates inspire more self-acknowledgment than other campaign forums and (2) debates cut back somewhat on affability. These are different tales. According to debate theory, the first is especially important because true dialectic should create conditions of self-risk for an arguer, a willingness to genuinely explore an issue even if it means eventually recanting one's original position.[39] In 1992, Bill Clinton had one of these self-reflexive moments in the third debate: "If I had it to do over again, I might answer the questions a little better. You know I've been in public life a long time and no one had ever questioned my role, and so I was asked a lot of questions about things that happened a long time ago. I don't think I answered them as well as I could have."[40]

The cynic will seize on these findings as evidence of mere self-worship or gut-spilling but that seems too harsh a judgment. A more parsimonious explanation is that debate—even in its atrophied, political form—issues a special invitation to the Self. In 1996, both Bob Dole and Bill Clinton accepted these invitations. Mr. Dole was especially affecting when doing so:

> I'm running out [of time] here. It's a very proud moment for me. And what I want the voters to do is to make a decision. And I want them to be proud of their vote in the years ahead, proud that they voted for the right candidate, proud that they voted, hopefully, for me. And I'll just make you one promise. My word is good. Democrat and Republican groups have said Bob Dole's word is good. I keep my word. I promise you the economy is going to get better. We're going to have a good economic package and we're going into the next century a better America.

Debates cut back somewhat on Human Interest, a measure of how often "people words" are used. It is impossible to think of political speech devoid of such words, so it is not surprising that debates are filled with them. But debate's intellectual agenda—matters of public policy—leaves less room for such tokens. That absence signals a difference in degree bordering on a difference in kind between debates and the other campaign forums.[41]

5. *Debates establish a common meeting place.* Some of my most important findings regarding debates are the nonfindings: Few important differences can be attributed to either (1) incumbency or (2) party, suggesting that formal debate levels the playing field between contestants, ensuring that the perquisites of incumbency do not become determinative. Debate's agendas, its moderators, and its formalities do what they are designed to do—provoke clash among contestants on a limited set of issues. As a result, debates ensure rhetorical coordination among opponents as they circle around each other's points. This, too, is part of debate's lore—the establishment of an agora so that the issues of the day can be put before the people under conditions of equal advocacy. To establish such conditions, a common language must be found, and this produces rhetorical interlacing and cross-referencing. Snippets from the first debate of 1996 exemplify:

- "The Senator mentioned the trial lawyers. In the case of product liability. . . ."
- "Mr. Lehrer, I hope well have a chance to discuss drugs later in the program. . . ."
- "Notice again, you're very selective, Mr. President. You don't want to . . ."
- "You talk about the Brady bill. There's been only one prosecution under . . ."
- "Well, I failed to mention North Korea and Cuba a while ago. You look at . . ."

Debates also cut back on the candidates' partisan styles. Political parties, it seems, can produce sinecures, forestall social reforms, and raise money like hooligans, but they seem unable to materially affect the course of a presidential debate. The story on the campaign trail is quite different. When DICTION was used to analyze stump speeches, thirty-eight of the forty-seven variables (81 percent) produced main effects for Party, but only seven variables (14 percent of the total) reliably separated Democratic from Republican debaters. Cynics will attribute such nondifferences to a kind of institutional collusion (Republicrats and all that), but a happier interpretation is that the rigors of the debate format override partisan differences. Yet another possibility is suggested by debate theory itself: when people engage in a spirited exchange, a natural learning effect occurs—a heightened awareness of interpersonal differences but also an ability to understand and articulate the position of the Other. Slowly, irresistibly, this places a Democratic overlay on Republican rhetoric (and produces the reverse effect as well). Little wonder, then, that it is hard to identify the speaker's party of origin in the following passage:

> But I think first, you should . . . I should understand that the question on your mind is, do I understand your problem? But I understand that if it occurred to me, and I might just say that I'm from a large family. I got lots of relatives. And they're good, average middle-class, hard-working Americans. They live all across the country. . . . I understand the problems. Whether it's two parents working because one has to pay the taxes and one has to provide for the family, whether it's a single parent who just barely pays the pressing bills, or whether you're worried about

an education for your children, going to the best schools, or whether you're worried about safe playgrounds, drug-free schools, crime-free schools. This is what this election is all about.

Although disguised here, this is Bob Dole the Democrat. And here is Bill Clinton the Republican, disguised as Herbert Hoover:

First of all, we have a big plan to reduce capital gains. . . . Part of my tax package, which is paid for in my balanced budget plan, would exempt up to half a million dollars in gains from people when they sell their homes, which I think is the biggest capital gains benefit we could give to most ordinary Americans. We also have a capital gains now for people that invest in new small businesses and hold the investment for five years, that was part of our other economic plan. And these are things I think that will go a long way toward helping America build a stronger economy and a better tax system. I think the most important thing to emphasize though is that we also have to help people in other ways to build a stronger economy, and we can't have any tax cut that's not paid for.

Perhaps the most remarkable thing about the findings reported here is that they largely reinforce traditional, but untested, lore about debate. As we have seen, debate gives equal footing to incumbents and nonincumbents, Democrats and Republicans, Clintons and Doles. Debate does not completely obliterate the differences among them (that would surely be impossible) but it does insinuate a common language into what is often a discordant political environment. This does not make debates models of intellection but it does mean they are neither ersatz forms of advertising nor shards of discourse scooped up from the hustings. Presidential debates are comparatively sober, comparatively focused, comparatively plainspoken, comparatively self-risking encounters with some potential to create genuine dialogue. Or so my data show.[42]

POLITICAL ADVERTISING

Political advertising inspires a long list of detractors. Here are some reasons why: (1) advertising, most famously, degrades the political

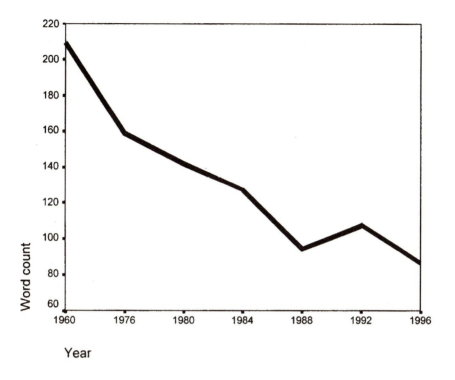

Figure 5.2. Length of Advertisements in Sample (n=553).

process by merchandizing candidates as if they were bars of soap;[43] (2) so much money is now spent on creating national ads that no funds are left to engage the electorate in local venues;[44] (3) advertising's visual endowments cause even serious news programs to feature them, thereby compromising traditional standards of reportage;[45] (4) the constant onslaught of negative advertising disillusions the electorate, making them reject all campaign communications and, even, making them not vote;[46] and perhaps most damaging, (5) political ads cheapen the quality of campaign discourse by trading on unsubstantiated claims and the basest of human instincts.[47]

This bill of particulars is but an abbreviation of the larger case made against campaigns in general: they are too superficial, too expensive, too degrading, too long. Political ads can at least plead innocent to the latter charge since, as figure 5.2 indicates, they have gotten shorter over time.[48] With the 1996 ads averaging only eighty-six words in length, is so slim a reality worth the vitriol directed at it? Even asking such a question will be heresy for many: for Common Cause, which wants to enact campaign finance reform to limit the egregious amount now spent on advertising; for Project VoteSmart, which wants to increase the supply of political information now being suppressed by advertising-driven campaigns; for the League of Women Voters, which sponsors advertising's great rival—campaign debates. None of these groups would be surprised to learn that voters frequently depend on advertising for their political information.[49]

But if advertising is a swamp, it is at least an interesting swamp. I find political ads to be complex despite their brevity (or perhaps because of it) and to provide certain benefits that have heretofore gone unappreciated. For some it will seem odd that I devote time here to the language of political commercials since advertising is such a visual medium. But as experts in the graphic arts tell us, an "integrated" medium like advertising, in which words and pictures are wound around each other tightly, cannot be understood if one of its components is ignored.[50] To observe that advertising has pictures is to say too little; to assert that pictures are more memorable (or more influential) than the words used to frame them is to allege realities not yet proved. So, for example, to see a tall stranger come riding out of the sunset only to jump off his horse next to a roaring campfire surely makes us feel we are in the presence of majesty. But it took language to explain that that stranger was Clayton Williams and even more language to explain that he was a Republican, that he was running for governor, and that he wanted the votes of urban Texans in 1990. Pictures are impressive, but they come to mean specific things only when viewers are guided toward those specificities. Language helps do the guiding.

Despite the great amount of research now being done on political advertising, few have stopped to ask what makes it special. One way of answering that question is to compare ads to other campaign outlets (like speeches and debates). Doing so reveals some obvious and nonobvious things. To wit:

1. *Political advertising is effusive.* Compared to the other campaign forums, political ads are highly Embellished and contain more Patri-

otism, Inspiration, and Praise (*bold, brave, good, glorious*) as well. That is, advertising can be thought of as the poetry of politics, a device for saying things that are hard to say face-to-face. Advertisements use pictures because pictures (at least the best of them) are overdetermined with meaning—the American flag, two children selling lemonade, the lead-off hitter sliding into second base, unemployed workers waiting for their welfare checks. Political artists gobble up these images and put them to work in behalf of their candidates, thereby turning pictures into arguments. The precise ontology of these images does not matter, only their forward thrust. This makes advertisements surreal in the extreme, a place where figments from different eras, different axiologies swirl about one another, asking viewers to submit. Even without the pictures and swelling chords, that is, a Reagan commercial still has perfect pitch:

> *Reagan voice*: Just across the hall here in the White House is the Roosevelt room; draped from each flag are battle streamers signifying every battle campaign fought since the revolutionary war. My fondest hope for this presidency is that the people of America give us the continued opportunity to preserve a peace so strong and so lasting, never again will we have to add another streamer to those flags.[51]

It is useful to look carefully at the language of advertising and then to look again. As the ancient rhetoricians would say, advertising is aggressively enthymematic. It is never complete unto itself but only becomes complete within its audience. It trades on viewers' fundamental assumptions, their unspoken hopes and worries, and then asks that these be contributed to its own half-logic. When reminiscing above, that is, Mr. Reagan transcends the polis. He makes no distinction between grand and foolish wars but instead makes a salad of the many emotions conflict produces—pride, history, triumph, fear. In so doing his ad becomes a prayer, not a self-endorsement. He asks for no votes, only for agreement on certain fundamental premises and then, silently, for the application of those premises to his personal candidacy. All of this happens by indirection, making the logic of advertising a highly emotional logic.

2. *Political advertising is implicative.* Compared to campaign speeches and debates, political ads are surprisingly understated. They score considerably lower on Certainty and Activity and are especially low on Insistence, meaning that they do not, contrary to stereotype, hammer the same point over and over again. Instead, political ads wander among a thicket of images and ideologies, deftly brushing up against all of them but never grasping them brutishly, completely. When advertising was a younger art, it behaved differently. Note, for example, how clear and assured political advertising was in 1960:

> *Kennedy voice*: Mr. Nixon has said that our prestige is the highest it's ever been. I don't agree. This is a strong country, but it must be stronger. This is a powerful country but it must be more powerful. We must build a strong America in a world that is free. I ask you to join me in building that America.[52]

By 1988 things had changed. In part this was because political ads were no longer manufactured out of pastiches from the stump. Instead, they contained the kinds of "production values" Madison Avenue prefers. Replacing the straightforward, declarative arguments of the Kennedy advertisement were thirty-second playlets artfully scripted by a new breed of campaign advertisers. Narrative is useful because it lets advertisers make claims without having to account for those claims and it is powerful because its dramatic personae and twists of plot and pacing are so distracting. With narrative, arguments are no longer delivered in Gatling gun style. As a result, viewers are encouraged to defer policy considerations to some later date. A Dukakis narrative from the 1988 campaign illustrates how intriguing these deferrals can be:

> *Bush crony #1*: Oh, jees. They're going to kill us on this Noriega thing. Look at the headline—Panamanian Drug Lord . . .

> *Bush crony #2*: Yeah. It's a picture of Bush with Noriega. Just won't let it go, will they?

> *Bush crony #1*: No. We need a lot better answer.

> *Bush crony #2*: Something better than I don't remember.

Bush crony #1: Well, I'm working on it. I'm working on it.

Bush crony #2: You better be.

Bush crony #1: Maybe we should just stick with "I don't remember." Ha, ha.

Announcer: They'd like to sell you a package. Wouldn't you rather choose a President?[53]

Advertisements like this keep us from feeling pestered. The ad makes its points but also lets the viewer feel like an autonomous creature capable of independent thought. Viewer and narrator team up here, producing a quintessentially postmodern effect—a Dukakis dramatization of Bush strategy-making that does not acknowledge its own rhetorical status. By now viewers have learned to take this legerdemain in stride, thereby marking the emergence of a mature art form.

3. *Political advertising is telegraphic*. To say that ads are telegraphic is not to say they are short. In fact, telegrams are dense with information: "John died. Stop. Funeral Friday. Stop." What telegrams do not supply is interpretation and that is how it is with ads as well. Campaign advertising puts things on the agenda and then quits the scene. That is why advertising's low Insistence scores are so important: commercials embrace no issue for very long; they hit and run. Notice in the following ad, for example, how each sentence is an entity unto itself and could easily be rearranged without great conceptual violence being done. The interdependence among the topics vanishes almost as quickly as it appears:

Governor: I'm Dick Riley and I want to talk with you for just a moment about my friend Jimmy Carter. I was for him four years ago. I'm for him today. The textile industry is important to our state. Exports are up. Fort Jackson is still open and the President helped with both. Jimmy Carter is a widely respected man who's good for South Carolina and good for the nation. I'm voting for him on November 4th and I invite you to join me.

Announcer: Re-elect President Carter.[54]

Ads have become the primary repository, and delivery system, of a campaign's "talking points." Ads contain what Raymond Williams might call the "keywords" of a campaign [55] and so it is not surprising that compared to speeches and debates, ads score much higher on Complexity (and much lower on Familiarity), largely because they index the topical issues of the day. In addition, ads are higher on Concreteness (to add solidity) and Numerical Terms (to create a sense of magnitude). These four features produce a string-of-beads effect, as issue after issue is momentarily exposed to the viewer and then secreted away. Ads do not, as a result, ever complete arguments. They only start them. Two ads from the 1996 Clinton campaign show how much can be packed into a very small space:

> *Announcer*: Imagine if *Dole and Gingrich* were in charge. A hundred-thousand more *police*. The President's doing it; Dole and Gingrich would undo it. *Family and medical leave*. The President did it; Dole/Gingrich against. *College scholarships* strengthen education. The President did it; Dole wants to eliminate the *Department of Education* and undo it. Banning *cigarette ads* that target *children*. The President did it. Dole would undo it. Dole/Gingrich. Wrong for our country. *President Clinton*. Protecting our *values*.[56]

> *Announcer*: The Oval Office. If Dole sits here and Gingrich runs Congress, what could happen? *Medicare* slashed. *Women's right* to choose, gone. *Education*, school *drug programs* cut. And a risky $550 billion plan *balloons the deficit*, raises *interest rates*, hurts the economy. President Clinton says *balance the budget, cut taxes* for families' *college tuition*. Stands up to Dole and Gingrich. But if Dole wins, and Gingrich runs *Congress*, there'll be nobody there to stop them.[57]

It is hard to imagine these spots working any harder than they do. It is also hard to imagine how advertising could be better suited to the demands of a postmodern age. Ads like these revel in their plurality, spitting out issue after issue without even a tissue of integument between them, thereby demanding only half-listening from their viewers. Such ads depend for their effects on viewers' abilities to instantly recognize the key political terms of the day (*drugs*, *taxes*) and to be impressed that so many issues have been addressed ad seriatim. Busy voters have many things on their minds. Political ads do as well.

4. *Political advertising is compensatory.* Advertising also gives the campaign a "second voice," one that says things the candidate cannot say personally. Bill Clinton is a case in point. As we see in the ads above, the Clinton campaign was more than willing to name names and to pin Bob Dole to the mat (it added Newt Gingrich for good measure). Not surprisingly, then, Clinton's ads were much more negative (low Optimism, low Commonality) than his speeches and far more ideological as well (low Realism). In addition, the Clinton ads had none of the Human Interest for which he was famous, nor did they make the great number of Voter References he used on the stump. Instead, his ads were filled with Leader References (as can be seen above) as well as Party References. Ostensibly, Mr. Clinton thought it untoward to do the party-baiting himself so he ceded the job to his advertisers:

Dole: You're gonna see the real Bob Dole out there from now on.

Announcer: The real Bob Dole? He's voted for 900-billion in higher taxes. Fellow Republicans call him the "tax collector for the welfare state." The real Bob Dole? The real Dole opposed higher minimum wage ten times, voted to slash Medicare, raised premiums, weakened nursing home standards. The real Bob Dole? The real Bob Dole? The real Bob Dole, against 100-thousand more police, against a drug czar to fight smugglers. The real Bob Dole? The real Bob Dole, wrong for Kentucky, wrong for America.[58]

There are other ways in which advertising is compensatory. A national political campaign is a complex undertaking involving hundreds of thousands of people. They work for months on end, hustling the candidate to and fro, adjusting to countless exigencies between March and November. The candidates themselves can only be in one place at one time and, while there, can only respond with their native wit. Ads, on the other hand, are a team affair. They can be created quickly and satellite-fed even quicker. They can adjust to new circumstances instantly, squelching dangerous rumors or correcting a candidate's misstatements. Most important, advertising can conduct many conversations simultaneously.

The 553 ads gathered here were categorized into six main topics and then analyzed for distinctive language patterns. The categories included human services (13 percent of the sample), the economy (29 percent), foreign policy (13 percent), law and order (6 percent), ethics and morality (25 percent), and multiple topics (14 percent). Most of the stylistic patterns were unsurprising. And that is important. Each topic provided the candidate with a predictable, but different way of reaching the voter. When addressing human services (disaster relief, Aid to Dependent Children, the nation's schools), for example, campaigns loaded up on Optimism and Inspiration. When discussing the economy, they used Commonality, Accomplishment, and Realism to generate a "can do" spirit. Law and order provided a sterner option, with candidates issuing dire warnings (low Optimism) to stiffen the nation's resolve (low Realism). Ethics and morality permitted a happier preachment: high Commonality, Optimism, and Religious References. But foreign policy ads varied considerably from campaign to campaign, sometimes adopting a reassuring tone and sometimes becoming apocalyptic. Two advertisements from recent George Bush campaigns illustrate these options:

Historical voiceover: Just two hours ago allied air forces began an attack on military . . .

News report: President Bush said today that he reassured Mr. Yeltsin the United States would stand by democracy. If revolutionary terrorists are armed with nuclear and chemical weapons it may pose new challenges to the president.

Announcer: In a world where we're just one unknown dictator away from the next major crisis, who do you most trust to be sitting in this chair?[59]

Announcer: On an August day in 1988, an historic event took place. It didn't happen on Main Street or in any American town, but in Russia, when soldiers began destroying hundreds of nuclear missiles with the understanding that we've destroyed some of our own. The first disarmament treaty of its kind—and though most Americans were unaware of the significance of the moment or realized it was George Bush who led the way—some day their grandchildren will.[60]

The conventional view is that political ads are surgical strikes designed to deal with special campaign problems. My data suggest another function: they let candidates speak in a range of voices. Advertising opens up a candidacy whereas speeches and debates are more constraining. In these latter forums, the candidate performs. But advertising reverses that process: it performs the candidate. Through its images and contrivances it sends messages that the candidate did not have time to send or, for strategic reasons, could not personally send. This makes advertising "false" in the extreme: few people pontificate for fifteen seconds at a clip or spend their days standing next to an American flag while tousling the hair of a six-year-old. In its own defense, advertising makes this implicit pledge: the candidate would have done such things, organically, if time and circumstance had permitted.

5. *Political advertising is contrary.* Many people are transfixed by negative advertising. Voters despise it; the press decries it; and candidates are defensive about it. Somehow, though, the genre endures. Indeed, despite their antipathies, voters watch enough negative advertising to be influenced by it;[61] the press focuses heavily on it via their ad watches (a tactic that may advance, rather than retard, advertising's effectiveness);[62] and even candidates who enjoy the privileges of incumbency and a stupendous economy—candidates like Bill Clinton—use negative advertising extensively. Studies by Lynda Kaid,[63] Darrell West,[64] and Kathleen Jamieson and her colleagues[65] show that the 1996 presidential campaign used more negative ads than any campaign since 1952 and that the Clinton campaign was fully implicated in these trends.

How much negative advertising is there? Karen Johnson-Cartee and Gary Copeland report that more than one-third of all presidential ads these days is negative,[66] and my sample roughly conforms to those figures. Of the 553 ads studied here, 50 percent could be reliably classified as Promotional (straightforward endorsements of a candidate's positions), 23 percent Comparative (Candidate A versus Can-

135

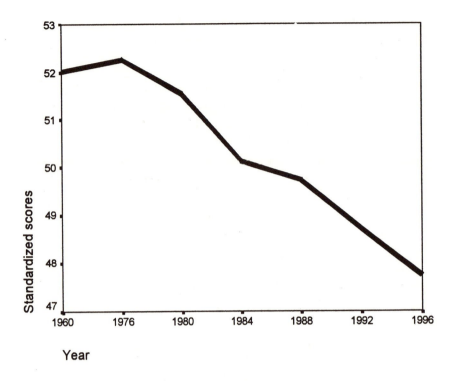

Figure 5.3. Optimism in Political Advertising over Time.

didate B), and 27 percent Reactive—sustained attacks on an opponent or responses to charges made by that opponent. But when the advertising was broken down by year, the Reactive ads ranged from 11 percent in 1960 to 43 percent in 1996, with the intervening years seeing a stair-step rise in negativity.

Structurally, then, political advertising has become more negative. As we see in figure 5.3, that has been true stylistically as well. Should these findings depress us? Some scholars think not. Bruce Gronbeck, for example, argues that character attacks may actually draw the electorate into the public square. "Voters are not very confident of their own knowledge of issues," says Gronbeck, "nor do they think much of solutions proposed in the heat of a campaign."[67] As a result, says Gronbeck, negative ads may give the voter the gumption to participate in the political process. And such extra participation can be important, says Kenneth Goldstein, who finds the effects of negative ads most pronounced in races decided by a mere percent or two.[68] Kathleen Jamieson makes an even more important point: negative ads usually contain more policy information than the better-liked promotional spots.[69]

Consider, for example, the following ad produced by the Reagan campaign during the 1980 presidential race:

> *Voice #1*: The League of Women Voters invited President Carter to join the 1980 debates. He refused the invitation. Maybe it's because during his administration inflation has gone as high as 18%. The number of Americans out of work has reached eight and a half million. Housing starts have hit a new low, while interest rates have hit a new high. Maybe he won't debate because he knows the real question is, "Can we afford four more years of this?"

> *Voice #2*: The time is now for Reagan. Reagan for President.[70]

Despite its distemper, it is hard to fault this ad for efficiency. Like most Reactive ads, it (1) covers a diversity of topics (high Variety scores), (2) provides specifics (Leader References, Numerical Terms), (3) keys on policy matters rather than general human emotions (low Familiarity scores), and, most intriguingly, (4) contains no Self-References. In other words, negative ads have a remote-control quality to them. Rarely does one find a candidate personally addressing the flaws of his or her opponent. Instead, the job is left to an omniscient narrator who uses "a report format"[71] to deliver the coup de grâce.

This rhetorical distance may be important. By using third parties to throw the brickbats rather than having the candidate do it personally, negative ads may actually contribute a tincture of civility to politics. The American people might even appreciate such restraint. When the Reactive ads of winning and losing candidates were compared, for example, the "winning" ads were shown to be (1) fairly impersonal (low Self-References and Human Interest), (2) business-like (high Insistence, Accomplishment, Temporal References, and Numerical References), and (3) straightforward (they did not back into their positions via Denial statements). In other words, negative advertising may not be as monolithic as some have assumed. As we see in the following ad, overstatements can always be substituted for empirical claims but it may not be functional to do so:

> *Voice #1*: I think Governor Reagan in a crisis situation would be very apt to use military force.

> *Voice #2*: We really have to keep our heads cool. And I don't think that Reagan is cool.

> *Voice #3*: He's sort of like the old western movies; you know, go out and shoot 'em dead type attitude and I think that could really get us into a lot of trouble.

> *Voice #4*: Reagan doesn't stop to think of things before he does it.

> *Voice #5*: That scares me about Ronald Reagan. It really does.

> *Voice #6*: My decision is made. I'm going to stick with President Carter.

> *Announcer*: On November 4th re-elect President Carter.[72]

Despite negative advertising's high profile, the majority of political spots made for presidential politics are Promotional and Comparative. This does not make political commercials a boon to the democracy but it does suggest they have some prosocial value. Although Ronald Reagan's "Morning in America" ads were greeted with derision in the academic community in 1984, for example, there is little doubt that they tapped into powerful cultural myths and deeply felt human emotions and hence brought (many) Americans together. While political ads will probably always be the id of campaign communication and political debates the super ego, one must never underestimate the importance of that which advertising most reliably delivers— political emotion. The crush of modern life now makes it hard for voters to head to the voting booth on a crisp November morning. If political advertising puts a spring in their step on that occasion, can it be entirely loathsome?

CONCLUSION

The three campaign forums analyzed here are quite distinct. Their distinctiveness is important. Together, they offer the hope that enough different forms of communication can make the overall campaign productive for the citizenry. The language of conventioneering, for example, shows that campaigns are both a time of remembrance and a time of decision-making and that American politics is as hortatory as its functionality permits. For their parts, presidential debates level the playing field among opponents, inject a modicum of sobriety into a campaign process that often gets out of hand, and force candidates to be more introspective as well. Given these qualities, one can only wish for more debates.

Of advertising we probably have enough. The negativity of campaign commercials is disturbing and their fatuousness cannot go unremarked. But we need to know more about their effects. Some researchers claim that obnoxious though they are, political ads may be informing the electorate and, in certain circumstances, helping to get out the vote. The findings reported here suggest that political ads are more complex than most people suppose. They often have inspiring themes, they place new items on the national agenda, and they provide a way for candidates to deal with complex, or touchy, issues. This does not make political ads commendable but it does make them interesting.

The theme of this chapter is that political campaigns can best be seen as a kind of national conversation. To be sure, the conversation they inspire is often superficial and occasionally degrading. No doubt we can do better. But campaigns do not fail when they make people uncertain, because uncertainty leads to discovery. And campaigns do not fail when they make people angry, because anger can be motivating. Campaigns, and conversations, only fail when they forestall genuine engagement. The data in this chapter show that campaigns produce engagement—sometimes. One can only hope that that sometimes becomes always soon.

CHAPTER 6

The Political Voice

W HEN actors become old and tired, they can always play politicians. The scripts for political films are easily mastered and the dramatis personae rarely complicated. Politicians on screen are often morally shallow—such as Bill McKay in *The Candidate* or the title character in *Bob Roberts*—when they are not being malign, such as Willie Stark in *All the King's Men* or Lonesome Rhodes in *A Face in the Crowd*. Whether it is Otto Preminger in the 1960s or Sidney Lumet in the 1980s, Hollywood directors have learned the political routines implicitly. Even when dramatizing admirable characters like Jefferson Smith in *Mr. Smith Goes to Washington* or Dave Kovic in *Dave*, the directors also highlight the baleful hangers-on who become the heroes' foils in the films.

There is a message in this predictability: political behavior has become tacit knowledge for most Americans, making a film like *Primary Colors* familiar to them even before they have seen it. Most Americans quickly recognize the political voice—its coarseness, its velvet intonations—even though Hollywood sometimes makes their lives more complicated by portraying complex characters like Frank Skeffington in *The Last Hurrah* or Jordan Lyman in *Seven Days in May*. While less common, these characters are more representative of the real world because they are complex. This chapter's theme is that the political voice is complicated because it contains all of our hopes and dreams, all of our denials and repressions as well.

Sigmund Freud knew something about repression, and, according to historian Carl Schorske, he knew something of politics as well. Schorske tells the story of Freud, who, at the age of forty-five, was finally given an associate professorship. For Freud, this was an honor much delayed, a sentiment he revealed in a letter to a friend:

With Tony Bernal and Sharon Jarvis

The public enthusiasm is immense. Congratulations and bouquets keep pouring in, as if the role of sexuality had suddenly been recognized by His Majesty, the interpretation of dreams confirmed by the Council of Ministers, and the necessity of the psychoanalytic theory of hysteria carried by a two-thirds majority in Parliament.[1]

Freud's burlesque has intriguing conflicts. On this most personal of occasions, he sought out the most formal, the most public, of rewards. Or at least part of him did. The other part, the mocking part, knew that such a great huzzah was incommensurate with the honor he had won. As any good analyst might observe, Freud's humor thereby revealed an emotionality that his cold, Viennese exterior was obliged to reject. The scientist in Freud laughed at the sight he had constructed but the child in Freud demanded recompense. To find it, he turned to Mother Politics.

Freud's double-meaningness is the double-meaningness of us all. Politics is powerful, irresistible, because it contains both the maternal principle and the paternal principle. That is, even though government collects our taxes, paves our roads, and sends us to war, its ceremonies and traditions also fill us with feelings of destiny. This duality cordons off politics, making it an arena of contradictions. Hollywood capitalizes on these contradictions when it shows great leaders undone by simple flaws or eternal truths sacrificed to the raw expediencies of the day. Hollywood enjoys using political plots because it does not have to invent the drama found there.

This chapter looks at campaigning in light of other societal discourses—particularly corporate advocacy, religious preachment, and social activism—to discover what makes politics special. It also examines what politicians say during a campaign compared to what the press and the people say, and it concludes that politics is an inherently fractured discourse. In addition, it looks at the role played by political parties and finds a surprising symmetry, and durability, to partisanship in the United States. Ultimately, if the data in this chapter are to be believed, civic wisdom lies not in blindly accepting or rejecting politics but in coming to see its complications as our own. In such a frame, political understanding becomes a kind of self-love. This is a frame Dr. Freud himself would have understood.

COMPENSATORY POLITICS

To say that politics is compensatory is to be polite about its most maddening feature. Politics is compensatory in both senses of the word: (1) it offers imperfect solutions to human problems and (2) it grounds those solutions in the world of barter and commerce. So, for example, the U.S. Congress only considered antitobacco legislation when other, less arduous methods of dealing with the problem had failed. But even then it factored in a host of issues: payment for some, but not all, tobacco-related illnesses; restrictions on tobacco marketing at some public venues but not at others; subsidies to farmers who would no longer grow tobacco; due regard for the resulting price increases on a pack of cigarettes. It is often said that watching legislation being made is like watching sausage being made. What is not said often enough is that a democratic society serves only sausage.

Comparing the many thousands of texts collected in the Campaign Mapping Project inevitably produces many differences but nowhere were these differences more stark than when the three campaign voices were contrasted. Table 6.1 sketches out the most important of these differences: political campaigners are more buoyant, more grounded, and more relationally concerned than either the people or the press. Does this make politicians weather vanes? It does. Their discourse points in three directions at once: to the concrete, to the human, to the possible. Does this make politicians facile? It does. Campaigners eschew genuinely philosophical discussions by offering solutions to problems they can solve rather than discussing those they cannot. If given the choice, politicians would rather discuss national values than anything else. Does this make politics imperfect? It does. It also makes it politics.

Members of the press enjoy detailing campaign banalities. For them, banality is the most grievous charge that can be leveled at anyone or anything, the eighth of the deadly sins. For politicians easily intimidated by the press, a charge of banality will usually send them scampering. Ross Perot cared little for the media and, had he known what it was, he would have thought banality a virtue. He proved that during both of his runs for the presidency:

TABLE 6.1
Politicians vs. Other Campaign Participants

Political Dimension	Language Variables	Campaign Voice		
		People	Politicians	Press
Spaciousness				
	Optimism	Low	High	Low
	Patriotism	Medium	High	Low
	Insistence	Medium	Low	High
Directness				
	Realism	Medium	High	Low
	Accomplishment	Low	High	Medium
	Complexity	Medium	Low	High
Relationship				
	Self-References	Medium	High	Low
	Human Interest	Medium	High	Low
	Present Concern	Medium	High	Low

We've got to eliminate—we've got to *eliminate the hatred* and stress that divides us. We've got to become a *united team* working together to make the century the *greatest in our history.* As your president, I will use *the bully pulpit* of the White House to keep the American people focused on *these important issues* that only you the people can deal with. I'll create and support an environment that keeps us focused on *being good people* that love and care for one another, because we must be good people if we want a *great country for our children* in the 21st century. Remember, it is *better to light a candle than to curse the darkness.* The *shadows will fall* behind you if you walk into the light. And if all the darkness in the world cannot put out *the light of one little candle*; and as all this odd stuff happens, focus on that and *just keep marching* toward the light.[2]

Here, Mr. Perot sets a record for banality. He says old things in old ways and new things in old ways. That he does so is remarkable given his high-technology background and his brilliance as a financier. But the language of campaigning came naturally to him because he habitually treated concrete problems as the only problems that counted. An American empiricist, he, but one with a certain jauntiness, a quality that impressed many and that made him seem dangerously hyperactive to others. But few could gainsay him completely because he humanized issues so well. Billionaire that he was, Perot spoke as if he lived in South Dallas, a place he had never visited, a place he would never visit:

> Everywhere I go, *people ask*, "Ross, do we have *bad people* in Washington"? I reply no, we have *good people* in Washington, but they are trapped inside a bad system. Political campaigns go on too long and cost too much money. It costs an average of $800,000 to run for the House, $4 million to run for the Senate, and a $100 million to run for the presidency. *The large contributors* who fund these political campaigns control our government instead of *the owners of the country, the people.*
>
> We must shorten elections to four months. This would dramatically reduce the cost. We must pass laws requiring candidates running for the House to get all the money from *people in their districts* and candidates running for the Senate to get all the money from *people who live in their states.* Get rid of PAC money, foreign money and all soft money. This is wrong. We must stop it. In addition, nearly *half of our people don't even vote* because it's *hard for working people* to get to the polls on Tuesday. Hold elections on Saturdays and Sundays so that *everybody can vote.* In addition, get rid of the electoral vote for the presidency. It's as obsolete as a dinosaur.[3]

Figure 6.1 shows that Perot's enthusiasms were not unique to him. Throughout the last fifty years, the gap in Optimism between campaigners and the people/press has never closed. Given the diverse personalities represented in my sample, and given the nation's vicissitudes during this time—Korea, Vietnam, continuing threats from the Soviet Union, periods of economic distress, a volatile Middle East—that consistency is all the more impressive. It is almost as if we pay our politicians to make us happy.

Such a notion is not completely far-fetched. It may even be true that we lampoon our politicians out of pure defensiveness. Perhaps if they suddenly began speaking like us we would all run screaming

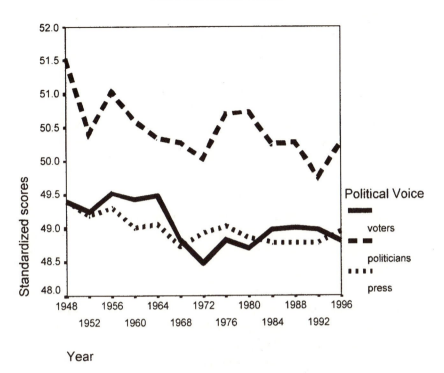

Figure 6.1. Optimism Scores over Time.

into the night. Some such notion lies at the heart of Warren Beatty's humor in *Bulworth*, the story of a politician who said exactly what was on his mind and who was, as a result, dyspeptic. Such movies resemble the pile-ups on the interstate—they fascinate us because they are dramatic, because they do not affect us personally, and because they are rare. Movies like *Bulworth* are to be witnessed, not to be lived.

Politicians' optimism may even engender a contagion response. Martin Wattenberg finds that between 1952 and 1988 voters consistently voted for candidates rather than against them. "Contrary to popular wisdom," says Wattenberg, "the like/dislike data provide excellent evidence . . . that American voters cast their ballots with a focus more on the positive than on the negative."[4] That is clearly not how the press operates. The data I have assembled here, corroborated in very different fashion by other researchers, show that the press tells a far more somber story.[5] It drops out the patriotic allusions, the bon mots, and the familiarities and concentrates instead on campaign personalities rendered in historical perspective. It is enough to bring a tear to Ross Perot's eye:

> While President Clinton and Republican nominee Robert J. Dole whirl around the country by train, plane and bus courting voters, Reform Party presidential candidate Ross Perot avoids personal contact with voters, preferring to remain at his desk in a Dallas high rise and communicate via television commercials.
>
> Perot has had a couple of close encounters with voters. He reluctantly shook hands with a dozen leaders of the American Legion when they formed a receiving line after his speech to their convention in Salt Lake City on Wednesday but for the most part, he seldom ventures beyond his Dallas command post.
>
> Perot has had even less contact with the news media. When three reporters followed him backstage after his Legion speech, he sent word via a club wielding security guard that he would not shake hands with the Legionnaires unless the reporters left.
>
> All of this is reminiscent of 1992, when Perot, running as an independent without a party affiliation, made only one in person appearance before Oct. 1, and that one was a mid summer disaster. He told the NAACP convention of his cotton broker father's affection for black sharecroppers in his home town of Texarkana, Tex., and referred to blacks as "your people."
>
> Yet by comparison, Perot's schedule this year is a veritable talkathon. In the three weeks since his nomination, he has delivered his folksy view of the world to two national veterans groups and has two more speeches scheduled this week.[6]

Although press discourse will be examined more carefully in chapter 7, several of its features can be noted here. Most obvious are its distanced quality (versus the candidates' interpersonal flourishes), its emphasis on campaign processes (versus candidates' focus on values), and its tendency to feature the downside of politics. But even more distinctive are its high Insistence scores. Note in the passage above how the reporter commits to a single topic, boring ever deeply into the Perot campaign, each paragraph adding detail to the reporter's overall thesis. When it comes to politicians, however, theses are hard to find. Instead, discussions begin and end quickly and transitions typically take the form of "Now this . . ." The politician presumes an impatient listener.

Indeed, the political voice's low Insistence scores are its signal feature. That quality produces the openness many find so frustrating in politics—the sudden renegotiations of just-completed compacts, the unsteady search for something agreeable to say, the impertinent amalgamations and transmogrifications. Low Insistence scores mean that politicians negotiate the intellectual terrain moment by moment. Some years ago, critic Richard Weaver described such "spaciousness" as endemic to mid–nineteenth century oratory, a time when issues of authority seemed settled, allowing an orator to speak with a "declamatory quality" and assume that "he was speaking for corporate humanity. . . . Oratory of the broadly ruminative kind," said Weaver, "is acceptable only when we accredit someone with the ability to review our conduct, our destiny, and the causes of things in general. . . . If we reach a condition in which no man is believed to have this power," Weaver concluded, "we will accordingly be impatient with that kind of discourse."[7]

Weaver's predictions about impatience have come true, but the rhetorical qualities he identified have not in fact waned. Politicians continue to look for "room" sufficient for their purposes. But today their low Insistence scores suggest a difficult pluralism, not a cultural uniformity. Their license to use a presumptive discourse may have been revoked, philosophically, but its rhetorical attractions still beckon. And so when he spoke, Ronald Reagan knew that he was no Rufus Choate but he still managed to cover the waterfront in five minutes:

American values

> You know, it is tragically easy today to forget the spirit of America four years ago. We united to salute two hundred years of human liberty. We stood on the threshold of our third century, confident that we'd kept faith with our heritage, certain of our capacity to build on that heritage in shaping our future. The eyes of the world were upon us. No

147

ally but knew we were reliable; no adversary but knew the full measure of our devotion to democracy and our commitment to freedom around the world.

Economic prosperity

We were prosperous, our economy, was sound, our leadership was trusted and respected, our people faced the future with a robust faith. As I say, it's easy to forget. It has been a long four years.

Foreign entanglements

The bright promise of a new century slowly dimmed and we slipped into a long twilight of doubt and confusion. Our prosperity was squandered in economic mismanagement. Today, the average American's real spendable income is less than it was in 1976. Our strength was diminished. We no longer possess the means to deter a serious challenge to our allies or ourselves. Our credibility was wasted. Today, our allies cast about for ways to accommodate to a world without America's leadership. Our adversaries cast about for new adventures, probing the frontiers of freedom in some places, penetrating them in others.

National restoration

And we're told that to think of other times is simplistic, that to wish for our restoration as a great nation is simplistic, as though we hearkened to some distant golden age existing only in myth and legend. But, what we are talking about is America four years ago. We are talking not of reaching for myth; we are talking rather of restoring the reality of an America that was for 200 years and that can be again.[8]

The seamlessness of Reagan's remarks is noteworthy. His hortatory first and fourth paragraphs sandwich practical fears but the junctures between them are not obvious. Reagan shows why political discourse is high on both Realism and Patriotic Terms, perhaps attesting to Ambrose Bierce's observation that politics is "a strife of interest masquerading as a contest of principles."[9] But for many Americans the masquerade has become naturalized—they expect national values and GNP data to be served up simultaneously.[10] This makes something of a religion out of modernism but that, too, is the American way. Campaign oratory emphasizes clear, practical action (i.e., high Accomplishment scores) even as it deploys the nation's reliquary. If this be a contradiction, so be it. Politics, too, is multitudes.[11]

Politicians' heavy use of Self-Reference and Human Interest is also one of its most characteristic features. Journalists decry such cozying-up, finding Bill Clinton especially irksome in that regard. Academicians also denounce it as a dangerous diversion from the structural logic that ought to guide decision-making. But the politicians offer a strong rebuttal. By placing people (and themselves) at the center of things, they underline the fact that nothing happens in a democracy unless the people will it. In arguing thusly they reinscribe the ancient Greek tradition in which, according to philosopher Sheldon Wolin, the political "comprehended all of the significant area of life in the community: family, religion, education, poetry, drama, and the fine arts as well as the functions usually associated with government in the narrow sense—for example, lawmaking, administration of justice, war, diplomacy, etc."[12]

Even though the U.S. population has increased exponentially during the last fifty years, thereby making face-to-face campaigning difficult, candidates have compensated by increasing their Human Interest terms steadily. In addition, the natural campaign cycle (from late August through early November) finds a consistent rise in Self-References. As the candidates approach election day, that is, they give evidence that a campaign is ultimately a referendum on themselves as people. All of this makes the political voice anthropocentric. The press instinctively resists that style and a vivid contrast results:

Chicago Tribune

The most recent trustees' report, in June, projects that Medicare, a $181 billion program in 1995, will be bankrupt in five years unless benefits are restrained or the payroll tax, which funds the program, is increased.

Dole has called for creation of a bipartisan commission after the election to recommend steps to shore up the program.

Until he left the Senate, Dole supported the GOP plan that would have cut the projected rate of growth in Medicare over the next six years by $167 billion through reducing benefits and making policy changes that save money.

According to the Congressional Budget Office, the Republican plan would reduce the average yearly Medicare benefit in 2002 from $8,100 to $7,000.[13]

Bob Dole

I want to strengthen and save Medicare. I don't see any senior citizens here, but if one shows up, I want to be sure they understand this. Don't be frightened by all the ads from the labor bosses and the Democratic Party. They're trying to scare senior citizens. Don't believe it. Under our plan, Medicare grows 7 percent a year—twice the rate of inflation, 39 percent over six years. We're going to preserve and strengthen Medicare just as we did back in 1983, when I was on a commission that rescued Social Security from bankruptcy—and I will be known as the president who saved Medicare.[14]

To say that politics is compensatory is to say several things: (1) because the population is large, campaigners blend the institutional with the social; (2) because politics is conflictual, campaigners try to accommodate all who care about an issue; (3) because politics is part cost-accountancy, part religion, campaigners balance the empirical with the axiological; (4) because life is hard, campaigners try to stay upbeat. As Gerald Bruns notes, "the discourse of governance is rooted in the essential weakness of the one who speaks . . . because reality is intractable, or has a will of its own."[15] In other words, politicians talk as they do because they have no other choice. But by taking on so much, asks Gary Orren, is politics now stretched out of shape?[16] By constantly overpromising, have politicians contributed directly to the cycles of discontent now affecting the nation? Knowing how crucial civic hope is to a culture, the political voice responds with a question of its own: If not me, who?

Synthetic Politics

Despite its willingness to bear such burdens, politics is in some trouble. Studies show that political cynicism has never been higher or turnout rates lower. Judging by book titles alone (*Why Americans*

Hate Politics), politicians are held in contempt and the press is not far behind (*Breaking the News: How the Media Undermine American Democracy*).[17] Numerous explanations for such attitudes have been advanced—poor economic conditions, a decline in candidate quality, a raft of political scandals, the rise of the mass media, New Class attitudes, and so on—but rarely is an inherentist answer given. I advance that claim here. When examined closely, I argue, politics can be seen as an inherently unstable discourse. Its borders are constantly being violated, leaving it with nothing to call its own. Politics is a liminal place, a space between. A person-on-the-street's comments illustrate:

> Well, you know, like [politicians] will tell you one thing, then they'll turn around and stab you in the back. And they'll tell somebody else something else. But they [politicians] couldn't care less. They're looking out for number one. They'll do whatever they have to do to make things easier for them or to benefit them. I don't know, it's just a political thing. And I disagree with that policy 100%, you know. So I just stay away from it. I'll tell you, I don't even vote. Because I, to me, they're all just a bunch of power-trippers. Bunch of liars is all. I mean, you know, I don't like a liar. To me that's the type of person that'll stab you in the back the first chance they get. And I just don't like it.[18]

Our interlocutor provides at once a moral, a pragmatic, and a relational critique of politics. In one breath he speaks like a spurned lover ("they'll tell someone else something else") and in another like Parson Weems, consigning all politicians to the hotter portions of hell. But he also speaks a functional language—"they're looking out for number one." The complexity of this critique is suggestive. It is doubtful, for example, that our interlocutor would react personally or morally to General Motors' sudden recall of Chevrolets. Similarly, if his pastor's morals were suddenly found wanting, he would not use that occasion to criticize the cleric's driving habits as well. Most people, most days, react compartmentally to life. But when it comes to politics they use all of themselves all of the time.

Table 6.2 suggests why. Compared to other public discourses, politics is an admixture. The comparisons made here were intentional: because politics is a social text it was contrasted to activists'

TABLE 6.2
Campaigning vs. Other Discourse Domains

Comparisons	Rhetorical Features of Campaign Speeches	
	Similarities	Differences
vs. All Domains	————	High Realism
		High Self-Reference
vs. Corporate Advocacy	High Commonality	High Patriotic References
		High Party References
		Low Certainty
vs. Religious Preachment	High Human Interest	High Activity
vs. Social Protest	High Voter References	High Optimism
	High Leader References	

protest statements; because it is an institutional text, it was also compared to corporate advocacy; because it is a moral text, religion was its third foil.[19]

Politics' most unique tokens turned out to be Realism and Self-References, for many of the reasons already addressed. Bottom-line analyses are normally not requested of preachers or protestors, and, when requested of business executives, they are normally requested in private, not in the luncheon speeches, public announcements, and mission statements studied here. On the campaign trail, however, politicians have no privacy. While the Amdahl Corporation may speak in generalities, Bill Clinton must have a more limited agenda. The resulting contrast is stark and it asks us to rethink what we know about political discourse:

Bill Clinton

And when we were expanding Head Start and passing that School-to-Work program Senator Kennedy talked about to help young people who don't go to four-year colleges get good training and good jobs, when we improved the college loan program by cutting the cost and improving the repayment terms—when we did these things the other guys, they tried to stop us. But John Kerry helped us pass it. He's on the right side of history, and he's on the right side of history in making college available to all Americans. We'll do it if you give us four more years and if you give us John Kerry back to the United States Senate.[20]

Amdahl Corporation

It is vital to our success that the communities in which we operate grant us the ability to prosper, an environment in which to attract outstanding people, and give fair consideration to our plans. In return we strive to be good citizens and to contribute to every community where we do business. This means that we must: (1) Conduct our business with the highest ethics and integrity. (2) Contribute our resources, time, and talent to community improvement. (3) Offer equal employment and advancement opportunities. Quality, innovation, and caring are the hallmarks of the Amdahl philosophy. These characterize our dealings with our employees, customers, stockholders, and the communities where we work and live.[21]

The Amdahl statement is boilerplate, the sort of text that brings a knowing smile to any good Marxist. Indeed, its breast-beating makes campaigners seem almost restrained in contrast. Like politicians, corporate speakers emphasize Commonality but actually outstrip them on this dimension, seeming almost collectivist at times. That too is an irony. But the greatest irony is that corporate representatives exceed the politicians on Optimism, constantly downplaying such matters as production foul-ups, union unpleasantries, corporate crime, and the like. Campaigners are surprisingly more forthcoming, perhaps because the journalists swarming about them leave them no other choice. And so, remarkably, politicians' Realism grounds them in a way not demanded of their corporate counterparts. Because they must deal with a diverse constituency, politicians also cut back on Certainty, resulting in a more tempered discourse. In contrast, the industrialists are often eloquent when describing problems that politicians, not they themselves, must solve:

Another sign of corporate commitment is the creation of ethics training programs—and even departments—by many companies, including some that have been rocked by scandals. In the past few years, we've seen companies like Union Carbide, Boeing, McDonnell Douglas, and Chemical Bank set up programs to help employees deal with ethical conflicts. These activities show that—despite the headlines we occasionally see—ethics plays an important role in business. . . . And that brings us to the second concept of ethics that I'd like to talk about—character. . . . That's why we become concerned when we read about talented athletes who die from a drug overdose. Or about well-educated Wall Street workers who go to jail for insider trading. These are the choices—the values—of individuals. And they raise a logical question: do we see a shift in the values of young men and women entering the work force today?[22]

This is an admirable discussion of corporate ethics but it is also circumspect. No charges are leveled here, no names named. Instead, the speaker covers the terrain broadly, ending on an interrogative, not a declarative, note. In the passage below, however, Bob Dole is more candid. His charges are clear and pointed. He does not wax sociological:

I have never questioned anyone's private character, and I will not start now. People are not perfect, and public service does not require them to be. But there is a difference between private character and public ethics, because public ethics is a public trust. When it is violated, the damage is done to our nation, our institutions and our idealism. Confronting it directly and forcefully is not a personal attack, it is a public duty.

The problems of the Clinton administration have become a pattern. A habit of half truths. An atmosphere of evasion. And what bothers us most is not just the wrongdoing but the excuse-making. In every case this administration has refused to take responsibility for the mistakes it has made and the harm it has caused. The goal is always to conceal ethical failure, not confront it. We hear, not apologies, but alibis. The buck stops nowhere.[23]

The campaigners' high use of Self-Reference may signal a dangerous megalomania on their parts or it may simply show that the buck always stops with someone in politics. The campaigners outstripped the corporate spokespersons four-to-one on this variable, two-to-one for the preachers and social activists. These findings suggest a transparency to American governance that often goes unnoticed. Politicians can be imperious from time to time, turning their staffs into praetorian guards (as did Richard Nixon), but they cannot hide for long. Thus, their Self-References can be seen as a truly democratic token, a sign that issue and image are usually conjoined in American politics.

Viewed through such a lens, Ross Perot's little soliloquies are more charming than dangerous. He may have been a Democrat or he may have been a Republican but mostly he was a small-d democrat, one willing to step away from his corporate shield and present himself to the American people directly:

> People constantly ask me, particularly since yesterday, why are you willing to endure all of this bitter, negative, mean-spirited stuff? Here's the reason. I consider myself the luckiest man alive in this country because of my parents, my wonderful wife and five children and 10 grandchildren. I've certainly had more than my share of business good fortune.
>
> I want you to know I am not campaigning to be president to live in the White House, to ride in a limousine, or to hear the band play "Hail to the Chief." I want to be your president for one reason: To face and solve the problems we discussed today, and pass on a better, stronger country to our children. It's going to be a tough challenge, but we can do it because of our devotion to our children and grandchildren. And when the job is done, and we know we're leaving them a better, stronger country, I will look all of you squarely in the eye and say, "I just got paid for the trip."[24]

It is not surprising that human relations would be emphasized in both American politics and American religion. Americans have never been attracted to meditative practices and they like their politics convivial as well (witness the growing use of talk-TV, a forum that stresses interpersonal matters, during presidential campaigns). But politicians go even further by emphasizing Activity—salvation now, not later. Thus, if American politics is a religion it is an odd one: it is confessional, not contemplative, and it is vigorous, not contemplative. These features explain why "politicized" clergymen like Pat Robertson and James Dobson are so distinctive. The Activism, Realism, and Self-References they habitually use are normally found on the campaign trail, not in church.

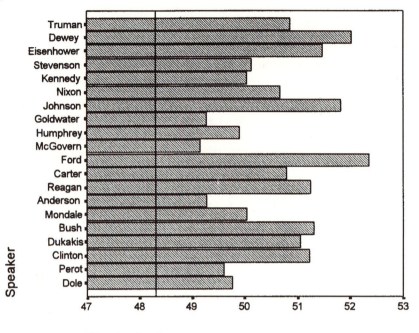

Figure 6.2. Optimism Scores for Campaigners
(vs. mean for social activists).

DICTION would be a sorry tool if it did not find major differences in Optimism between politicians and social activists, the former being Establishment types and hence protective of the status quo. But a campaigner is also something of an insurgent, especially the nonincumbents among them, persons who are rarely satisfied with the way things are. Besides, politicians deal each day with environmental degradation, the denial of women's rights, the indignities of racism, substandard housing, the threat of war, and the thousands of other problems with which social protestors also deal. So why are politicians' Optimism scores so much higher?

Figure 6.2 shows that not one of the twenty politicians studied here even approached the social activists' mean on Optimism. And this is not just a function of electoral enthusiasms, for none of the noncampaigning presidents did either, even though they discussed war, poverty, disease, and sundry other calamities. These data suggest a kind of insulating function to politics. It is as if the American people want a fire wall built between them and the essential darkness. As we saw earlier, neither the press nor citizen letter-writers have been willing to provide that service, so politicians pick up the slack.

When all of these data are reviewed simultaneously, it is clear that politics is patchwork. It is part public relations, part civil religion, part pragmatic planning, part social healer. It is also activist, upbeat, and reasonably personal. It resembles no other discourse specifically because it has all other discourses deposited within it. The result is pure syncretism. Politicians play a hundred roles; they speak with a thousand voices.

The work of Michael Oakeshott helps explain why. In his magisterial work, *The Politics of Faith and the Politics of Scepticism*, Oakeshott argues that politics has never been simple. "No doubt our political vocabulary is corrupt," says Oakeshott, "but it is an illusion to suppose that [it ever had an]'original meaning' which has become debased." For Oakeshott, ambivalence lies at the center of democratic politics. "It is our predicament," Oakeshott says, "to be able to enjoy a complex manner of government only at the cost of an equivocal political vocabulary,"[25] or, as I have argued here, a dense political vocabulary.

Why is this our fate? Because politics is the offspring of both faith and reason. Its optimistic strain derives from the church: "In the politics of faith," Oakeshott opines, "the activity of governing is understood to be . . . the perfection of mankind." Such perfection cannot be left to Divine Providence but can only come from the "unrelaxed efforts" of the human community. On such a view, people "are the creatures of their circumstances," thereby giving government a direct and obvious role: "the control and organization of human activity for the purpose of achieving human perfection."[26]

But there is another voice as well—that of skepticism—which takes "the radical belief that human perfection is an illusion" or, in its less radical form, that "we know too little about the conditions of human perfection" to pursue it directly. Thus, for the skeptic "the maintenance of order is the first object of government," thereby requiring a more plebeian view of social possibilities (high Realism scores, in our case). The skeptic achieves that goal by removing "religious 'enthusiasm' from politics," a task that became the work of Hobbes, Hume, Burke, Paine, Bentham, Calhoun, and Macaulay, according to Oakeshott.[27]

Two additional aspects of Oakeshott's model are that (1) Faith and Skepticism must be balanced for a society to prosper and (2) each brand of politics contains an "uninhibited version" which, if unchecked, threatens to devour the culture whole. Oakeshott worries that an unbridled Politics of Faith (radical environmentalism, for example, or the Religious Right and Black Separatism) can impose on state affairs "a counterfeit simplicity" and an overweening will to rule. Skepticism, too, has its nemesis—cynicism, perhaps, or mindless scientism—and that imperils a society as well. "When either of these styles of politics claims for itself independence and completeness," Oakeshott concludes, "it reveals a self-defeating character."[28]

Oakeshott asks us to accept politics on its terms, not on our own. The data I have gathered here speak to that point: politics is built out of several subdiscourses and achieves its distinctiveness thereby. The sad version of this story is that politics becomes everything to everyone and hence unmoored. The happy version is that it allows politics to stay in touch with all sectors of society. On his best day, that is, Al Gore can talk with Billy Graham in the morning and Bill Gates in the afternoon and still have dinner with Jesse Jackson. Such a schedule requires inventiveness on his part but, according to Michael Oakeshott, Mr. Gore's acculturation should have equipped him with the proper instruction: "Neither Dionysus nor Apollo, but each in his place and season."[29]

DIRECTIONAL POLITICS

To say that politics is directional is to say that it gives voters clear ideological cues and directs them to specific policy positions. Throughout American history, those jobs have fallen to the political parties. Recently, however, the American people seem to have gotten lost, with over a third of them now declaring themselves Independents. Jack Dennis and Diana Owen report that partisan identification has decreased markedly in the last two decades, a phenomenon connected to "a gradual disappearance of mass support for the institution of the political party in the United States."[30] Martin Wattenberg argues that these declines amount to a political "dealignment"[31] but Dennis and Owen see the issue in more cultural terms—increasingly negative feelings about government in general, rejection of all "special interests," a national decline in patriotism, and, in some cases, genuine interest in third-party alternatives.

Whatever the reason, dealignment has had consequences: divided government in Washington;[32] an increasingly imperial presidency;[33] more and more split-ticket voting;[34] insufficient party discipline to pass needed legislation.[35] Why have the parties's fortunes run so low? There are several answers: the increasing importance of presidential primaries has made the regions, not the parties, determinative as to candidate choice; the increasing clout of consultants and PACS has made candidates more responsive to them than to party officials; the rise of candidate-centered electioneering has changed how campaigns are financed, with the parties no longer being the only power brokers.[36] Russell Dalton adds still other factors: voters are more mobile today (and hence do not join organizations, political organizations included); they are also better educated (and hence unwilling to take directions from party officials); and they are less likely to become party volunteers (thereby ceding power to political professionals).[37]

As I have argued elsewhere, television may also be part of the story since television gives viewers a sense of effectivity, making them less dependent on party coaching.[38] Robert Putnam goes further when declaring that television keeps everyone at home, thereby lowering citizens' rates of joining all groups, political parties included.[39] Scott Blinder shows the inevitable consequence of this retreat: those who watch an excessive amount of television are especially unlikely to identify with a political party.[40] And there is yet another relationship between television and politics: the media are not mentioning a candidate's party as frequently in their reportage, thereby depriving voters of the partisan cues needed to stabilize their political choices.[41]

When a political party is no longer a reliable source of partisan cues, says Gerald Pomper, it has lost its most potent electoral weapon.[42] Indeed, as we saw in chapter 3, political candidates themselves no longer emphasize their party connections, thereby making it more "costly" for voters to discover the candidates' allegiances.[43] But not all scholars are ready to announce the death of the parties. The parties may have declined in salience, says Michael Hagen, but that does not mean they no longer perform important functions.[44] Indeed, John Zaller reports that party loyalty has not dropped precipitously over time;[45] Paul Abramson and his colleagues show that party identification still predicts electoral votes quite well;[46] Joseph Schlesinger remarks that parties are still well financed and highly professional, while David Rohde reports that Democrats and Republicans still organize the U.S. Congress and still produce party-line votes when needed.[47] As Nelson Polsby has said, the "parties still have work to do and were they not to exist, something very like them would have to be invented."[48]

My question differs from the research done to date. Here I ask: do parties have distinctive political voices? I find that they do. Their voices are not completely unique, of course, and the campaign process no doubt blurs party differences as candidates cater to middle-of-the-road voters. But Democrats and Republicans do talk differently and these differences may well "prime" voters in predictable ways. More intriguing, these language patterns relate quite well to the specific ideologies undergirding the two parties.

In a brilliant set of essays, Richard Weaver counterposes liberal and conservative beliefs by focusing on their distinctive rhetorical manifestations. "The proper aim of a political party is to persuade," says Weaver, "and to persuade it must have a rhetoric." Treating Edmund Burke as the quintessential liberal, Weaver shows how he habitually used the argument from circumstance. Revealing his own ideological leanings, Weaver was not much impressed with Burke's brand of argument since it accepted "the facts standing around" to coerce political decisions. "Such argument savors of urgency rather than perspicacity," says Weaver, "and it seems to be preferred by those who are easily impressed by existing tangibles. . . . "By thus making present circumstance the overbearing consideration," Weaver continues, "it keeps from sight even the nexus of cause and effect. It is the least philosophical of all the sources of argument, since theoretically it stops at the level of perception of fact."[49]

The DICTION program allowed me to put Weaver's theory to the test. When the campaign discourse of Democrats and Republicans was compared, Democrats were found to produce (1) *a grounded rhetoric* (high Realism, high Familiarity), (2) *a humanistic rhetoric* (high Commonality, high Voter References), and (3) *an institutional rhetoric* (high Leader References, high Party References). Surely this is Weaver's argument from circumstance gone statistical. Note, too, how the component parts of liberalism work in tandem: abstract truths are not allowed to countermand the forces of everyday life. The job of government is to make the empirical world a better place for the people who inhabit it. Because life can be hard, government must intrude and, when it does, organizational encrustations develop. But one principle should guide political action: The collective, always the collective, must be its own salvation.

While Weaver was not much impressed with the argument from circumstance, he acknowledged that it "undeniably . . . has the power to move."[50] Indeed it does. The quintessential liberal, George McGovern, demonstrates:

> The president must not only exert personal supervision over his most important subordinates, he must also have personal contact with rank and file Americans. I find my opponent's conduct of the presidency cold and aloof. He deals too much with the power brokers and too little with the people. As president, I will go to the country several times a year for town meetings in school auditoriums, factories, and neighborhoods. I will listen as well as speak and hopefully, I will learn what the people are thinking and feeling. There will be no more White House indifference to the poor and oppressed among us; to the women who are seeking a more fulfilling role in society; to the young who are in a hurry for change and to the black or brown or red who can wait no longer for change. And the White House will not be deaf to the plight of blue collar workers who find that the system created to serve them exhausts them, bores them, uses them up, and exploits them. No citizen of this country should have to suffer in silence; no single voice can always be needed. But every voice must be heard. As president, I

161

will hear the voices of dissent and discontent, and the needs a president will never know if he hides in the White House. The president is a person, and the presidency is a personal as well as a political institution.[51]

McGovern uses all of the partisan cues here: a people too long ignored; a people that works too hard for what it gets; a people with the right to depend on the government it has created. For McGovern, the political cosmos was set in motion by a participant God, not by a watchmaker God. McGovern is one with his moment here, standing among the people because the people stand within him. He resists the regnant hierarchies and he repairs to the places—the schools, the factories, the neighborhoods—where political reality is most real. Wilson Carey McWilliams outlines the liberal credo in more conceptual terms: "American democracy needs, and can stand, only so many stanzas of epic poetry; contemporary politics calls for the more prosaic effort to protect and rebuild locality, association, and party, the links between private individuals and public goods."[52]

Republicans do not produce epic poetry but they are attracted to it. Epic poetry is replete with larger-than-life individuals emboldened by some grand vision, some grand adventure, some grand idea. This is the conservative's mindset, one who uses the argument from definition, a dependence on what is ineluctably true. Weaver uses Abraham Lincoln as his exemplar (a not uncontroversial choice) and defines his style thusly: "the argument from definition . . . includes all arguments from the nature of the thing. . . . The postulate is that there exist classes which are determinate and therefore predictable. . . . The evidence that Lincoln held such beliefs is overwhelming. . . . "The true conservative," Weaver continues, "is one who sees the universe as a paradigm of essences, of which the phenomenology of the world is a sort of continuing approximation."[53]

The conservative is an aggressive theorist, an idealist; hence the Republicans' low Realism scores. Time, space, the present, people's feelings, concrete objects—these cannot sustain a worthy argument, according to Weaver. Such phenomena are too rooted in the world, too pliable. Far better is discourse that transcends the moment, that reaches deep for unchanging truths. When he gave his election-eve speech, Tom Dewey did exactly that:

We will follow the strong, clear policies I have set forth in the course of this campaign. The world will know at last, know where we stand, and it will be the same every day. We shall be all out on the side of human freedom. We will work for peace through the United Nations and by every honorable means wherever the peace is threatened. We will wage the peace in solidarity of purpose with every other free people—and we will wage it without hatred of any people. We will wage the peace knowing that by the verdict of history and in the eyes of God, justice and freedom and human decency have always been and will always be the right cause.

Tonight we are called, not to pride and boasting, but to humility. In this momentous time our country is called to renew its faith so that the world can begin to have hope again; to renew its strength so the world can begin to be of good courage again; to renew its vision so that the world can begin to move forward again out of this present darkness toward the bright light of lasting peace.[54]

The easy gloss here is that Dewey's speech is purely ceremonial, not a Republican master-statement. In part that is true; the speech is formulaic. But a deeper read finds an ideological shadow. For one thing, this is a static address, one where entities hover (*justice, freedom*) rather than march forward with purpose. The *burden of history* hangs heavy here as well. The *new* never amounts to more than *renewal* and even *vision* becomes *renewed vision*. Too, *freedom* is revered for its own sake, not as a prelude to behavior. This is also an obdurate address (*where we stand*), a text where all motion is potential motion or, just as often, motion denied. Things perseverate in this address (*lasting peace*); they do not spring from the moment full born. Time is therefore glacial (*the same every day*) and judgmental (*the verdict of history*). People are not flesh-and-blood creatures but instantiations (*human decency, human freedom*). This is, in short, not a casual text.

Argument from definition is essentialistic argument. Republicans scored significantly higher on Inspiration, Liberation, Patriotism, and Passivity than did the Democrats. The Republicans used slightly more Religious References as well. The result is a rhetoric of icons, one that causes the head to tilt upward. These features, says Joanne Morreale, make Republican convention films especially powerful, as their videographers gaze over the nation's civic touchstones looking for emotionally satisfying scenes and remembrances.[55] The Democrats, in contrast, produce a rhetoric of narrative, a rhetoric grounded in the lived moment, in people's experiences. Both parties use both approaches from time to time, of course, since each rhetoric has its obvious attractions. Ronald Reagan was a master narrator and Jimmy Carter a good preacher (his race in 1976 produced less Realism than any Democrat before or since). But the parties' internal similarities were generally greater than their differences.

How sturdy are these party voices? To answer that question, a subset of language variables was assembled to produce two paradigm styles—Republican and Democratic—and then a number of tests made to see which circumstances affected them.[56] Interestingly enough, the styles continued to distinguish sitting presidents (those not on the campaign trail), although the differences were smaller. In addition, the closer a race became (as measured by polling figures), the more likely the candidates were to revert to their respective paradigm styles. This was especially true for the Democrats. By looking at their relative use of the Democratic style one could predict with some accuracy how close their race was (the Republicans were a bit more curvilinear in this regard). Democratic incumbents and challengers used their paradigm style equally, but Republican challengers used theirs more faithfully than incumbents (perhaps because their style has such hortatory qualities). Neither paradigm style, however, insured victory—both winners and losers used them with equal intensity.

Have the paradigm styles held up over time? As figure 6.3 reports, they have waned somewhat, especially since 1980. Why? A number of possibilities exist. Ideological differences between the parties may have diminished, as witnessed by the debt-permitting Ronald Reagan and the debt-denouncing Bill Clinton. Another possibility is suggested by the work of Anthony Downs, whose "spatial" theory of politics holds that voters prefer candidates closest to them on a left-right scale.[57] As more and more people move to that scale's midpoint, the reasoning would go, candidates drift there as well, moderating their rhetorical styles in the process. Yet another possibility features the growing power of television. As candidates adapt their campaigns

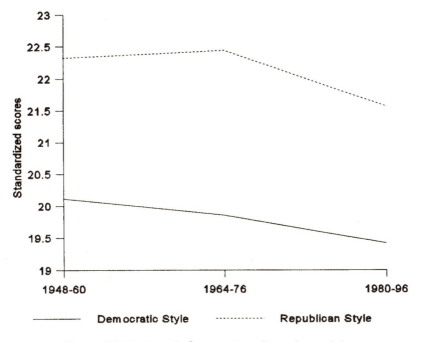

Figure 6.3. Partisan Style over Time (Speeches only).

to the tastes of a mass audience, they naturally seek out a more generic style.

And what of the Independents? Political theorists are unsettled on that question. Some argue that independent voters reject both parties equally while others argue that they have no preference one way or the other. Still others feel that Independents are less involved politically than party-line voters.[58] All three explanations may be correct at some times for some independents. And with only John Anderson and Ross Perot in my sample, these matters cannot be settled here. But the Independents did score significantly lower than the party candidates on both paradigm styles. That was especially true of Ross Perot (Anderson used the Republican style more often than the Democratic style), surely the more intriguing of the two candidates.

Perot's special preferences were for Denial, Human Interest, and Past Concern, a complex trinity. The first two features depict Perot as a classic populist, one who rejects institutions in order to do the will of the people. That was certainly his campaign theme—the scrappy little fighter who knew what the American voter truly felt. Perot's heavy use of the Past may have been an idiosyncracy (a characteristic he shared with Newt Gingrich) or it may have been his attempt to ground his populism in the salvific myths of the American experience. And then there is this possibility: Perot was a true eccentric. His stylistic patterns may have been his own. They may have emerged from no special political tradition and may have had no particular ideological trajectory. They may have merely been the tokens of an unbuttoned American original. Illustrations of that hypothesis abound:

> Now, keep in mind—who is the greatest fighter pilot that ever lived? Tom Cruise—can't fly. What about Robbie Reisner? Never heard of him. What about Chuck Yeager? Yes, he's an old guy. I kind of remember him. The point being—we are so twisted up. It's bizarre.
>
> But isn't it interesting—everybody rushes to Hollywood for makeup, for acting, for haircuts on the runway—because you've got to just be looking good. The fact that you don't say nothing doesn't matter. The fact that you say stuff that doesn't make sense doesn't matter. The fact that you say things and do things that damage the country don't matter. It's just important to get out there, tap dance, chew gum and juggle, and entertain them.
>
> And the next time you watch a State of the Union message, I hope you'll just sit at home and whistle "There's No Business Like Show Business Like No Business I Know." "Everything about it is appealing." You follow me?[59]

According to Gerald Pomper, "partisanship can be understood as a quick cue, readily available to the voter" that can serve as a "means of simplifying the potentially overwhelming complexities of casting a ballot."[60] As we have seen here, language may be one of those cuing devices. Both Republicans and Democrats have unique political vocabularies, although it remains to be seen whether their styles will survive the increasing pressures of the mass media or the changing ideological tastes of the American voter. These are matters that bear some watching. As George Stephanopoulos has opined, "you *need* a partisan campaign to get [candidates] on record for what they want."[61] Equally important, partisanship is needed to frame options for voters and to help them clarify their own political values. If political language can help promote that clarity, so much the better.

Conclusion

Politics is a difficult business and the data reported here show why. Partisanship is a double-edged sword: a democracy needs a sharp dialectic to formulate intelligent plans but partisanship can also frustrate achievement when its practitioners posture instead of lead. As we have seen here, the two major parties foster language conforming to their ideological traditions—Democrats are "compassionate empiricists" and Republicans "philosophical patriots." If E. J. Dionne is correct, however, the fact that these differences are abating somewhat may be even more important. Says Dionne: "To reengage members of the broad middle class, liberals must show more respect for their values, and conservatives must pay more heed to their interests."[62] Given the internecine struggles now being waged in both the Democratic and Republican camps, the future of American politics may be determined by how well they approach Dionne's ideal.

We have also seen that politics is a distinct domain. But its distinctiveness lies in its ability to blend other societal discourses. This lets politicians have commerce with a great many people but it also makes politics frustrating since it must do so much at once. The result is an imperfect synthesis: if politics is a religion, it is a noncontemplative religion; if a business, an ideology-based business; if a brand of social action, one that foreswears pessimism. And to the extent that politics is an institution it is an institution built out of people, not abstractions. Because these demands are so conflicting, a campaign commands the full attention of those seeking office.

But politicians do not campaign alone. They are besieged each day by media personnel and the importunings of the electorate. Campaigns therefore become a dense fog of discourse, with the press trying to focus on ideas and the politicians trying to erect as large a canopy as possible over themselves and their supporters. At the risk of sounding theological, a political campaign therefore permits as much transcendence as its immanence will allow. Because campaigns last so long, candidates can never really hide; because they must speak so often, candidates inevitably become part of the social conversation. All of this cross-purposing gives politics its uniqueness. It would be nice if it were prettier but, then, it would not be politics.

CHAPTER 7

The Media's Voice

THE news is a complex thing. In reality, it is not one thing but many things. It is both herald and critic, soothsayer and cultural historian, and its text contains a congeries of voices—baseball players and rock stars, the nation's leaders, the proverbial person on the street, young celebrities-in-the-making, a great variety of news anchors and beat reporters. Whether or not these voices produce harmony or cacophony remains an open question. With so many organizations now in the news business, with newspapers and magazines doing daily battle, with both of them competing against television, and with all three now confronting the Internet, we may have finally entered a postmodern space containing more news than reality.[1]

Some scholars argue the opposite, contending that the news is a single, monolithic entity because its personnel are socialized by corporations more responsive to market forces than to people's everyday experiences.[2] Marxist critics like Stuart Hall push the matter further, arguing that overriding political structures—late capitalism, in the case of the West—have turned reporters into cheerleaders, making them incapable of discovering "news" unless it has been foreordained by society's overlords.[3] In such a scenario, the media feature the economy rather than social policy during elections, and centrist candidates rather than third parties, because newsworkers are controlled by base-superstructure relationships.

My concern here is with humbler matters. I ask: What is the news? A basic question like this is not asked frequently enough. One basic fact is that print news stories about presidential campaigns have gotten steadily longer over the years. In my sample, this was true for the *New York Times*, the *Washington Post*, the *Los Angeles Times*, the *Chicago Tribune*, the *Atlanta Constitution*, and the AP/UPI wire stories.

With Jon Rutter

It was also true for the *Christian Science Monitor* but only during the last thirty years.

Why the increase? Indeed, why the increase when newspaper readership is declining, not advancing, when advertisers are finding other venues for promoting their wares, when more and more (nonpolitical) topics are vying for media coverage, when some news organizations are struggling to meet their payrolls and, indeed, when overall lineage in many newspapers has been either holding steady or going down?[4] One obvious explanation is that the congressional press corps has grown exponentially over the years, thereby placing increased pressure on editors to include more political news.[5] Another possibility is that campaign stories are longer because they have become more complicated, with reporters having learned how to wring more news out of the news. So, for example, a political profile of Texas governor George W. Bush now becomes a commentary on family ties and on changing cultural patterns in the Sunbelt. New York mayor Rudolph Giuliani's drive to clean up Time Square is linked to the gentrification of Italian Americans and to economic relations among multinationals. In short, we are now in an era of luxuriant reporting, an era in which one story tells all stories. Politics has become a metaphor for life itself.

That, at least, is my suspicion. I explore that suspicion here by (1) outlining the unique features of the news as social discourse, (2) asking if the media are fulfilling their traditional mandate of objectivity, and (3) examining what distinguishes the print and broadcast media. Assembling basic data about the news is especially important because, when it comes to the mass media, facts are so often overshadowed by opinions. As Bartholomew Sparrow observes, the news is what economists call a credence good, "a product that has to be consumed on *faith* since it is difficult for the customer to evaluate the quality of the commodity *even after consuming it.*"[6] Because that is so, the credibility of the news is its most important quality.

But that quality is sorely lacking, according to many. The Pew Research Center conducts periodic surveys of opinions about the press but rarely reports heartening results. One of their recent studies shows that only 15 percent of the American people have a "very favor-

able" opinion of networks news, that viewership as a result is dropping, and that people generally see little fairness, accuracy, or help-
fulness in the media.[7] Other research shows that broadcast news
"presents the viewer with a singular, cynical image of presidential
politics and the political system"[8] and that it also equips viewers with
"significantly more negative emotions" about politics than do alternative sources of information.[9] And then there is the issue of bias: Robert Lichter and his colleagues show that George Bush received 20
percent fewer positive stories than did Bill Clinton in 1992, a fact
that is met with a sizeable yawn by most reporters since Mr. Bush did
little to advance his own cause during that campaign.[10] Still, charges
of news bias are persistent. The American people know what they
know and, when it comes to the media, they are not pleased with
what they know.

They need to know more. For one thing, they need to know that
consuming political news builds "diffuse support" for the political
system even though it can also turn voters against specific candidates
and parties.[11] They need to know that heavily reported stories are best
remembered by the electorate, suggesting that the mass media have
considerable influence even when reviled.[12] They need to know that
news reports can significantly affect voters' evaluations of candidates'
"viability"—their possibility of winning—an outcome of considerable consequence in a crowded electoral field.[13] And they need to
know that the mass media have especially powerful effects among
undecided or marginalized voters.[14] In short, the American people
need to think in more complicated ways about the mass media. Only
by knowing what the news is can they help determine what it can
become. This chapter tries to head them in that direction.

What Is the News?

A basic question is whether or not the news should have a voice of
its own. If the news is a mere conduit, after all, a neutral medium that
passes along the nation's dialogue, its texts should be self-denying. As
with the smile on Alice's Cheshire, the news in this model would be
first a transparency and then a nothingness. Consumers would have

no need to kill the messenger because there would be no message. The reporter would be little more than a scribe.

None of my findings substantiate this theory. Instead, I find the news to be persistently rhetorical, a powerful, self-aware text that paints a consistent view of politics. Newsworkers not only know who they are but also have a clear sense of mission. Scholars have recently made a great deal out of the shrinking sound bite in the news but that is but one manifestation of a larger model: the press as political superintendent. Operating in that role, the press assumes these things: that facts are inchoate, inexpressible on their own terms; that politics dies unless dramatized; that political ideas are dangerous when floating freely, undisciplined; and that traditional news norms ensure an enlightened polity. Operating on these principles, news organizations produce a predictable product.

The product they produce is an adjunct to democracy, although some will blanch at that claim. So many Americans now hate the news that they ignore it completely. Even more hate media personnel who, in their eyes, are overpaid and pontifical, persons who do not know what it means to earn an honest dollar and who are unpatriotic in addition. These are strong charges but they are also understandable given the textual features of the news:

1. *The news is skeptical.* As we saw in chapter 6, the media are considerably more negative than politicians and those differences have not abated during the last fifty years. If anything, the media's pessimism has increased. Again, one can recite the recent litany in these matters—Vietnam, Watergate, Iran-Contra, Whitewater—but the simple fact is that the press has always reported what is going wrong and the American people do not like it when things go wrong. Studies continually show that many Americans would, if they could, place severe constraints on the Fourth Estate, even as they embrace its First Amendment protections. People become especially discomfited with the press during election season when, as we have seen, voters habitually become more buoyant. Politicians abet them in these ways but the press refuses, churning out endless stories of campaign misdeeds and malignant political motives. Although many Americans lose their footing from time to time, for example, it took

but one stumble from Bob Dole during the 1996 campaign to produce a "news peg" for a month. Ordinary people seethe at such overreporting. They find it uncharitable in the extreme and they find it lazy journalism as well.

When the press makes light of a seventy-three-year-old falling off a dais they cordon themselves off from the citizenry. Such coverage makes the press seem an alien thing, even a European thing—a gaggle of overly wordy, unappointed oligarchs who gleefully report the nation's bad news. The simple, American agrarian resists. He resists the bad news but especially the glee. He finds it a cowardly emotion, the secret handshake of a secret fraternity that is elitist to the core. For these reasons, one almost never hears an American child wish aloud to become a journalist. In the United States, to aspire to journalism is to declare oneself better than one's neighbors:

> I am sick and tired of your daily "Bush bashing." Your daily negative political cartoons aimed at the president, misnamed headlines, left wing commentary and biased reporting in regard to the presidential race smack right in the face of fairness and objectivity. As a public trustee, you have an obligation to be both fair and objective. It seems, however, that there is a conspiracy in the media, and that the *Roanoke Times & World News* is actively campaigning for Bill Clinton. This might sound ridiculous to you, but it sure seems very real to me![15]

Political news is reliably negative. DICTION found no important differences among the seven print sources and five broadcast sources on Optimism. In addition, Optimism scores did not vary during the course of the campaign; they did not change from region to region; they were no higher in stories about incumbents than in stories about challengers; both Democrats and Republicans received the same, sour, coverage between 1948 and 1996. Using an entirely different set of measures, Robert Lichter and Ted Smith found a similar pessimism when they compared campaign reportage to the remarks of political candidates.[16] To understand the press's negativity, however, one must distinguish between (1) the partisan negativity objected to in the quotation above and (2) the universal negativity of the press. Complaints about partisan negativity come and go. During the Monica

Lewinsky scandal of the late 1990s, for example, one almost never heard Republicans complain about media bias even though that debacle produced some of the worst forms of pack journalism. Similarly, when the press refused to pursue rumors of extramarital relations on the parts of George Bush in 1992 and Bob Dole in 1996, no hosannas were sung by Democrats.

But universal negativity, gratuitous negativity, is something else. It is the press's consistent refusal to lift the nation's spirits that people find obnoxious. They found it odd, for example, that so much attention was focused on contretemps within the Royal Family during Princess Diana's funeral, or that locker room hatreds in Chicago received star billing when basketball's Bulls were winning their sixth world championship. "Why bring it up?" the American people ask. "Because you will read it," the press replies. "Besides," the press continues, "it happened."

Much happens. But journalism is an art form because it is a *selective* discipline, because someone, somewhere, declared one event worthy of coverage and another unworthy. Consider, for example, a standard piece of news discourse:

> The Bush campaign dismissed one of three campaign supporters accused of anti-Semitic or fascist involvements. A campaign spokesman said he was dismissed after it was learned he had been active in efforts to defend a man condemned to death over atrocities at the Treblinka death camp.[17]

Here is a synecdoche for virtually all campaign coverage. The report appeared on 9 September 1988 in the *New York Times* and then vanished forever. The Bush campaign moved on to other matters and the *Times* did so as well. Even the Dukakis campaign made little of it. And so this story never had the "legs" needed to become a full-fledged pseudo-event, which is to say it was never given the legs by the press.

But the story sits there nonetheless—in the pages of the *New York Times*—and it sits there surrounded by other morsels of negativity. Stories like these are consistently overincluded and eventually become a torrent, causing some citizens to rush past them to the sports page . . . where they read about a potential baseball strike.

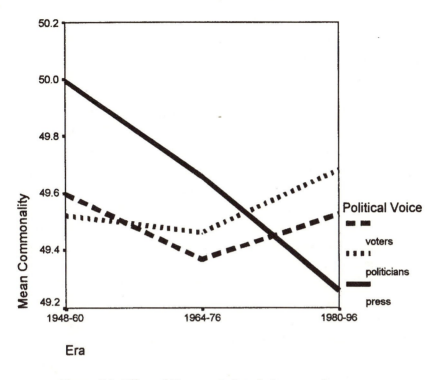

Figure 7.1. Effect of Time on Political Commonality.

From the press's standpoint, such stories are part of life's dialectic. "How can a democracy succeed," the press asks, "if it turns its back on trouble? . . . "If further investigation found the Bush campaign to have been a haven for neo-Nazis," the press would continue, "would you not want to know about it?" Surprisingly, many Americans would not.

But an "organic" defense of press negativity goes only so far. The media also produce what Timothy Luke calls "artificial negativity" when it makes bad news out of nothingness or, at least, out of very little.[18] Figure 7.1 provides a vivid illustration of that tendency. The language of commonality has dropped steadily downward in press reports over the years, suggesting an increased fracturing of the American electorate. When the twenty-five news reports with the lowest Commonality scores were extracted from my database, every one featured public opinion polls (who's up? who's down?), a brand of reportage that has now become a staple. Because polls are now so plentiful—in part because news organizations themselves are in the polling business—there are always enough data to support any claim the press wishes to make. So, for example, a news story entitled "Clinton Has Edge in 3 Polls; But Figures Vary Widely"[19] has something for everyone: Clinton voters can take heart but Bush voters need not despair. Four years earlier, a carefully phrased headline like "Bush Makes Up Ground"[20] could stir up Republicans, while a story entitled "The 1992 Campaign; Clinton Poll Lead Narrows" could motivate the faithful in both parties.[21] Polls are now so omnipresent that meta-polling has become a cottage industry ("In Judging Polls, What Counts Is When and How Who Is Asked What").[22] Even when the race has yet to be run, a race can be run in the newsroom ("Comparing the Post-Convention Polls").[23]

Polling stories can also make local things national ("Poll in Minnesota Shows a Neck and Neck Race")[24] and add nuance to a campaign that may have become bloated ("Poll Finds Most Americans Back Grants for Parental School Choice").[25] Given the rhetorical attractions of polling stories, it is not surprising that they become increasingly popular over the course of a campaign, as we see in figure 7.2. Such trend lines show how the media work to keep the campaign interesting, even though candidates' remarks showed no significant drop in Commonality during the campaign. In defense of its negativity, the press would argue thusly: (1) the people of the United States have always disagreed with one another; (2) political campaigns naturally bring these disagreements to the surface; (3) the strength of the nation lies in its pluralism, not in a feigned homogeneity; (4) the press has a positive obligation to report on the nation's fault lines; (5) it is the job of the politicians, not the press, to bring us together.

The media have always defended themselves on these grounds and their argument is not without merit. Lately, however, some members of the press have decried their profession's ingrained negativity. Journalist Paul Taylor left the *Washington Post* after many years, in hopes of finding a more positive way of fostering democratic dialogue.[26] James Fallows took over the editorship of *U.S. News and World Report*

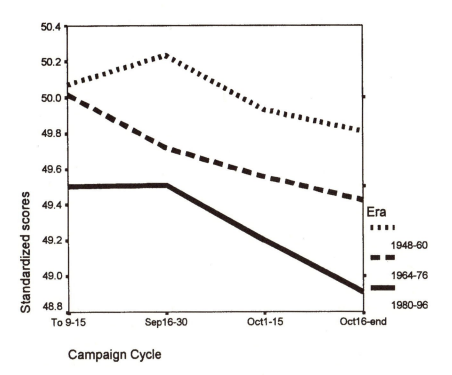

Figure 7.2. Commonality across Campaign Cycle (Media only).

in part because he hoped to change the formulas of standard political reportage.[27] The "public" or "civic" journalism movement, an attempt by Ed Fouhy and Jay Rosen to goad the media into assuming more responsibility for building social capital, was also a reaction to the media's negativity.[28] Fine efforts all, but one wonders whether journalism will—or should—bend to its critics. The world has always been an imperfect place and politics is most assuredly an imperfect profession. Someone, most likely a journalist, must shed light on these imperfections, for in light there is truth. That is a bromide, but probably a necessary one.

2. *The news is energetic.* If world history books were written by reporters rather than historians, few seventh graders would fall asleep. For the press, politics is a whirlwind within a whirlwind. Press coverage far outstripped political and lay discourse on Activity and

did so consistently throughout the thirteen elections studied here. These differences never really abated, suggesting a truly generic quality. In one sense that is not surprising since journalism is supposed to relate the events of the day. But the Activity found in news coverage far exceeds mere motor description. Rather, it creates a suggestive, involving narrative in which all action, both empirical and psychological, and all experience—including thought itself—have dramatic consequence. A rather breathless CBS news report from the 1996 campaign shows how carefully chosen language can give energy to an event that otherwise had none:

> Bob Dole is personally *ratcheting up* the attack on President Clinton's character and ethics. His campaign operatives *opened fire* on several fronts over the weekend including accusations about overseas contributions to the Clinton campaign. Today Dole himself *picked up* on that *line of attack*. . . .
>
> Campaign staffers also handed out a press release with five questions directed to President Clinton and Vice President Gore regarding campaign contributions from Indonesian banking interests. We were told Mr. Dole would raise this issue in his speech, but he didn't. However, at the airport, after a *quick strategy huddle*, he decided to *personally weigh in* on what he called the Clinton-Gore Indonesian connection relating to campaign contributions. . . .
>
> With the *gloves and coat off*, Mr. Dole basked under the Missouri sunshine before *heading off* to San Diego where he's indicated he will say these same things to the president in Wednesday night's debate. . . .
>
> The Democratic Party's success at collecting huge campaign contributions from foreign sources has raised questions about the legality of its fund-raising operations and given the Republicans *an issue to jump on.*[29]

Filling in the ellipses of the network's commentary were a series of rather aimless remarks by candidate Dole. At one point he is shown asking, "Now has anybody got any . . . advice for the debate on Wednesday night? Should it be tougher or softer?" and a voice from the crowd came back, predictably enough, with "tougher." A bit later, Mr. Dole is quoted more substantively: "About 30 people who worked for this administration are already gone. They are in jail, or they're indicted, or they're out of there. Then he talks about an ethical administration. He does not have an ethical administration and we're going to go after that in the debate Wednesday night." But Mr. Dole's remarks here are pedestrian, not sulfuric. If they had not been preceded and followed by the Nightly News's own dramatic flourishes they would have died a quick death on the editing bench. Precious little in the Dole campaign galvanized CBS viewers in 1996, but because the show had to go on, it did.

The news's dramatistic mandate also works in the opposite direction. Candidates now build their speeches out of highly extractable sound bites, snippets that retain their dramatic punch even when shorn of their original context. What is an extractable sound bite? One with considerable linguistic Activity.[30] For example, although George Bush was quoted only twice in one news clip (one which declared his 1992 campaign deeply troubled), it is significant that both extracts were chosen for their sense of dynamism: "2.7 percent is darn good growth and it *pulls the rug right out from under* Mr. Clinton, who is telling everybody how horrible everything is. And the economy of the United States led Europe, led Canada, led Japan and *we grew* at 2.7 percent." After again declaring Mr. Bush's electoral chances grim, ABC's newscasters allowed the president one more chance on stage and, again, he found the requisite verbal energy: "And we're *closing the gap.* And in seven days, we are *pulling ahead at the finish line* to win this election."[31]

Given the media's appetite for political energy, the 1996 campaign was a special disappointment. Said news commentator Jeff Greenfield: "This is the most uninteresting election of my lifetime. You don't have a cutting-edge candidate putting anything on the table. Clinton is *running out the clock.*" Greenfield's use of a dilatory metaphor is interesting, especially for a profession so attracted to kinetics. The choice of images of NBC's Tom Brokaw is equally uninspiring: "We're *turning over every rock* we can without just making it up."[32] But despite their disappointment with the campaign's raw materials, the press's Activity levels in 1996 were no different than in previous years. That is, the news formula is set and its mandate clear: A campaign will have energy. When the empirical falters, rhetoric will compensate.[33]

This is not to say that campaign coverage is either mechanical or unknowing. It is simply to say that journalists have perfected a technique that give the news a certain look and feel, markers that tell us we are watching the news rather than a soap opera. One interesting adaptation found in news coverage emerged when quiescent moments in political history were compared to troubled times. To track the media's responsiveness to periods of high unemployment, economic fear, or people's feelings of well-being, DICTION probed the news texts for their relative sense of urgency.[34] Urgency was measured by how the passages tacked back and forth between Spatial and Temporal language. Texts high on the Space-Time variable were assumed to be more grounded, concerned with stable, physical realities, in a sense, more deliberate. Texts low on that variable featured time at the expense of space. They were more reactive, concerned with immediate or impending matters.

Figure 7.3 tells three versions of the same story: when conditions are hard, the media produce more urgent coverage; under favorable conditions, they are less time sensitive. No doubt this is an unconscious response on the media's part but, statistically, it is not an insignificant effect. One senses that reporters become caught up in the challenger's rhetoric of change during certain elections. In 1976, 1980, and 1992, for example, when all three prosperity indicators were sagging, the media became especially time anxious. This makes sense since journalists visit with voters so much during a campaign and hence may transfer voters' concerns to their own news stories. But when viewing the reporting on election eve 1992, one senses that the Clinton campaign had a special hand in its creation:

> *Tom Brokaw*: NBC's Andrea Mitchell who has been on the Clinton campaign *from the beginning* still is *on the job tonight*. John Cochran is with the president in Houston. The president will be *arriving later.* Andrea, the Clinton people are confident, but they're not taking it for granted *at this point*.

> *Andrea Mitchell*: Tom, the journey Bill Clinton *began 13 months ago* when he announced his candidacy in Little Rock is *now down* to one *endless final day*.

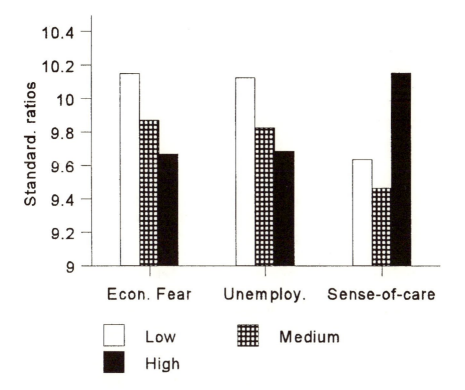

Figure 7.3. Space-Time Ratio and Political Conditions (Press only).

Bill Clinton: One more day.

Mitchell: It's a good thing, because his voice was all but gone as he *started a 4,000 mile trek* to try and nail down key states like Pennsylvania. Actually, Clinton's *final day* of campaigning *started after midnight* at New Jersey's Garden State Race Track where a long shot named Bubba Clinton came in first last week. Clinton is anything but a long shot. . . . Leaving nothing to chance, Clinton will have hit nine cities in eight states on his *final 27-hour quest.*

Clinton: We—we need to carry every state we're visiting. And if I work *all day long*, maybe that will increase the likelihood that the people who are supporting our ticket will *vote tomorrow.*

Mitchell: After a *year of speeches*, his message has been brought down to this:

Clinton: Never forget, never forget *in this last day* what *this last year* has been about—a fight between hope and fear. . . . I'm hopeful and determined. You know, I was thinking about, you know, I take this race *one day at a time*, and to those who are still trying to make up their mind, I ask them to go with us. . . . And I am going to work as hard as I can to challenge you to assume responsibility, to *build a new future*, and then to empower you to seize control over *your own destiny*. That's what this election is all about. . . . If you will be *my voice tomorrow*, I'll be *yours for four years.*[35]

Both NBC and Bill Clinton send the same message here: Time is of the essence. Both actors play their parts well, completing one another's lines, complementing one another's emphases. The resulting dialogue is seamless. Even in printed form there is an unquestioned energy here, a sense of impending change. There is also a sprightliness, a youthfulness. One wonders whether such temporal collusions sent a metamessage in 1992: that George Bush was a man of the earth, not a man of destiny, a man whose time had come and gone.

The mass media commit no crime when using drama to make politics interesting. Some would argue they actually do the nation a service when transferring the energy of the campaign trail to viewers at home. A utilitarian might even claim that any rhetoric that succeeds in increasing voter turnout is helpful in the long run. As I and my colleagues have argued elsewhere, the news media may do "an important social good when using the techniques of dramaturgy to make governance more interesting to people than it would be otherwise." At the same time, however, "there is an important difference between drama and democracy, with the former requiring spectators and the latter participants."[36] Indeed, some researchers have found that dramatic news presentations can actually decrease viewers' recall of political information and negatively impact their overall political sophistication as well.[37] In short, it is still too early to know which kind of news is a blessing and which a curse, although it is not too early to worry about such matters.

3. *The news is interpretive.* Figure 7.4 shows how relentlessly interpretive news coverage has been over the last fifty years. As we saw in chapter 6, politicians refer to tangible realities far more often than

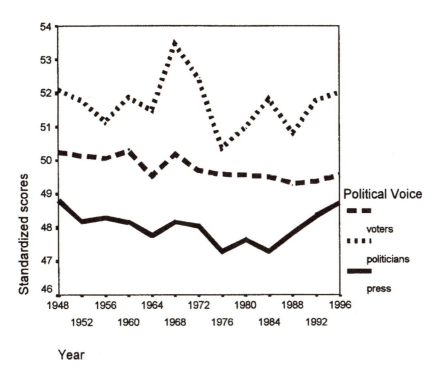

Figure 7.4. Realism Scores by Voice over Time.

the press. This is a rhetorical marker of kind, not degree. At first blush this may seem odd since one tends to think of the newspaper as a depository of facts and figures, a catalog of the day's events. And the parallel expectation is also attractive—that politicians bloviate. But the trend lines are obdurate: none of the twenty-one politicians studied came even remotely close to the press on abstractness.

Does this mean that the press does not deal with facts? No, it just means that people do not read an entire newspaper or watch a thirty-minute broadcast just to find out what happened. They can do that in far less time. Instead, they want to know what it means that something happened. The *New York Times* does not offer all the facts fit to print; it offers all the news fit to print. It offers interpretations: the history and location of the World Trade Center, the philosophy of the Islamic fundamentalists, the logic behind the building's security system, the feelings of the bombing victims, the relevant laws that apply to a capital crime, and, once again, the feelings of the bombing victims. By definition, the news deals with the unexpected, the serendipitous. It takes but a minute to learn that something new has happened but it takes much longer to understand an event in its totality. The bombing of the World Trade Center is still discussed many years later because its meanings have not yet been exhausted.

In other words, the media's interpretations are not confined to the editorial page. They are insinuated into every column inch of newsprint, in every arched eyebrow in the television studio. Journalists are lay philosophers; they read entrails. They do not superimpose meaning on the world (although they are often accused of doing so) but they recover it instead. In that sense they are children of the Enlightenment. They assume that all events, no matter how cosmic, are part of a pattern, that they can be explained. They assume that all official decrees have a motive and they seek it out. And they are addicted to reasons—sociological reasons, political reasons, psychological reasons, geographic reasons, economic reasons. As with their Enlightenment forebears, journalists are impatient with all forms of madness and with many forms of religiosity. Because they do not posit a mystical world they do not find one. Journalists are skeptics not because they love facts but because they love so few explanations.

It is this interpretive bias that sets journalists apart. It particularly sets them apart from politicians, who have a policy bias. The politician really only asks one question—what should we do?—while the journalist asks many questions. The interpretive bias also sets the press apart from the laity who usually do not want a great many explanations, just the ones that apply to them. For these reasons journalists become objects of distrust. Politicians treat them as diddlers who would rather study the world than change it. Citizens see them as persons who refuse to accept things at face value and who, as a result, live in a world of dankness and cynicism.

But the press operates as it does for a reason—because the world refuses to interpret itself. Consider, for example, a thoroughly ordinary news story about a political debate. We have here a classic invitation for reportage: three important people talked to one another for an hour and a half and then stopped talking. End of event. Then the journalism began, and it began with a headline: "Most Viewers Think Clinton Won Debate, Polls Say." Notice in the following story the paucity of facts. Notice that the victory was not Clinton's until someone declared it so:

> Polls taken after the third presidential debate suggest Ross Perot won some hearts and minds, and maybe a few votes, although more viewers thought Bill Clinton won the debate.
>
> In four sets of ratings put out by the networks Oct. 19, Governor Clinton came out on top in two polls, Mr. Perot in one, and they tied in the fourth. President Bush got the best rating from 1 in 4 voters in each poll.
>
> In an NBC News poll, 31 percent said the debate made them think more favorably of Mr. Bush, compared with 36 percent less favorably. Clinton's numbers were better: 36 percent more favorable, 29 percent less favorable. For Perot, 60 percent said they think more favorably of him, 12 percent less favorably. In a CNN-USA Today poll, 12 percent said the debate made them switch their preference, and for more than half the switch was to Perot. Re-interviewing voters who had been polled before the debate, Gallup found significant increases in their view of Perot as the best candidate to handle the economy and budget deficit. An ABC News poll measured preferences before and after the debate. Bush's support was unchanged at 29 percent; Clinton's dropped from 52 percent to 48 percent; and Perot's rose from 11 percent to 19 percent.
>
> ABC asked "who won?" and 36 percent said Clinton, 26 percent Perot, 21 percent Bush. Twelve percent called it a tie. "Who did the best job?" was the question posed by CBS, CNN-USA Today, and NBC. CBS got a Clinton-Perot tie at 30 percent, with 23 percent for Bush. CNN-USA Today came in with 37 percent for Perot, and 28 percent each for Bush and Clinton. Clinton had 35 percent, Perot got 30 percent, and Bush 23 percent in the NBC poll.[38]

This article is at war with itself: some say Clinton won, some Perot; going from 11 percent to 19 percent is not bad but it is also not great; Bush looks better in some polls but looks like a loser in others. That so many different surveys have been quoted here is itself an admission of defeat since, if one brawny fact had been found, the story could have been far shorter. But in politics there are few brawny facts until election day, and so, despite the brave headline, the Associated Press is really only guessing here. The article bristles with numbers but the numbers lead everywhere. At one point the reader is told that Clinton won the debate and at another that his percentage dropped—what is one to make of that? No bench scientist would know what to do with phrases like "think more favorably" or "best candidate to handle the economy" or "won some hearts and minds." This is pure effluvia, but it is also what life provides.

In some ways, journalists are heroes. They reach each day into the buzzing confusion of the world and extract a shard of evidence. Then they mount their Olympus to get some perspective on it and ultimately issue a guess as to what it means. Given the awesome power—and secrets—entrusted to the State, no democracy could survive without the journalists' guesswork. But all is not perfect. Studies show that "almost half of all reporting was punditry and analysis" and that "80% of the public felt that there was too much commentary in the coverage."[39] Numerous studies confirm those suspicions. Using very different methods than those used here, Catherine Steele and Kevin Barnhurst found a steady increase in opinionizing in broadcast news between 1968 and 1988,[40] and that proved to be true for the print media as well.[41] (My findings show exactly the same trend.) Other studies reveal that in their rush toward commentary the media fail to cover candidates' issue positions adequately.[42] Also, the press is sometimes too creative in their interpretations: Matthew Mendelsohn reports, for example, that when a conservative wins an election it is likely to be described as an "ideological mandate," while a victory by a political newcomer will be treated as a "personal mandate," not a philosophical one.[43]

The media's interpretations are often misguided but one must also consider life without the press: facts without meanings, speculations without data. Journalists take the time to pause, to sift through the details of our lives, to make sense of them. The sense they make is sometimes wrong, as is true of all interpretive work, but that hardly means the quest should be abandoned. Sometimes the press becomes too caught up in its narratives but such narratives are absolutely required if a large and diverse polity is to be reached. That journalism is imperfect goes without saying. That it is a necessary imperfection cannot be said too often.

IS THE NEWS WORTHY?

No discussion of the media's voice would be complete without asking whether that voice has become compromised. The question of media bias has been persistent and it is still a major area of research. For many, however, there is no need for further study. Beginning some thirty years ago with Edith Efron's *The News Twisters*, conservatives especially have decried the media's politics.[44] Operating on the (correct) assumption that most journalists are registered Democrats, they conclude the inevitable—that the press's sole purpose is to undermine the Right. Such critics note that Richard Nixon's descent began at the hands of two journalists and that Jerry Ford's intelligence and George Bush's manliness were constantly the butt of media jokes. Lyndon Johnson, Jimmy Carter, and, recently, Bill Clinton might well disagree with this analysis, and even Ronald Reagan might attribute some of his Teflon qualities to his media-centric personality. But anecdotes alone will never resolve this particular debate for it is a war in which all parties have sufficient ammunition.

Scholars have broadened the discussion in recent years. Herbert Schiller, most famously, has argued the opposite case: that the press has been captured by a set of interlocking directorates. In his book *Culture, Inc.: The Corporate Takeover of Public Expression*, Schiller cites case after case in which the press has held its fire when facing the avatars of capital.[45] As Timothy Cook documents, the fact that newspapers and television networks are increasingly being folded into information conglomerates makes Schiller's concerns especially worrisome.[46] Such scholars note that the genuinely radical voices of the Far Left are never really treated seriously in the mainstream press, and that third party and independent candidates never really have a national platform from which to air their views. In the United States, they argue, only money buys an audience.

Because the issue of media bias is a Rorschach experience in which people see what they expect to see, a number of content-analytic studies have been launched. But even here the results have been equivocal. A study by Dennis Lowry and Jon Shidler is typical: they find that Democratic and Republican candidates received the same number of sound bites during the 1992 presidential campaign but that the Republican sound bites were somewhat more negative—score one for both sides of the argument.[47] David Woodward, on the other hand, found that over a twenty-year period Democrats tended to get more press coverage during primaries but that Republicans got more during the general election—another draw.[48] Many of these studies have focused on questions of proportionality, on which party has received the most media attention. But for most people the real argument lies elsewhere, in the innuendos and snide interpretations reporters use to sway people's perceptions. These subtle kinds of bias are more damaging, critics note, because they are omnipresent, hard to discern, and genuinely pernicious.

DICTION is too crude an instrument to detect perniciousness, but some of my findings are relevant to the question of media bias. Generally, the news text looked like it should. Compared to politicians and the citizenry, the news was low on Embellishment, suggesting that it did not use coloration to send subtle political messages. In addition, it was not given to overstatement, being far lower on Leveling Terms (allness statements) and Tenacity than the other campaign voices. Instead, it was fairly precise (high Numeric Terms) and it deployed Leader References and Party References constantly—exactly what one would expect from a journal of record. Finally, and unsurprisingly, the news used virtually no Self-References but instead employed Communication Terms (*said, advised, demanded, mentioned*), thereby putting politicians, not reporters themselves, on stage.

Overall, then, the news seems to have the qualities taught in the J-schools. The average newspaper is filled with good, workaday journalism that advantages neither party and that still manages to explain what is happening in the world. There is virtually no stylistic flourish in the following passage, and, in that sense, it represents its genre:

George Bush, the Republican Vice-Presidential nominee, told the nation's bankers today that a Republican Administration would get "the professional regulator off the backs of American industry."

Mr. Bush, speaking to 2,000 delegates at the American Bankers Association convention, attacked President Carter for failing to keep campaign promises.

Mr. Bush said he agreed with Treasury Secretary G. William Miller's remark to the convention Monday that voters should not listen to false promises to provide quick cures.

"For once I agree with the Administration," Mr. Bush said. "Carter four years ago offered precisely the kind of false promise to solve inflation that this convention was warned against two days ago."[49]

To explore the question of media bias further, the basic textual qualities of the news were fashioned into a Detachment Index and then a number of subanalyses made.[50] Detachment is not quite "objectivity" but it is as close as an instrument like DICTION can get to that quality. A detached text makes careful claims, focuses on concrete political entities, and adopts a third-person perspective. By way of contrast, the text scoring lowest on Detachment in my database was a quotation from Daniel Webster lovingly resurrected by a citizen of Wichita Falls, Texas, in a letter-to-the-editor written during the 1964 presidential campaign:

I am an American—These duties I share with my fellow citizens: It is my duty to obey my country's laws. It is my duty to vote, so my government may truly represent the will of the people. It is my duty to keep informed as to the honesty and ability of candidates for public office. It is my duty to pay such taxes as have been devised by representatives elected by me, to defray the cost of government.

It is my duty to serve on juries when called on. It may sometimes become my duty to hold a public office for which I am suited, so my government may function efficiently. It is my duty to defend my country, if need should arise. It is my duty to abide by the will of the majority, to stand behind my government, so my nation may be unified in time of crisis.

I am an American—I take pride in my country's Declaration of Independence. I am a believer in the American Creed.[51]

In stark contrast is the text with the highest Detachment score, supplied, not surprisingly, by the Associated Press:

Here's a state-by-state (plus the District of Columbia) assessment of where the presidential race stood before Sunday's debate. The number of electoral votes in each state is in parenthesis:

ALABAMA (9): Polls make it close, elevating Ross Perot's importance.

ALASKA (3): Surprising tossup in usual Republican stronghold.

ARIZONA (8): Surprising lead for Bill Clinton in state Democrats haven't won since 1948.

ARKANSAS (6): Clinton leads comfortably at home.

CALIFORNIA (54): Big Clinton edge in the biggest state.

COLORADO (8): Clinton ahead.

CONNECTICUT (8): Clinton leads in the polls.

DELAWARE (3): Surprising edge for Clinton.

DISTRICT OF COLUMBIA (3): Clinton way ahead. . . . [and so forth through the alphabet].[52]

The most important result from the Detachment analysis was what was not found: (1) as we see in figure 7.5, there were no great differences in how the two parties were treated by the press in the thirteen presidential elections; if anything, Republicans were treated slightly better; (2) Third Party stories scored well above the mean for Detachment in 1980, 1992, and 1996, suggesting a respectful approach toward them on the part of the press; (3) there were no pronounced differences in Detachment among the six newspapers—they tended to follow the same journalistic formula; (5) no important differences could be detected among the five broadcast sources either; (5) Detachment did not vary in meaningful ways across the campaign cycle (from the convention through election day).[53] While these data hardly settle the question of media bias, they are interesting. The sanguine interpretation is that over the long course, the press gives the candidates an even break. Less optimistically, one could conclude that bias cannot be isolated in word

190

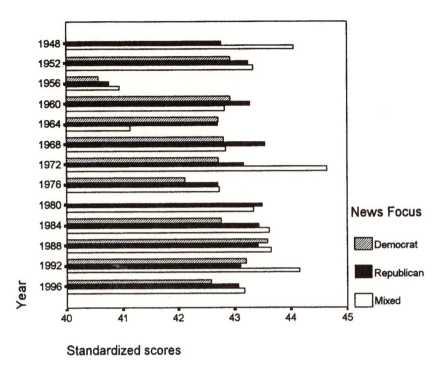

Figure 7.5. Detachment vs. News Story Focus.

choice alone and that more sophisticated instruments are needed to detect it.

More specific analyses showed that Detachment has actually gone up over the years for print coverage, suggesting that news norms are now being followed somewhat scrupulously by members of the press. These increases in Detachment held for each of the print sources studied here. In addition, when presidential elections became especially close, the media increased their Detachment, again suggesting deliberateness on journalists' parts. Also, when prosperity indicators sagged in the United States (unemployment, economic worry, a sense of uncertainty toward government), journalistic coverage became more detached, ostensibly an attempt to get judicious interpretations on the table when the nation most needed them. Finally, and at the risk of undermining the Liberal Bias explanation, when stories focusing on Democratic front-runners were compared to ones featuring Republican front-runners, the "cheerleading theory" of press coverage failed. Republicans were treated with greater Detachment than were Democrats.

The news, in short, seems worthy, or at least much of it does. Even with the admittedly limited measure of Detachment employed here, none of the traditional sources of bias could be detected. And with the large number of texts examined in this study, those differences were given ample opportunity to present themselves. They failed to do so, and they failed to do so consistently. These findings do not suggest that political news is perfect but they are encouraging. The cloud darkens somewhat when the issue of modality is considered. Print news was far more detached than broadcast news and that is a fact of some consequence. Because televised news is such a complex stimulus, media bias takes on very different dimensions in that venue. Print and broadcast differ in other ways as well and those differences complicate things yet again.

What Are the Words For?

Because television news is both visual and verbal, DICTION tells only part of its story. But that is not to say it tells us nothing. For example, even though broadcast texts were less detached than print texts, they were far more detached than either lay commentary or politicians' remarks. That is, broadcast news is still news; it draws on the same basic formulas inherited from its print forebears. But the matter cannot be left there, for television adds a whole new dimension to campaign politics. Larry Bartels reports, for example, that consumption of network news is systematically related to decreased regard for political candidates. In addition, he reports that watching television news tends to decrease viewers' abilities to correctly identify candidates' issue positions, especially during the last, crucial, days of the fall campaign.[54] Compounding these findings are those of Shanto Iyengar and Donald Kinder who report that "Americans believe by a wide margin that television—not magazines, radio, or newspapers—

provides the most intelligent, complete, and impartial news coverage," thereby giving it special political authority.[55]

One cannot discuss broadcast news without discussing its pictures. They are what give television special command over our perceptions. Beyond Tom Brokaw, beyond Dan Rather, there are the pictures: clear, real, forceful, authentic. Despite the arbitrariness of the pictures its videographers create, despite the hundreds of editors and splicers on the networks' payrolls, despite the thousands of faces lying on the cutting room floor when the news program begins, television constantly makes this promise: you do not have to take our word for it; you can see it for yourself.

Pictures also give broadcast news its pace and variety, its psychological force, its humanity. Given the power of television's pictures, then, what are the words for? One finding that is at once predictable and curious is this: television news uses considerably less Activity than does print news. Why? Ostensibly because pictures provide the action for viewers, thereby releasing the network reporter to attend to other matters. To say that the president boarded Air Force One is to waste time when the boarding can be easily shown. For print reporters, however, the absence of pictures taxes their prose significantly, requiring them to create a more complete verbal narrative. What can be shown (or implied) in a twenty-second video montage on television, takes considerable effort in the newspaper:

> President Nixon will make his next campaign trip Monday when he will meet supporters from 11 Eastern states at the home of New York Gov. Nelson A. Rockefeller and take part in a motorcade and rally.
>
> The White House announced that the President will motorcade through ten communities in Westchester County, and then go to a reception at Rockefeller's home near Tarrytown.
>
> After the reception, to which campaign leaders from 11 states are invited, the President will address an evening rally at the Nassau County Coliseum in Uniondale, L.I.
>
> With the election now less than three weeks away, Democratic efforts to force the President on to a stump campaign and to engage him in debate show no signs of success.

No other campaign trips have been announced. The President is scheduled to go to Philadelphia Friday to sign the revenue-sharing bill in Independence Hall, but the White House describes that trip as "non-political."[56]

Another difference between print and broadcast news is television's low Insistence scores. The broadcast transcript roams freely, bringing up more topics per unit time than print. That makes television news seem fluid, even languid, as it drifts effortlessly across the political scene. Because television news is so fragmented, one does not feel hectored when watching it. One feels participatory instead, emergent, constantly ready for the new twist, the new turn. Watching television keeps one in a constant state of anticipation.

Print news, on the other hand, is Thomistic. It tells you where it is going, it takes you there, and then reminds you three times where you have been. On television such an approach would be tedious in the extreme. But because print is, in Marshall McLuhan's terms, a "hotter" medium, we expect it to do more of the work for us.[57] The conclusion to the Nixon travelogue presented above shows how that work is done:

> Despite his limited campaign schedule, the President said yesterday that the last three weeks "are always the most important weeks of a campaign."
>
> Mr. Nixon was addressing a group of labor leaders from 24 countries who are spending a month in the United States observing the campaign.
>
> The last three weeks are "the most important, because that is when the people are listening, that is when the people are going to make up their minds," Mr. Nixon said in welcoming the group to the White House.
>
> Referring to the fact that American campaigns last eight to 12 weeks or longer and wear out the campaigners as well as the voters, the President said that "the British have a much better system."
>
> The British limit a campaign to three weeks, he noted.[58]

This sort of thematizing is rarely seen on television (except, perhaps, in its news magazines or documentaries). In part that is because television uses a gaggle of voices to tell its story while print coverage has a unitary authorial sense. The result, says Shanto Iyengar, is that television news becomes episodic, focusing on specific persons and events, not sociopolitical abstractions.[59] Kevin Barnhurst and Catherine Steele report that the episodic pace has picked up recently, with television now using more pictures with shorter exposure times than in the past.[60] These decisions produce linguistic consequences: television news is dramatically higher on Realism, or, to frame it in the reverse, it is far less interpretive than print. Television eschews grand theory and works instead to maintain "flow"—the news anchor introduces the acts and then steps aside. Perhaps because television news is so underinterpreted, researchers find that those who watch it tend to learn about candidates as people, while newspaper readers gain more general political knowledge.[61] Similarly, television news is less critical of the political system than are newspapers, perhaps because "the political system" (and most other abstractions) are so hard to depict for viewers.[62]

The issues of pace can also be seen in this finding: television news employs more urgent language than does print, with television emphasizing Time and newspapers emphasizing Space (although the gap has narrowed a bit recently). When one takes all of these findings together—television's focus on the here-and-now, its preference for the concrete, its open agenda, and its more cavalier approach to Detachment, one discovers a people's medium. Thus, it is not surprising that broadcast uses Human Interest language heavily and is also high on Cognitive Terms (*believe, consider, decide, speculate*), creating an unmistakable emphasis on the psychological. As Doris Graber reports, with television featuring close-ups 70 percent of the time, its text naturally takes on an interior feel.[63] Perhaps that is why the political interview has become a staple; it lets reporters get inside candidates' heads rather then allowing them to drone on endlessly about their policy positions. Television, in short, helps viewers make contact. While network news is more subdued than *Jerry Springer*, its style is still up-close-and-personal. So, for example, after one of the 1992 presidential debates, NBC brought together a panel of voters to get their reactions. Needless to say, the interviews did not focus on global warming or the Japanese yen:

Respondent #1: I think [Perot] did better than I expected him to do. He did a great job of delivering exactly what he stood for.

195

Correspondent: Are you going to vote for him?

Respondent #1: I'm—I'm close to closing my thoughts on voting Perot.

Correspondent: And Mrs. Kagan, what about you? What did you think of Ross Perot last night?

Respondent #2: Well, I thought he did a good job. I was surprised. I thought maybe he—there would be a definite difference between his not—not looking as polished as the politicians and experienced, but he held his own in there.

Correspondent: And Dennis Vandiver in Peoria, when we talked last Friday on NBC Nightly News, you seemed to be leaning toward Bill Clinton. What happened after last night?

Respondent #3: Well, at this point, Mr. Brokaw, I really haven't decided. I really enjoyed the debate last night, and if anything, it really left me undecided as to who I'll vote for.

Correspondent: Well as a fellow salesman, I'm sure that you admire his style, but once you get beyond the snappy one-liners, do you have a full understanding of what he really wants this country to do?

Respondent #3: I'd like to think I do. I—I tried to absorb as much as he's delivered these last few months. Ross Perot is the only candidate who hasn't sent me a letter to come to a thousand dollar a plate dinner. So I know he's not going to owe anybody anything when he gets there, and I really feel he's sincere in his efforts.

Correspondent: Mrs. Kagan, how did you think that President Bush did last night?

Respondent #2: Well, he—he was steadfast. He held his own. I believe he was a little bit too repetitive for me. He used some cliches and the tax and spend, and I—it was a little bit too much repetition.

Correspondent: How about Bill Clinton—what did you think of his performance?

Respondent #2: Well, he was—he looked good, but I thought his—he was too programmed. He had the pat answers and that kind of both-ered me about him.?[64]

In a most direct manner, then, the language of broadcast news captures its essence. Its pictures are unquestionably important, and we need to understand them better, but a purely linguistic analysis also tells us much: that print and broadcast news differ in important ways but that they follow the same basic script. It has become popular to decry broadcast news for being too frothy, for distracting the electorate from the serious business of choosing their leaders. But the NBC interview hardly seems toxic. It depicts three American citizens struggling with the most important decision they will make as citizens. It is the story of this interior struggle that television tells so well. Newspapers do a better job with the details, with the candidates' platforms, with what it all means. Television news, in contrast, is the perfect consumable—it gives the general lay of the land and does so with lightning speed. When it works well it brings politics to life and makes governance less an abstraction. For a nation of busy people, that hardly seems a crime.

Conclusion

There are enough data in this chapter to support anyone's theory of political news. Those who dislike the press will seize on its busy narratives and declare it facile. Those who hate journalists' negativity will argue for a more buoyant alternative. Those who object to the press's interpretations will call for a blander medium. In response, the press would argue that while a great many facts are always available, that is usually the problem—it takes people to sort through them and to draw prudent conclusions. Reporters feel they are trained to do that, and, while they sometimes get things wrong, their track record is probably no worse than that of any other interpretive craft—stock brokerage, for example, or venture capitalism. Journalists call them as they see them, but because they make their calls in public, we tend to remember their mistakes more than their rectitude. When one takes the grand view, however, the rectitude seems obvious.

But these data pose questions too: If the news were less dramatic, would we still pay attention to it? If the news were more saccharine, would we be forewarned when we needed to be forearmed? If the news were less interpretive, could we make sense out of the things that happen each day, each month, each year? The answer to all three questions is no. We need reporters because we do not have the time to govern ourselves and because we dare not trust our representatives to govern us in private. If the world were not complex and if power were not corrupting, journalism could be declared a luxury. Until those conditions obtain, we must adjust to its fallibility.

Besides, the media are not as bad as some claim. I could detect no overarching favoritism here. Instead, the press adhered to news norms with considerable dedication. Admittedly, one rough examination like this one cannot exonerate the press completely, but a great many texts were studied and a great many language patterns searched. If systematic bias existed it would have shown itself somewhere. But it did not. DICTION is a crude tool but it is not so crude as to miss important differences between print and broadcast news. These differences are important because the two media serve such different constituencies: television delivers quick, digestible bits of information to a great many people while newspapers slow their readers down, focusing on ideas rather than personalities. This latter function seems an especially important one.

The news, in short, is a complicated text. It provides facts but also offers interpretations, and that conjunction (or disjunction) upsets many. The news explains what is wrong with the world, and that upsets still more, especially when the press delights in hanging the crepe. The news, especially televised news, puts us in personal touch with our leaders, and that seems like a good thing except when it seems like a bad thing. Because the news is so complex, and because it is so vital to democratic life, it will probably always make us quarrelsome. One can imagine worse fates. Somnolence, for example.

CHAPTER 8

The People's Voice

Those in the polling business are fond of saying that any generalization made about the American people is correct. To help produce that effect, a different politico each day launches into some brave declaration with the phrase "the American people demand . . ." and thereby becomes a ventriloquist for the nation. The press, too, conjures up a different electorate with each new headline—"The American people are in a sour mood," "Americans have become oblivious to market trends," etc. In being described in these ways, the citizenry is essentially being invented as well. Demographers add to the confusion (or richness) when reporting that the American people are obscenely rich or desperately poor, avant-garde or numbingly traditional, depending on the sample drawn. The electorate, it would seem, is kaleidoscopic.

Capturing the voice of the American people is not easy today but it has never been easy. Historically, political sociology was the venue of the ward heeler who knew how and why people voted as they did and who turned that intelligence into a career. Journalists and other popular writers (Upton Sinclair comes to mind) also took a community's measure. Their special understandings were often used to right social wrongs or deflate trial balloons sent aloft too quickly by some politician. In the 1930s a new rival emerged—the opinion-takers—and by the end of the century they had become the first among equals. Polling in the United States has since become a multi-million-dollar annual business and it now guides the futures of both Microsoft and Dan Quayle. The media also conduct their own polls, as do candidates and political parties. But so too do special interest groups, academic consortia, international conglomerates, and Hollywood Incorporated. Because of polling, everyone now knows what everyone else believes.

With Jeffrey Jones

Or so it would seem. I have not relied on polling here to capture the people's voice. Respectful as I am of such methods, they tend not to feature citizens speaking in their own words. To be efficient, survey researchers force respondents into restrictive locutions—"strongly agree," "mostly true," "more often than not." To be even more efficient, surveyors then scale these responses so that a number of mathematical things becomes possible—frequency distributions, chronological trends, centroids and outliers, stochastic predictions. With each such transformation, with each new level of abstraction, the voice of the individual becomes fainter even as the people en masse becomes a grand and impressive thing.

My approach here is to inspect a large sample of letters-to-the-editor written during presidential elections between 1948 and 1996 and then compare these texts to those of other campaign actors. I take this approach because so much is revealed when people speak for themselves. I agree with Robert Huckfeldt and John Sprague, who observe that voters' attitudes "are tied directly to the composition of particular locations,"[1] and with Susan Herbst, who says that "conversation is essential to good citizenship and that it can thrive even in a mass democracy."[2] If these scholars are right, some efficient way of monitoring these local conversations must be found. I agree especially with David Thelen who observes that political leaders overly depend on what the media think the people think. Thelen tells the story of Senator George Mitchell who admitted he based his understandings on the *Washington Post*'s stories (rather than read the five hundred citizens' letters he got each day) but who also understood that "journalists reported as a pack, telling the same stories" rather than reflecting the "wide range of experiences from [people's] daily lives."[3]

I try to capture some of that experience in this chapter. After explaining my particular way of assessing the people's voice, I discuss what that voice sounds like when contrasted to what politicians and the mass media say. I report an eerie constancy to the people's voice, as if citizens ran their own, separate campaigns every four years. My data also suggest that the American people are quite functional in orientation even though it is the passionate among them who receive most of the publicity. Finally, I examine how people's language changes when they reflect on themselves. While I readily admit that finding an authentic voice of the people may be impossible, it is a possibility that must be tested, as David Thelen eloquently reminds us:

> Citizens and politicians have become increasingly invisible to each other because the cultures and institutions where they used to meet have lost their authority and because the practice of opinion management and interpretation has transformed the ways citizens and legislators talk and listen to each other. . . . By denying the voice of authority of everyday experience—of home remedies, folk wisdom, word of mouth, and firsthand experience, by which people have long made sense of life—experts have concluded that everyday talk is ignorant. By narrowing the range of experience worth learning from, experts have simultaneously made only a tiny fraction of life visible and eroded the confidence people bring from their intimate worlds to public conversation.[4]

FINDING THE PEOPLE'S VOICE

Locating a reliable source of lay opinion without using polls is not easy. Surveys are popular for a reason, actually, for several reasons: (1) the stimulus can be controlled by the researcher, with the same questions being used from place to place and from era to era; (2) responses can be readily transformed into quantitative indices, thereby making tests of difference possible; (3) respondents can be selected with demographic care, thus insuring generalizable findings; (4) polls can be administered in a straightforward and efficient manner. But surveys are not perfect. How one phrases a question, for example, may well influence the kinds of responses one receives. Too, the surveyor, not the citizen, typically determines which political topics will be included in the poll and which will be left out, thus preserving the surveyor's (not the voter's) perception of the political agenda. Other issues confront polls as well: voters are increasingly disinclined to answer the questions, thereby making random samples harder to find; few survey items have been repeated during the past fifty years, thus making comparisons difficult. Even when the "same" question is repeated across different administrations of the instrument, people in one era (or social group) may interpret that question quite differently from those in another era or social group.[5]

Given these difficulties, there is probably as much art as science in polling. Most good survey researchers acknowledge that fact, although few of them would trade the method's rigor for the deeper resonance afforded by other methods—focus groups or in-depth interviewing, for example. But these latter techniques are relatively recent phenomena (thus negating historical comparisons) and they are often designed for expedient (and proprietary) reasons, with data typically being collected for particular races and particular candidates, thereby making cross-comparisons difficult.

Selecting any research method introduces liabilities that would be avoided had another method been chosen. Mindful of this trade-off, I have taken to letters-to-the-editor for several reasons: (1) letters are written by citizens themselves—on their own topics, in their own language; (2) as such, they reflect the people's agenda, which is not to say they are uninfluenced by other agendas; (3) letters are extant, thus permitting longitudinal analysis and reanalysis of the same materials when new questions present themselves; (4) letters can be self-interpreting—their authors usually say why they hold a particular opinion, a service not regularly provided by surveys; (5) letters are also self-interpolating—writers are self-conscious political actors (e.g., "as an eighty-year-old, I feel we must . . ."), thereby providing personal data about the data they provide. In short, as with any organic form, letters have a nuance not found in even the best-designed surveys.

Deciding to use letters was not an easy decision, however, since so much folklore exists about letter-writers. They are often thought to be overly excited at best, partisan cranks or political "plants" at worst. They are also thought to be chronic complainers, persons whose lives are so unsatisfying that they spend their time in lonely garrets scratching out their vitriol. Also, because letters columns are so popular, it is assumed that letters are carefully vetted by the newspapers, thereby perpetuating yet another form of media gatekeeping. Finally, letter-writers are thought to be kin to ultraconservative talk-radio participants.[6]

Because these stereotypes are hardy, I chose my sample of letters carefully: (1) to ensure some measure of representativeness, the collection was restricted to newspapers in twelve small cities (averaging around 100,000 persons each) spread evenly throughout the United States; (2) these cities were each large enough to incorporate some of the diversity found in the nation itself and yet small enough to represent political opinions formed outside the nation's dominant media centers; (3) in composite, these twelve cities are a microcosm of the United States; whether one looks at voter turnout rate; partisan affiliation; racial, educational, or economic data; media habits or demography, the million or so residents in these cities, when taken collectively, represent the nation generally; (4) surveys of the newspapers' editors conducted in 1993 and again in 1997 revealed that the papers exerted virtually no editorial control over the letters; they published 90 percent of those received, altering them only for reasons of libel or excessive length; (5) because the twelve cities generally lie outside the nation's metropolitan centers and because my sample contained no more than one letter written by the same person, the effects of organized mailings were minimized and, most likely, eliminated altogether.[7]

To answer some of the nagging questions surrounding political letter-writers, two separate surveys were run after the 1992 and 1996 elections. In each case, a group of letter-writers and a random sample of residents were drawn from the above communities and their political and social attitudes then assessed by a mailed, paper-and-pencil survey. In addition, a third survey was conducted in 1994 to get some idea of what local residents thought of those who wrote letters-to-the-editor.[8] This latter survey showed that the people in these cities held no monolithic views of letter-writers. Some respondents felt them too liberal and others felt them too conservative; letter-writers were not thought to be overly educated but they were thought to be community-minded; interestingly, respondents felt that the letter-writers resembled their friends and neighbors but not themselves (a displacement effect?). In general, then, stereotypes about letter-writers seem not to have taken hold among ordinary Americans.

What did the surveys show about the writers themselves? Generally speaking, letter-writing is a contrarian enterprise: Republicans write more letters when a Democratic president is in office and Democrats do the same with a Republican incumbent. Letter-writers were also somewhat older than the norm (fifty-four versus forty-seven years old) but otherwise they were quite similar to the general population: they reported the same average family income ($45,000), watched a similar amount of television (about three hours per day), subscribed to the local paper with equal frequency (73 percent), and were no more liberal or conservative than the average citizen. In addition, they were no more likely to own or rent a home than their neighbors and no more politically trusting or politically efficacious than the average citizen. Generally, that is, the writers resembled the other voters in their communities (who tended to be white, home-owning, middle-of-the-road, and somewhat educated).

But letter-writers were also different in important ways. They were much more politically involved than the comparison sample: they contributed more frequently to political campaigns, they consumed more political news, and they were more likely to volunteer for campaign projects. These general patterns held true for both surveys, although the 1996 race depressed consumption of political news for writers and nonwriters alike. The overwhelming sense one gets from the data, then, is that letter-writers simply cared more about their communities than did their fellow citizens. This was true despite their personal economic circumstances or where they lived (the writer/nonwriter differences could be found in each of the cities tested). The writers voted, petitioned, and affirmed the political covenant, precisely what Jefferson and his colleagues had requested of all citizens.

While the language of politics will be given special attention in this chapter, surveys have their uses. My survey data, as well as that gathered by others, suggest that if collected under the right conditions, letters-to-the-editor can provide a rich source of insight.[9] Letter-writers do not represent the great unwashed American because the great unwashed American does not vote with much regularity. But my studies show that none of the usual suspects—money, privilege, party, education, geography, era, occupation, socioeconomic status—predictably distinguished writers from nonwriters. Instead, letter-writers can best be thought of as reflective citizens, persons who have the same cultural residue deposited within them as other voters but who also have an idealized view of the civic compact. To read their letters is to examine these ideals, an exercise that becomes especially intriguing when they are read alongside those of other political actors.

LISTENING TO THE PEOPLE'S VOICE

While letter-writers may not be perfect representatives of the larger population, they seem worthy surrogates. In perusing the thousands of letters collected here, I have never had the sense of being among strangers. Rather, letter-writers just seem to have more gumption than most people:

> Reagan is a 'bad seed' completely without feeling or compassion. If we put this man in the White House again, for another four years, it will be the end of a democratic government. He lies to the American people and blames everyone else for his disastrous administration. I am sure the American people do not want to go back 200 years, when we fought and won our freedom, only to lose it again with this monstrous man.[10]

> I am a Roman Catholic. But I most devotedly hope John F. Kennedy is not elected President Nov. 8. If Kennedy is elected President everything that goes wrong, including chicken pox for babies, will be blamed on my church. No, thank you.[11]

> [I]n response to Bush's McCarthyistic tactics regarding Bill Clinton's visit to the Soviet Union, Clinton showed us how a true leader rises above the mudslinging to communicate his goals for our country's future. He is not afraid to identify problems and offer solutions for them. But most importantly, he is not afraid to run on his record as governor of Arkansas.[12]

People who write letters-to-the-editor are scolds. They use far more Blame terms (*angry, brutal, cowardly, deceitful*) than either politicians or the press and more Denial terms as well (*can't, shouldn't, wasn't, won't*). They combine these refrains with a good many Leveling Terms, thereby producing the kinds of overstatements seen above. But it is useful to reflect on the nature of a scold. A scold is neither a churl nor a villain. Parents tend to be scolds, as do grade-school teachers and Little League coaches. Scolds spend considerable time remonstrating young people but they also have a salvific impulse, some instinct for improving things. Although the writers in my sample were not as Optimistic as the politicians, they were much more positive than the press, often ending their letters with policy recommendations: "Kick [Panetta] into retirement and elect Bill McCampbell—for a change and a better system of government";[13] "It's a hard campaign. We all must make a hard decision. But to have tunnel vision is dangerous. It's not over yet, Mr. Bush. God bless President Dukakis."[14]

There is an indefatigability to the writers, a tirelessness that probably has many roots. While they quickly spot the nation's shortcomings (often spelling them out in exquisite detail), a kind of political essentialism buoys them up. This makes them the children of Tom Paine, firebrands-cum-idealists. It also makes them "system allegiant," persons who believe that the nation's blessings will secure its liberties if due vigilance is exercised. Thus, one of their standard moves is to contrast human shortcomings to the nation's durable political traditions:

> I have yet to meet anyone who does not consider their paycheck private property! Bryce McEuen, House of Representatives candidate for District 59, could take the same remedial course. He has the audacity to claim that the people do not have the right to "usurp the legislative authority." He could start his reading with the Declaration of Independence which states that governments derive "their just powers from the consent of the governed."[15]

> Stop and think, read if you can. Under President Clinton, the people of the United States have lost more of their freedoms and rights guaranteed under the people's Bill of Rights, the first 10 amendments of our Constitution, than under any president in the history of our nation. If nothing else, that should decide your vote.[16]

If writers like these are the children of Paine, they are also the children of Jesus, never completely ruling out the possibility of salvation. That is what makes them scolds rather than curmudgeons. One finds few letters that begin by predicting perdition and that end by recommending fallout shelters. Instead, they maintain the can-do spirit. Some writers ground their faith in charismatic force ("People criticized young Bobby Kennedy. Why? He has one of the best records ever accomplished by an Attorney General");[17] others find hope in communal alignments ("What most people fail to realize is that the prosperity we have enjoyed over the years and the buffer that protected us from the recession for so long is largely due to the strong unions that existed in our area.");[18] still others cling to redemptive possibilities ("If enough intelligent debate is stimulated, President Nixon might change his mind and stop pressing this legislation").[19]

The letters contained considerably more Religious and Irreligious terms than the politicians' texts, twice as many as media reports. These findings are hardly surprising but one must ask why. What is it about citizenship, or Americana, that makes it reasonable for 30 percent of the letters to contain such allusions? Why has there been no appreciable variation in the use of religious terms over time and why do writers of all stripes, not just conservatives, use such language? On the other hand, what is it about institutional governance (or institutional journalism, for that matter) that often makes them shrink from such language?[20] Is Stephen Carter right when arguing in *The Culture of Disbelief* that the American people are desperately seeking moral leadership, perhaps without realizing it?[21] Is William Bennett merely being polemical when arguing in *The De-Valuing of America*[22] that the nation's leaders have forgotten how to speak the language of values, a language that citizens themselves speak effortlessly and, often, injunctively:

It is ironic that the first avowed born-again Christian president, at least in recent history, should be under fierce attack by the right-wing evangelical Christian church establishment, including the Moral Majority movement. Why is this and what do these people want? Perhaps a clue can be gained by looking at the "sins" they stress and cite as evidence that America is dying. These sins include abortion, homosexuality, pornography, military weakness, ERA, the ban on religion in schools, divorce and humanism. The sins they do not stress, or seldom mention, are greed, violence, rampant materialism, dishonesty, intolerance, lack of human rights and compassion, a belligerent attitude, indifference (lack of love) toward our fellow man and lack of concern for resources to sustain future generations.[23]

As we see here, even a cursory glance at letters-to-the-editor finds a blending of political and moral issues. This author, for example, combines policy (the military, the Equal Rights Amendment) and axiology (greed, dishonesty, belligerence) seamlessly, even as he makes a point about the 1980 race. This boldness, this syncretism, is the writers' most natural mode of expression and it may explain why many of them are frustrated with the increasingly antiseptic discourse spoken by politicians and the media. These same concerns make them irrepressible, a fact evidenced by their highly embellished language (see figure 8.1). Perhaps because they are so constrained by space limitations, and because they feel their beliefs so powerfully, the writers use adjectives generously, as if their truths would go unobserved otherwise. Notably, these strategies are as available to the Left ("The Republican Party has never been more *narrow-minded, intolerant and out of touch* with the American people than it is today")[24] as they are to the Right ("The recent slander of Dan Quayle, and vicariously, the National Guard by his opponents and members of the press, is offensive to the great majority of the American people. Service in the Guard is *honorable, decent and patriotic*").[25]

Embellishment is almost always a sign of emotion. Eric Hoffer and Richard Hofstadter have argued that verbal habits like these can reflect a dangerous fanaticism.[26] While this may be true for some writers, it is hardly true for the majority (given the centrist locales from which the letters were taken and the thoroughly middle-class arguments made in the letters). For them, Embellishment had signal value ("pay attention to this") rather than ideological value ("I alone am right"), a conclusion that is reinforced by the letters' other features.

Figure 8.2 paints a stark picture of the people's voice: on a great many dimensions the writers produced scores equidistant from (and statistically separate from) the other political voices.[27] Each set of variables tells a different story: (1) *Realism*—the people are neither

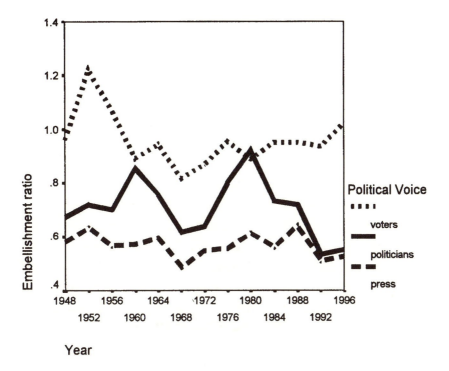

Figure 8.1. Embellishment Scores across Time.

as practical as the politicians nor as conceptual as the press. They have a foot in the former camp because they have real lives to live and in the latter camp because they also feel the need to rise above the quotidian, to be philosophers for a day. (2) *Self-Reference*—the writers do not imitate the media's objectivity (they write on the editorial page, after all, not the front page) but they are also not as self-absorbed as the candidates. This balance lets them be both position-takers and commentators, a synthesis denied political candidates who must stand with the ideas they present. (3) *Tenacity*—politicians are given to the strong declaration and so are letter-writers, but the writers also had high Ambivalence scores and so their words are at war with themselves. As a result, there is an equivocality (or multivocality) to the people's voice, a dialectical tension and a searching. When reading the letters, one often gets the sense that the author

209

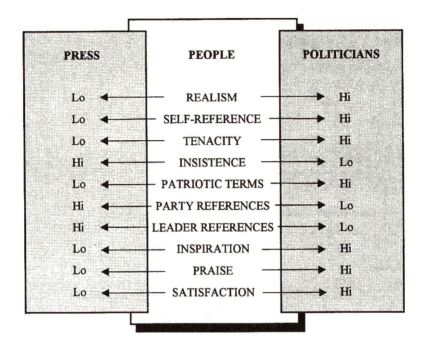

Figure 8.2. The People As Intermediary.

was still working out the ideas even as they were being set to paper. This quality gives the letters an energy and a restlessness and also an audience appeal:

> It's no longer speculation; Jim Baker will leave the State Department to run President Bush's campaign. At least he will be doing something that is possible, but I hope not probable! Has anyone every thought about the amount of our money it cost for the trips he has made trying to help bring peace to countries that have been under dictatorship since time began. This is not a probability. I know it, you know it and Bush knows it.
>
> What kind of campaign will Baker be running for Bush? Considering the shape our economy is in, the unemployed, the homeless etc., our economy doesn't seem to be on Bush's agenda. He is more concerned about the Third World countries than he is his own. We are not supposed to be the breadbasket of the world or make astronomical loans

to other countries. If the loans we made to other countries during World War II were repaid, we could not be in the economic slump we are in. France, England and all the others have made no attempt to repay these loans. Just because they were our allies doesn't mean the loans were a fight.

As always, I remain noncommittal on who I will vote for, if I vote. But I still remember how to spell Perot, Brown and Duke!![28]

The author here has adopted at least three personae: news commentator, partisan, and political diffident—all in two hundred words. It is hard to essentialize this letter but that is beside the point because such letters are often works in progress. As we see from their (4) *Insistence* scores, the letters-writers do not travel as far afield as the politicians but they do cover a good deal of ground in a short time. These midrange Insistence scores give the letters an effervescence that distinguishes them from the disciplined prose written by newspaper professionals.

In a survey of people's reactions to the news media, journalists were popularly viewed as arrogant, cynical, and unrepresentative of the average American.[29] Figure 8.2 helps explain why: the writers consistently outscored the media on (5) *Patriotic terms*, (6) *Inspiration*, (7) *Praise*, and (8) *Satisfaction*. While letter-writers are often cranky, they are far more upbeat than the average news story. Perhaps that is why, when pressed, voters identify more readily with political leaders than with media personnel, persons who seem unable to find good news to report. And so these two discourses meet each day in the newspaper, with the front page being resolutely glum and the letters sometimes sounding like sermonettes:

San Francisco is a lovely city. Delegates of the Republican convention proclaim it such. My concern is that they will remember how it was that it became so lovely, so great and so beautiful, even as our entire country has grown in beauty, strength and might. I have the same concern for the Democratic convention which will soon be held and I hope that all pettiness will be put aside as delegates are elected and platforms are adopted reflecting the desires of our people.

I hope that as our delegates square their jaws and make campaign promises they will also be prepared to square their shoulders in the discharge of their duties, and that we shall not be deceived when the voting is over in November. Honesty, sobriety, and fair dealings are words to be respected. Double talk and gobbledygook have no place in our society and weaken our moral fiber. In my consideration of candidates and party platforms I shall attempt to separate the wheat from the chaff and I shall be watching for it from this day forward to the election.

As our delegates view the lovely convention cities I hope that they see more than just the beauty of their cities. May they see the hands that built them. The great love, romance, work and sacrifice. The tears, the sorrow, the joy as they look out over the church steeples representing the many creeds and tongues of the people and their cultural and spiritual pride, I hope they are humbled to the knowledge that they have a grave responsibility before them. May they leave their conventions with an overwhelming love for their country and an honest, sincere, desire to serve it in the best way they can. And then, may each and every one of us do likewise.[30]

This letter was written over thirty years ago but those written today are still pinioned between the press and the politicians on Patriotism, Inspiration, Praise, and Satisfaction. They have also maintained this balance on (9) *Party References* and (10) *Leader References*: Voters are more interested than the candidates in horse-race issues but unwilling to turn the campaign into a narrow discussion of personalities and tactics.[31] These findings coincide with those of Judith Trent and her colleagues, who find across several elections that voters care more about the candidates' personal values than does the press.[32] Voters, in short, seem to have an agenda all their own.

Letters-to-the-editor have a bumptious quality. While often castigatory, they are rarely depressive; that gives them a liveliness and also a considerable warmth. Writers typically sketch out solutions to the problems they describe and then issue impatient pleas that action be taken immediately. Like the readers for whom they write, they are willing to call a spade a spade but they also work through their issues on the fly, rarely making a complete policy case. By concentrating so much on values, on hectoring, the writers produce a unique art form. On more than a dozen variables, they stand at arm's length from both

TABLE 8.1
Linguistic Variability in Political Campaigns

	Number of Differences Observed[a]		
Political Dimension	Voters' Texts (n = 6126)	Media's Texts (N = 8528)	Politicians' Texts (n = 3654)
Campaign Cycle	3	20	28
Campaign Era	24	40	35
Polling Spread	8	23	26
Unemployment Rate	18	36	27
Economic Anxiety	15	37	34
Sense-of-Care	18	39	34
Total Differences	86	195	184

[a] Out of 47 potential differences in each cell; $p < .01$ in all cases.

the press and the candidates. This makes them aliens in both camps, allies in both camps, or neither, or both. But it clearly makes them an alternative voice in the campaign.

DEPENDING ON THE PEOPLE'S VOICE

One reason for studying letters-to-the-editor is that even in an age of television and the Internet, 70 percent of adult Americans still read a newspaper every day. Indeed, Stephen Bennett and his colleagues report that while there has been some drop-off in readership over the years, Americans are still "wedded to their newspapers." They also find that using the electronic media during political campaigns actually stimulates newspaper reading on the part of citizens.[33] And so there is every reason to believe that letters columns become integrated into the voter's consciousness. There is another reason to believe that as well: letters are a stable political commodity that tells readers what they will get even before they get it.

Table 8.1 shows the letters' dependability: they did not change during the course of a campaign, nor did they vary according to the closeness of the race. Too, while the letters have changed somewhat over the years, they have not fluctuated as much as the other campaign voices. Most of the temporal changes—for instance, decreasing Familiarity, a modest drop in Realism, more references to Hardship, an increase in Numerical Terms—were conceptually unpatterned and often of small magnitude when compared to changes found in the candidate and media texts. In addition, the letters did not vary nearly as much as the other voices under changing socioeconomic conditions. Statistically, one should be able to expect many more such effects, especially since so many texts were examined (over six thousand), because so many different authors were involved, and because the letters were cobbled together from so many different geographic locations. And yet even regional differences were nonexistent; with the exception of three or four variables (out of forty-seven), one could not tell where a voter lived by reading his or her letter. Taken together, these findings suggest either that letters-to-the-editor are an unusually restrictive genre or that the People's Voice has a remarkable consistency.

My findings suggest that the richness of lay political expression lies not in its oddness but in its dependability. As if to improve on such conditions, the electronic media often select the exotic lay comment for reprise on the nightly news. But trying to understand who the American people are by watching them on television can be like looking for a coin where the lighting is good rather than where one has lost it. When reading the following letter, in contrast, a letter devoid of coloration or personality, one is taxed in a different way. Because it is impossible to tell where the letter was written or when, or what prompted the writer to write it, one is left to contemplate its essence:

> Sir: I believe that any loyal American citizen would expect an elected official of this country to be well-rounded, impartial, multilateral in his interests, and void of devotion to any special interest group. But shouldn't [the candidates] have the right to expect the same from the American public? I feel as if too many voters think only of themselves and of satisfying their interests and problems when voting. If the voter had a little more concern for his fellow man and made a decision which evaluated the "whole" candidate, rather than one phase of his view-

point, I believe America could be assured in most cases of getting the best man into office.[34]

To be told that this letter was written in 1960, in New Jersey, tells us little. It could just as easily have been written yesterday or a year from now. Our author, like many voters, is concerned here with enduring realities, and this fundamentalist strain distinguishes the people's voice. Missing here are the details of the Nixon-Kennedy campaign, its fireworks and spectacle. Missing too are references to the specific ills then affecting the nation. In their place is a faintly philosophical tone, one that looks broad and deep for truths that cannot be swept away in the morning. One finds no extractable quotations here; a harsh judge would judge the remarks banal. Most of the other letters deserve that apt, if ungenerous, characterization as well. To study them is to study why banality is important.

Even at the eleventh hour, even on election eve in 1976 in one of the closest presidential races in recent memory, even in the perennial battleground state of California, an American citizen can still take the long view and assume that his or her political lessons have a universality to them:

From the reports of apathy of voters to the general election this year, I am forced to break a long silence prior to Nov. 2. The Republicans are being labeled as the cause of all our troubles and debts! But remember: The Democrats have put us into every war since the Civil War! (See your history books.) That is what runs up the big debts that no one but the American citizens pay. Of course there is more employment during a war, but, when it is over the big demand for materials and personnel drops. Then, Republicans are elected to clean up the mess and the party gets the blame for all the debts and unsettled conditions. Immediately the Democrats promise more jobs if elected—bond issues and WPA type of work—which accomplishes nothing and runs the debt higher. Every congressman tries to prove his worth by the amount of legislation he turns out, very little of which is needed, but, causes more federal bodies to be implemented and administered. And we are stuck with them![35]

Not all letter-writers operate this transcendentally but the majority do. The letters were considerably less time sensitive than either the press's or the candidates' texts (as measured by the Space-Time variable), again suggesting a patience—and an essentialism—that keeps them focused on principles rather than practices. That the letters did not vary by region is particularly interesting. With the exception of a few variables—writers in the East used more "beltway" language, midwesterners were more colloquial,[36] and those in the West had marginally higher Certainty scores—the letters were largely indistinguishable as to origin.[37] For some reason, the writers consistently adopted a public voice, reaching past local concerns to leverage weightier matters. When social and economic times were difficult, for example, they adapted in only two major ways: (1) they became a bit more technical (less Familiarity, more Numerical Terms), perhaps in an attempt to document the country's travails, and (2) Party References dropped off somewhat, perhaps an admission that partisanship was no solution during hard times.

Generally, though, standard political factors did not explain variations in the letters. This suggests that an election is one thing for elites and an entirely different thing for the writers. Perhaps that is why voters so often report a "disconnect" between how a campaign is reported to them by the media and what they themselves see. Letters-to-the-editor are frequently bizarre and often strident, but if voters were asked which of the three voices most represented them they would probably choose the letter-writers. Some would be attracted to their bitchiness but more would appreciate their steadfastness. Even a fifth grader knows how to be steadfast:

> My classmates and I are really concerned about how few are voting. And do I mean a few. Only 55 out of 100 people voted in 1972. Some people say that there will be less this year. If the kids could vote I'm sure there would be more votes. But we can't so it's up to you. It's really important. It's our future.[38]

Another source of stability lies in the rhetorical roles the writers adopt. In an attempt to identify subvoices within the letters they were arrayed along two continua: one measured the extent to which the letters focused on practical politics (as measured by Party and Leader

References) and the other assessed their willingness to deal with axio-logical issues (a combination of Religious and Patriotic terms). Using a series of rough decision parameters,[39] three groups were identified: Pundits (those emphasizing "beltway" language), Traditionals (those who used axiological tokens heavily), and Functionals (those who avoided both kinds of language). Sixty-three percent of the cases turned out to be Functionals, no doubt the primary source of the stability identified above. The remaining cases were split equally be-tween Pundits and Traditionals.

These proportions did not vary over the years. They also remained constant across the four campaign cycles, in the four geographical regions, and in both close and distant races. Changing socioeconomic conditions had no effect on them either. Several conclusions can be drawn from these facts: (1) writers have one of three distinct political personalities—Traditionals guard national values, Pundits focus on campaign dynamics, and Functionals deal with community prob-lems; (2) the writers are overwhelmingly Functional, thus flying in the face of the stereotypes of letter-writers; (3) the remaining authors are more colorful but quite different from one another. For example, Traditionals tend to preach (high Certainty, Liberation, and Inspira-tion scores) and they worry about divisiveness (low Commonality). In contrast, Pundits use a more urgent language (low Space-Time scores), have a narrow agenda (high Insistence), and are consistently interpretive (low Realism), not unlike the press. Functionals focus on the here and now, use a good deal of colloquial language, focus on Accomplishment, and produce especially high Realism scores.

Data like these come alive when the letters themselves are examined:

Pundit

Jess R. Bushman's letter to the editor, which appeared with the headline, "Dole, Clinton differ" raised more questions than answers about the personal life of Dole. (1) Did he enlist or was he drafted? (2) Was he one of those 90-day wonders who were shaped up and shipped out in three months? (3) Was he wounded about the time Hitler' committed suicide and the war ended in Germany? (4) What happened to the first Mrs. Dole? Was she the nurse who was by his side during his miraculous recovery? (5) Why did he dump her? I've heard even she doesn't know. Was it for Elizabeth?

I'm having a hard time deciding if Dole is riding on Elizabeth's coattails or vice versa. She is a much better speaker and more interesting to watch than dull Dole. As to who I'll vote for, I think I'll write in Oprah Winfrey. Neither party has given us a super candidate if you delve into their personal lives.[40]

Traditional

To all the Pat Robertsons, Jerry Falwells and Pat Buchanans out there, I say: You will never impose your self-righteous, ultraconservative "ideals" on me or the majority of Americans. Your thinking is no different from that of the fanatical minds that plague the Middle East. You wish to force your ideas of religion, family values, morals, etc., on the rest of us. However, most of us are quite capable of thinking for ourselves; we're allowed to do that in this country, in case you've forgotten. For those of us who do not wish to be dictated to by the likes of religious fanatics, please don't sit idly by. Get out there and vote to protect our rights as individuals. Vote for Steve Musselwhite for Congress in the 6th District, for Rick Boucher in the 9th District, and for president, Bill Clinton![41]

Functional

There is a minor error in Robert S. Terry's letter to the editor (Aug. 26, "The economics of tax-slavery"). It claimed that each person's share of the debt is $4,000. This was true in 1982 when our national debt was $1 trillion. Now that our national debt has risen to $5 trillion, it's more than $19,000 "per every soul in the country."

The question that should be asked is whether this trend of rapid debt growth, if unchecked or reversed, will result in the destruction of our economy and our way of life. Unless taken care of quickly, I believe the rising debt and other national problems not being addressed by our current political leaders will result in the downfall of our present bountiful economic system.

This is why I support the principles of reform endorsed by the Reform Party, and why the Reform Party will be running an information campaign this fall rather than a competitive race with the Republicans and Democrats. The solution to these problems is not with which party controls Congress and the White House, but with an informed electorate.[42]

These are not just three ways of languaging but also three ways of seeing the world. Punditry, for example, is a deconstructive art. It presumes a world of stratagems and cabals, of false consciousness and malignant motives. People stand at the center of the Pundit's universe—candidates with their magnetism or hubris, pressure groups with their conflicting purposes. The Pundit posits a world of seeming in which that which should be known is hard to know. Hence the Pundit's purpose in life—to remove the scales from our eyes. The Pundit's world is a world of inconsistent binaries: image and action, language and intention, known and unknown, possibility and probability. The Pundit is also a master ironist.

The world of the Traditional is vastly different. It is a place of essences, not appearances, a place in which all can be learned if one has but the eyes to see. Truth lies not in the empirical world but in the world of faith, with its rights and obligations. Traditionals stand with one foot in the present ("vote for Steve Musselwhite"), but their other foot, their anchor foot, stands in the past ("we're allowed to do that in this country, in case you've forgotten"). Traditionals tend not to place their faith in institutional arrangements—parties, legislatures, bureaucracies—but in felt abstractions (love, honor, duty). Pundits and Traditionals are almost always disappointed by what they see about them, but Traditionals, at least, have hope.

Functionals come in many stripes. Some are self-appointed pedagogues and others are dialecticians, persons for whom the proper set of facts can set things straight. Functionals find it hard to converse directly with Traditionals who reduce everything to questions of fidelity. Functionals are averse to grand theory and so their letters tend to be quite direct. Because it is easier to be a Functional than a Traditional (for whom Truth is required) or a Pundit (for whom Sadness is required), they overwhelm the letters columns. Pundits, in contrast, come and go with elections.

219

The American polity derives much of its richness from this assemblage of characters.[43] They are hardy players, these three, and they emanate directly from the nation's cultural traditions. The American colonies began as a theocracy, soon became mercantile, and later developed democratic institutions. Each tradition has its own political temper and each endures. Letters columns have become a dependable site for their continued reengagement.

CONSTRUCTING THE PEOPLE'S VOICE

A capsule version of the three campaign voices would be this: Candidates address political initiatives, the press concentrates on political actors, and the electorate emphasizes political communities. Because these agendas are so different, democratic citizens often talk past one another, as we have seen throughout this book. A slender fact indicates that: letter-writers make more Voter References (*folks, voters, society, rank-in-file*) than politicians, far more than the press. These differences have been strong and abiding throughout the last fifty years.

It makes sense that voters would be self-interested in these ways given how often their concerns are disregarded by elites. To better study their attitudes, all texts (including those of the politicians, the press, and the letter-writers) with an exceptionally high number of Voter References were extracted from the database and analyzed separately.[44] The attempt here was to survey representations of or, perhaps better, "productions" of the American people. The assumption was that the electorate is not a stable, monolithic entity but a contested terrain. Even ordinary Americans understand this process of reification, a fact uncovered by Susan Herbst who quotes one fifty-year-old police commander as follows:

> Public opinion, generally, is what the media tells you. You have no way
> of validating the process. Generally . . . newspapers or television will
> report findings, and polls. If you accept that at face value—that every-
> thing is accurate and the poll's been conducted properly . . . you may
> or may not agree with the poll. The problem I have is that I don't like

to take things just on face value—just because it's in the newspaper or it's reported on television.[45]

This officer would not be surprised by my findings. Even in texts containing a high number of Voter References, the press emphasized the horse race: high Leader References, high party References, and high Activity. The citizen is less a citizen than a voter for the press, a variable in a campaign equation featuring demographic rather than psychological variables. The following passage, for example, focuses exclusively on human beings but not one of them is given a name:

> This year's presidential candidates are intensively wooing "the women's vote" as if there really were one. President Carter, supporting ratification of the Equal Rights Amendment (ERA), insists that what women really want is economic, social, and legal justice.
>
> Ronald Reagan is trying to tone down his hawkish image for women voters who, according to polls and research, tend to feel more strongly about pacifism than do men. He pledges to appoint a qualified woman to an early Supreme Court vacancy and asks the National Organization for Women (NOW) to reconsider its opposition to him.
>
> Perhaps never have women's issues and women's attitudes been so prominent a discussion topic in an election campaign. And polls indicate that more women voters, for whatever mix of reasons, tend to prefer Carter to Reagan as a presidential choice.[46]

The electorate is a different thing for political candidates. For them, people have relational value, which is why one finds a high number of Self-References and a considerable amount of Realism and Optimism in their texts. The American citizen is not an entity for the politician but an ally, a fellow traveler, a Thou needing an I. Negotiation, accommodation, and fealty lie at the center of the politicians' universe, but lying at the center of the center are human relationships. Lyndon Johnson specialized in such relationships. More than any other politician of recent times, he knew how to build bridges to people (and bridges to Texarkana as well):

> Most Americans want medical care for older citizens. And so do I. Most Americans want fair and stable prices and decent incomes for our farmers. And so do I. Most Americans want a decent home in a decent

neighborhood for all. And so do I. Most Americans want an education for every child to the limit of his ability. And so do I. Most Americans want a job for every man who wants to work. And so do I. Most Americans want victory in our war against poverty. And so do I. Most Americans want continually expanding and growing prosperity. And so do I.

These are your goals. These are our goals. These are the goals and will be the achievements of the Democratic Party. These are the goals of this great, rich Nation. These are the goals toward which I will lead, if the American people choose to follow.[47]

The writers' voter-centric texts were different still. Mostly they were angry: high Blame, high Denial, high Certainty, high Embellishment. Writers clearly become hortatory when the will of the people has been violated. But they are also canny rhetoricians, using ideological and emotional appeals to save the nation's souls:

- *The people have fallen asleep*: "I wish the American People would wake up. Doesn't everybody or most everyone know why Dole doesn't want Perot on the debates? Because Perot will tell it like it is and Dole doesn't want to hear the truth."[48]

- *The people must not be scorned*: "Quayle offends my sensibilities and my regard for the presidency. He must think that the American People are gullible. Somewhat, maybe, but not all that gullible. Wrong again, Dan!"[49]

- *The people must not be ignored*: "It is high time the voice of the American People was heard by national delegates and political leaders or democracy will be on its way out. Perhaps a national primary election would restore confidence, once again, in our democratic society. Do we dare wait much longer?"[50]

- *The people are not stupid*: "The American people know what the issue is in this important election. The American people remember the 21% interest rates that brought our economy to its knees and the double-digit inflation which is the most unfair tax on the poor and on the people who live on fixed incomes. We are not going to opt for the stagflation of the former administration."[51]

- *The people have shirked responsibilities*: "Citizens who vote for incompetent persons and entrust them with the interpretation of our laws show the greatest disrespect for law and order. It is not the youngsters who cry out for anarchy who are the criminals. It is we who permit unqualified people to hold office."[52]

While talk radio participants usually reserve their wrath for an imperious government, writers often include the people in their arc of blame. The trope of the lazy citizen is especially popular with them as is that of the benighted fool who has ignored basic political realities. But the letter-writers are children of the New Testament, not the Old, and so inevitably find the road to redemption—through greater political participation, most commonly, or through a heightened appreciation of democratic traditions. Some writers present a third alternative—a better cache of candidates—but that is less common. In this subset of letters, at least, one rarely finds a writer arguing that some politician has a special understanding of the American voter. Intelligence of that sort is alleged to lie within the writers themselves.

William Gamson has observed that media frames are often borrowed by voters to interpret the political world.[53] I find that less true of the writers studied here. Even when the Pundits reflect on the people, they are much less dispassionate than the press. Instead of treating the electorate as an electorate, they treat it as a citizenry. Their letters remain filled with the discourse of praise and blame.[54] In other words, the writers are constantly willing to become, in Rousseau's terms, "a spectacle to themselves."[55] They put the nation's strengths and weaknesses under the microscope and, in so doing, construct an electorate less utilitarian than that of the press and less cloying than that of the politicians. In viewing The People through a moral lens the writers perform an important kind of cultural reconnaissance. The accuracy of their surveillance is probably less important than their willingness to foster such a dialogue in the first place.

CONCLUSION

Do letter-writers really constitute the voice of the people? While my surveys show that they resemble their friends and neighbors on most objective measures, their friends and neighbors do not spend their idle hours straightening out the polity. But if they are not the people's voice, who is? The writers have real jobs, after all; they parent real children; they go to real churches; they die real deaths. They have their own names and they live in houses with unique addresses. They do not float about in cyberspace, nor do they gather occasionally for focus group sessions. Instead, they throw themselves into their communities and still find time to scold their fellow citizens. The writers have their peculiarities, to be sure, but they are not from Mars.

The acid test of their worthiness to serve as our spokespersons lies in what they say and if it sounds reasonable to us. DICTION shows that writers embellish their prose and so one must view their remarks as public discourse, not as talk designed for their intimates. But much of what they say still sounds familiar: they complain about government a good deal; they often speak in overstatements; at other times they reveal their uncertainties; they are not ashamed to speak of political matters in value-laden terms. Most important, they are different from both politicians and the press. They are not as caught up in the horse race as the media nor are they as negative. They also ramble less than politicians, are not as ego centered or as nationalistic, and, unlike politicians, they pay attention to campaign personalities. In rejecting both the media's and candidates' models, the writers introduce a third voice to the campaign. Given the popularity of letters columns, it is clearly a voice with which many can identify.

Overall, the writers churn out a predictable product that seems oblivious to changing political conditions. It is as if they live in a world entirely different from that of political elites. Whereas the media and political establishments are tied to the moment, writers focus on enduring (often less soluble) matters. The Traditionals among them are particularly willing to discuss moral issues but even the Pundits among them refuse to treat the campaign as a pinball game. Most of the writers are Functionals, however. That datum alone shows an important kinship between them and most Americans.

The United States may have become a nation where nobody can speak for anybody. But that does not prevent many from trying. More than either of the other political voices, the writers constantly interjected a grassroots element into the campaign. Their Voter References served as steady reminders that government is designed to improve people's lives. The media also spoke of the citizenry but usually did so in mechanical terms, while the candidates treated the same issue strategically. The writers chose a different path, goading their readers to become smarter and less apathetic, to renew the social contract, to become better citizens. In offering these injunctions they showed far more temerity than most Americans, more communal concern as well. Perhaps this means that writers do not represent the norm at all, only themselves. If that is so, perhaps the norm should change. Perhaps it will.

✻ CHAPTER 9 ✻

Campaign Reflections

IT IS customary to end a book on political campaigns with an apology for them. Most popular writers, as well as many serious journalists and academicians, come away from campaigns detesting them. They decry the politicians' manipulativeness, the press's negativity, the PAC'S ruthlessness, and the citizens' lethargy and then predict an imminent demise for the Republic. John Quincy Adams predicted these reactions more than two hundred years ago:

> This election of a chief magistrate for the whole Union will never be
> settled to the satisfaction of the people. The theory of frequent elections
> is that power cannot be trusted to the same hands, even of the wisest
> and the best. The two parts can be reconciled to each other only by the
> inconsistency and corruptibility of human nature in its best estate; and
> never, never will any great people be satisfied with the result of their
> own election of an Executive head.[1]

Because of such dissatisfactions, a cottage industry of election custodians has grown up in the United States, each with a special way of fixing what has gone wrong. I will not join that fraternity here, nor will this book end with a long list of suggestions for improving campaigns. Although I began this study with all of the usual biases intact, the more I learned about campaigns the more I have come to appreciate them. The more political texts I examined, the more computer power I expended, the more I have come to respect the complexity and subtlety of the work they do. When campaigns are taken as a whole—as they have been here—they take on an intricacy that makes one think twice before offering the easy bromide.

It is not easy to admit to such emotions since politics has been such a good whipping-boy for the academic community. Every four years, scholars parade before the television cameras deconstructing the candidates' ads and, then, deconstructing the media's deconstructions. But opening onself up to the complexity of a political campaign

226

arrests that impulse, much like intimate knowledge of a biographee opens up a biographer to truths he or she would have otherwise repressed. Monica Crowley admits to this process of transference when recounting her first thoughts about her subject, Richard Milhouse Nixon:

> When I first was preparing to meet him for the very first time, I was prepared to encounter the public image of Richard Nixon, which really is very one-dimensional. It's sort of a dark, brooding, serious, mysterious character. And the Nixon I knew, that part of him was just a fraction of who he was. And what surprised me so much and delighted me was that Nixon was so much more than that. . . The Nixon I knew was a brilliant man. He was a political mastermind, which even his detractors will concede. He was generous. He was thoughtful, thoughtful in the sense of compassionate. He was a warm person. He was a witty person. Nixon could be very funny at times, and that never, ever came across in his public image and I think that's a shame. I tried to get some of that humanity across in the book. I hope I succeeded.[2]

Other biographers report similar experiences. Edmund Morris, a Teddy Roosevelt and Ronald Reagan biographer, says that:

> In examining the lives of other people, one examines one's own. A biographer is, in a sense, a doppelgänger, a double goer; he becomes the shadow of his character. And an identity develops between the two, which may be loving, may be hypocritical. I think both these extremes are dangerous. If you love your subject, you end up writing soppy stuff. And if you hate your subject, it becomes unreadable for obvious reasons. So I think the best relationship that a biographer can have with his subject is one of mild affection. The interest must be there. One has to spend many years with this person, you'd better make sure, up front, that it's going to be a congenial relationship.[3]

This process of identification is often accompanied by one of transformation or, at least, of complexification. Ron Chernow, author of *Titan: The Life of John D. Rockefeller*, reports that "The image I started with was of this cold-blooded and rather monstrous figure." While that impression did not change entirely for Chernow, it was quickly supplemented by another: "He was both better and worse than I thought he was, as deeply involved with his philanthropy as with his business skulduggery."[4] Robin Wright, author of a book on Iran's Khomeini, lived in Beirut as a correspondent for the *Sunday Times* of London and saw two of her best friends taken hostage during the revolution. Says Wright: "I'd first been there during the Shah's era in 1973, and I kept going back, and back, and back; and finally I came to grips with why it was happening, what it meant, and answered some of my own questions. I don't have any sympathy for the revolution, but I certainly understand now."[5] Most transformative of all are the remarks of Nell Irvin Painter who had this daydream when she began writing her biography of Sojourner Truth: "I thought if I were sitting here and Sojourner Truth came and sat down, we could have a comfortable conversation. And it would just be hunky-dory and we'd get along just fine." But as time progressed, things became more complicated: "[A]s I learned more about Sojourner Truth herself . . . more about the period, her closeness to me receded and she became less and less and less familiar. And so now I think if she were sitting here, I would just have to listen."[6]

The data I have gathered here caused me to rethink campaigns rather completely. In the course of doing so I have been reminded of Alexander Pope's comments on Homer:

> His fable, subject, scope in ev'ry page
> Religion, Country, genius of his Age
> Without all these at once before your eyes
> Cavil you may, but never criticize.[7]

Given the tremendous amount of data that has passed before my eyes in this study, I now find it hard to cavil or criticize nonchalantly. Each time I confronted a disturbing campaign trend I quickly confronted another more propitious one, and this double-going made me question matters I had thought settled. Examining campaign texts microscopically also posed questions for which I had no easy answers: Why have Party References declined over the years even though the parties themselves are still robust and purposeful? Why can politicians no longer speak in the strong, stentorian voices of the past even though the New Left and the Radical Right have energized the ideological atmosphere in the United States? Why has all political discourse—

from citizens, from the press, and from the candidates—become more technical over time and why are people now so loathe to say things plainly? And here is the most curious thing of all: With politicians increasingly personalizing their remarks, why does the electorate not love the candidates? Indeed, why do they often hate them? Because campaigns are complex in these ways, I often found myself reduced to sitting and listening. An ideal posture for campaign reflections.

Admiring Campaigns

The language of elections has changed in important ways during the last thirteen presidential elections and these changes help explain why campaigns remain so controversial. The United States is a more complex nation than it was in the 1950s, and the politicians perform that truth every four years when decreasing the Certainty of their remarks. They quibble more today than before because quibbling is safe, if aesthetically unattractive, and because the details of politics now determine so much. They also resort to legalistic and scientistic language because modern life is so bureaucratized and because the mass media now follow the candidates around so doggedly. But all has not changed in politics: theological allusions continue to infiltrate political discourse as does the language of community. One can call this hyperbole but it seems a useful hyperbole. Its presence may explain why Kenneth Burke called politics secular prayer, an arena in which leaders rarely know anything for sure but still must act. Their language, their prayers, betray the uncomfortable duality of knowledge/action they face each day.

A good deal of criticism holds that campaigns no longer work well because they tire out the candidates as well as the electorate, resulting in a sour taste in everyone's mouths come November. No doubt that is part of the story, but I also found four quite useful campaign functions. For one thing, campaigns return a sitting chief executive to the people being governed—they re-democratize the presidency. A chief executive on the stump opens himself up to the people in a most direct way by speaking a more humane, less abstract, language. Equally important, the campaign brings out the optimist in the presi-

229

dent (it does the opposite for challengers), thereby insuring a clean, clear dialectic. The campaign also places issues of community at the center of the national discussion—incumbents emphasize the people's similarities while challengers do the opposite, thereby insuring a regular, calendrical discussion of whether or not the center still holds in the United States.

This study also shows that becoming enmeshed in the language of Washington, D.C., can spell political death. Sitting presidents who speak the language of the Beltway tend to lose, as do those who pursue an overly narrow, or overly passive, agenda during their run for reelection. All of these findings suggest that an ideal political campaign invigorates the nation, causing it to consider ideas and policies not previously considered. This function is especially well served when governors run for office. Surprisingly, the governors brought an entirely different style to the campaign compared to their federal counterparts. They tended to be more grounded (realistic, practical) and optimistic than nongovernors, as if grassroots politics were both a style of governance as well as a way of being. When running for office, the governors' platforms were positioned as alternatives to "politics as usual." Rhetorically, at least, they delivered on those promises, regardless of party or region.

One of the most intriguing findings of this study is that candidates who approximate the overall stylistic norm for politicians in the United States were most likely to become president. This suggests that American politics is somewhat centripetal in nature, that its people have a knack for identifying, and rejecting, political excess. Our evidence here is linguistic, not policy based, but the principle may well apply in both arenas. While the mass media tend to reward rhetorically precocious candidates (they are far more colorful, after all), the American people themselves listen for the middle ground. When they find it, they embrace it. That seems an important political effect in a nation of colossal, often troubling, diversity.

The American people have long been attracted to technological solutions and that has been especially true during political campaigns. Echoing those beliefs, CNN's Larry King has averred that the televison call-in shows made popular during the 1992 campaign were a dramatic adjunct to the democracy. "I think we've never had a year when we knew the candidates better than this year," said King, and all because Ross Perot and company were hooked up directly to the populace through the miracle of satellites.[8] Tracy Westen has embraced another technology—computerization—when publicizing The Democracy Network, a Website that encourages candidates to dynamically interact with the electorate and with one another as the campaign unfolds.[9] Through such procedures, says Westen, the American people can create a political agora for the modern age.

But the American people already have an agora and it is working remarkably well. With presidential debates now being all but institutionalized, only the most foolish candidate would shrink from them. And my findings suggest that debates do just what they are supposed to do—they decrease grandstanding, they keep the candidates focused, they make them more introspective, and they level the playing field between incumbents and challengers and between Democrats and Republicans. No other campaign forum reliably produces such benefits. No doubt, debates can be improved. Walter Cronkite has urged the adoption of a more "Oxonian" style, with formal resolutions and a limited menu of issues;[10] Bruce Buchanan has endorsed debates with nonexperts as interlocutors;[11] other commentators have urged that debates be legislatively mandated, scheduled weekly during the general election campaign, and open to all comers, including independent and third-party candidates.[12] While these suggestions might all be tried, presidential debates are already functioning quite well indeed.

While most people enjoy political debates, they detest political advertising. They hate its nastiness, its brevity, its inanity, and its plenitude. Ads allow candidates to say terrible things about one another and to criticize the status quo without having to provide a superior option. For these and other reasons, numerous proposals have been floated to ban political advertising entirely. But even ads are not without their benefits: They let a candidate broaden the campaign discussion, putting items on the agenda that other forums prohibit. They also let the candidates make a strong case for the issues dear to them, thereby adding an emotional dimension to the campaign that may actually help some citizens become better informed about the candidates' issue positions. Ads are often pessimistic, but a majority are promotional or comparative and not blatant attacks on an opponent. In short, my studies suggest that political advertising is rhetorically complex. That seems reason enough to examine ads more carefully before consigning them to the hotter portions of Hades.

The overarching theme of this book is that a political campaign is an extended conversation among three voices—the candidates, the press, and the people. When a campaign is viewed as a conversation rather than as a set of random behaviors, it takes on a special vitality. While politicians are never entirely forthcoming, for example, they are surely more forthcoming during a campaign than they are at other times. As for the people, who can deny that in 1964 they made it clear that they did not support extremism, or in 1980 that they hated feeling weak, or in 1996 that they liked having jobs? The press also speaks during campaigns, much to the dismay of the candidates. No doubt, the media indulge their tabloid tendencies too frequently, and their political cynicism is often debilitating. But the press keeps the candidates from floating off into the ether and thereby gives the campaign a discipline it would not otherwise have.

Most complaints made about political campaigns are criterial in nature. That is, each political voice demands that its standards be applied to all campaign discourse. The press is agenda driven, for example, and so it accuses politicians of being slippery and evasive when they are really trying to broaden the political dialogue. Politicians deal each day with a divided nation and so they feel a special need to buoy up the people whenever possible. They hate it when the press calls them windbags for doing so. Typically, the people are caught in the middle. They see the politicians as egotistical and the media as irresponsible and they find it shameful when both circumnavigate moral considerations. In short, whenever a campaign is run, three different campaigns are run simultaneously.

This book reports the results of those interactions. By knowing what distinguishes each voice, one can begin to see why there is an inevitable, democratic tension in the United States and why the ultimate wisdom may be to embrace that tension, not resist it. But that is hard to do. Because the three voices are so distinct and their self-understandings so enduring, they naturally resist easy accommodation. As with any criterial argument, solutions are hard to find because the problem is described so differently by the parties involved. Consider, for example, reporter Roger Simon's report of a presidential train trip in 1996:

> Nobody had to tell Bill Clinton to use the microphone on the rear platform of his train car to talk to the people who lined the tracks as he passed by. "We made sure we equipped the caboose so any time he wanted to talk to the people, he could," [Harry] Thomason said. "We knew he couldn't resist. . . ."
>
> "How you doin', man? Nice doggie! Hi, folks," Clinton says, his voice happy and buoyant. "Thang-kyew for sayin' hello. Good to see you running out there."
>
> *Snickety-snack* he travels along the rails. The light begins to fade, the sky turning from blue to black, but the president remains on his little platform, commenting on the passing scene, even on TV antennas.
>
> "That's the biggest satellite I ever saw!" Clinton calls out into the black of night on the way to East Lansing. A pause. He sees a clump of kids at a siding.
>
> "Nice bikes!" he shouts.
>
> *Snickety-snack.*
>
> "Hi. How are you? Nice garden. I like your dog!"[13]

Simon has a deft touch here. But buried within his reportage are two things: (1) fascination with Bill Clinton's irrepressibility and (2) a patent rejection of those instincts. Simon's needling of Clinton reflects an abiding democratic unease. Beneath Simon's smarminess, an old Puritan wishes to bellow out: "You're having entirely too much fun, Mr. President. A leader should be doing the Lord's business." In his defense, Mr. Clinton would detail the characteristics of the Political Voice described here: a president must speak the language of conviviality because otherwise the polity would become aimless. The press can indulge that ambiguity but a president cannot because the people cannot. A president must also be an embodiment of the nation's past and must use that past (via Patriotic Terms) to help the nation find a future. A president also tries to erect the largest tent possible, constantly broadening an agenda the press would rather keep narrow. And so they go back and forth, with the politician proclaiming "we must also consider . . ." and the press responding: "Mr.

President, let's go back to the point you made about . . ." More/less, breadth/specificity, emergence/convergence, individuality/multiplicity. These are the rhetorical tensions of a democracy.

Pundits call politicians empty but I find them quite full indeed. Like a preacher, a politician must be people-centered but, unlike a preacher, he or she can never be a pure idealist (John Andersen reminds us of that, as do Adlai Stevenson and George McGovern). A politician can speak like a business executive on occasion but is never really given the luxury of the corporate shield. Too, a candidate's constant Self-References show that issue and image are always conjoined in politics; this is a clear political asset when it is not a clear political liability. Like social protestors, politicians must address the people's business but, unlike the protestors, politicians must know when to pull back from the abyss. Politics is therefore a triangulated discourse. It appeals only to those with a knack for social geometry.

At almost every turn, the mass media reject the political voice, and it is perhaps good that they do. Their job, after all, is to inform us, not hearten us. Their language shows how they do just that: they tell us what is happening even when what is happening ought not happen; the press increases its rhetorical urgency when times are harsh but it generally tells a detached story (despite popular suspicions to the contrary). Politicians hate the press's relentless interpretations and would prefer that they merely list the events of the day in the newspaper. Citizens claim to prefer that as well. But facts mean nothing on their own, and so the press we most hate is also the press we most need. Politics is nothing if not a quest for meaning, and any quest needs a sentinel. That principle gives reporters employment.

Over the years, the press has told an increasingly disheartening story about politics. This either means that things have indeed gotten worse or that the press can no longer see past its own rhetorical traditions. A number of media doctors are worried about these tendencies, arguing that unless the press finds a more salutary posture, the democracy will not have the sense of community it needs to make decisions. Again, one must remember that politics is a conversation and that a conversation consists of many voices. The press's is only one of them. Indeed, as we have seen here, print coverage and television coverage report somewhat different campaigns, and so there is even a conversation within the media's conversation. Only one who hates pluralism could fault such an arrangement.

A unique aspect of this study is its focus on the People's Voice, a voice that has been submerged too often to polling data and the chance interview. The large collection of letters-to-the-editor assembled here changed that. The people, I found, carve out a "third way" in politics, one that rejects both the media's negativity and the politicians's glad-handing. The result is a self-reflexive voice that puts the people's agenda on the national agenda. While the citizenry is often treated as a political integer by the press and as a relational possibility by the politician, it is a moral and emotional factor for the people themselves. As a result, one finds a special passion, and intractability, to the People's Voice. When reading the people's letters, one had the feeling that the campaign they described was unique to them. This made their letters seem somewhat lonely. While that, too, is a democratic tension, it is a tension that bears watching.

When campaigns are viewed in-the-large, then, they take on magnificent scope and that makes it hard to decry them in the easy vernacular of the casual observer. Studying campaigns so closely constantly prompts this question: "Perhaps such-and-such a statement should not have been said but, if not that statement, what?" Because answering that question is hard, to call politicians vapid or the press a curse seems not just an empty expostulation but a dangerously empty expostulation. Political campaigns have developed as they have for many reasons, and every one of them is a human reason. To examine campaign language is to be reminded how elastic language is and also how important. Politicians depend on that elasticity but so do we all: The press retracts its misstatements of fact but its botched interpretations are covered under poetic license. The citizenry grazes over history opportunistically—"Bill Clinton is no Harry Truman"— but a judicious analysis finds that Harry Truman was no Harry Truman either (looking at letters-to-the-editor from the 1948 campaign is evidence enough of that). In other words, we resort to language each day to protect us from the things we cannot control or understand. A political campaign is a similar carnival of language but it is no less human because of it.

FIXING CAMPAIGNS

The American style of campaigning has reliably produced the intended result—a new president of the United States. One of those new presidents, George Bush, declared just after having been elected that "A campaign is a disagreement, and disagreements divide. But an election is a decision, and decisions clear the way for harmony and peace."[14] My findings suggest that political campaigns function pretty much as Mr. Bush envisioned. Consider the forces that threaten a democracy: (1) hopelessness—to which the candidates' Optimism and Commonality become antidotes; (2) aimlessness—to which the media's Insistence scores respond; (3) contentedness—a condition offset by the people's Blame and Denial scores and by their unwillingness to adopt either political or media scenarios; (4) rigidity—countermanded by the constant evolution of political discourse during the last fifty years; (5) anomie—offset by the institutional regularities of party, region, incumbency, and campaign forums; (6) hegemony—undermined when the campaign shakes a president out of his Oval Office routines, when the press reminds the candidates of their several failures, when the print and broadcast media vie with one another when telling the campaign's story, and when voters, or at least the articulate among them, demand that the people's agenda be honored.

These observations are based on linguistic behavior but other forces are of course at work in a campaign. Money and demography drive elections, as do the issues of the day, so one must not overstress the rhetorical. The 1980 presidential campaign provided an interesting lesson in this regard. Ronald Reagan's confidant, Michael Deaver, for example, argues that Jimmy Carter would have been reelected—no matter how he campaigned—if the American hostages in Iran had been released on election eve.[15] Ed Meese, another Reagan apologist, argues differently. He discounts the image of President Regan as a "Great Communicator" and says that it was the issues he ran on—American strength, free enterprise, a return to basics—that made him popular. "To cut him off from his convictions," says Meese, is "to disconnect him from the source of his political power."[16] Yet another take on the 1980 campaign is psychobiographical: Patrick Anderson argues that Jimmy Carter "could moralize but he couldn't shoot the bull. He ran brilliantly against the ghosts of Nixon and Watergate, but once they faded we tired of his preaching and stopped rooting for him."[17] Ronald Reagan, on this account, was all man, the sort of person whose strength overwhelmed his detractors and even let him reach young people: "The college students liked feeling good about America as much as their elders. They liked chanting *U,S,A,* and they liked the man whose administration had given them some reason for doing it."[18]

In many ways, then, a political campaign is a Rorschach onto which people project their own visions of reality. That is also true of campaign critics. The structuralists among them, for example, feature contractual forces and so they recommend more liberal, or more draconian, voter registration laws;[19] more liberal, or more restrictive, campaign financing; a shorter campaign, a longer campaign, a better shake for third parties. Other observers emphasize ideas: saturate the airwaves with issue advertising; require all citizens to have basic political literacy; make the media offer more substantive campaign coverage; require the parties to take their platforms seriously. And then there are the New Millennialists: gut the Electoral College; invigorate local access cable stations; wire up every house in the nation so that an instant plebiscite is formed; give every candidate's spouse a Web page. Those of a quantitative bent also have suggestions: free air time carefully apportioned among the candidates; term limits of eight years so the revolving door in Washington turns faster; computer data banks bulging with legislative voting records. Finally, there are the dialecticians: one ad watch for every advertisement aired; citizen forums in every village and hamlet; a gauntlet of two dozen debates for each candidate; a prohibition on polling during the last month of a campaign.

Underlying all such suggestions, however, are the technocratic assumptions of a technocratic people: if a thing is in trouble, and since all things are things, campaigns can be fixed. From such a perspective, rhetoric also becomes a technology. Says one of this ilk: we "have got to find a way of making issues as sexy as sex."[20] Other media technocrats—people such as CNN's Larry King—feel that the real action lies in television formats: Via talk shows, says King, "the public has become part of the story and that can't change. It's like showing freedom in the Soviet Union. . . . It is vox populi. It doesn't matter that only twelve guys call in. What does matter is, is you feel, 'I could call this guy.' "[21]

For their part, academics urge more and better forms of information. Elections commonly fail, they declare, because people do not know enough when voting. And so they advocate making the electorate sit in their respective seats, straight-backed and purposeful, while watching PBS documentaries. They also advocate producing more voter guides, more substantive political debates, fewer empty campaign commercials, and so forth. For academics, proper political decisions are driven by creating the right informational bandwith—the wider the better.

Counterposed to the technocrats are a ragtag assemblage of naturalists who admit that while law, media, and money are powerful, other forces must be reckoned with as well. The moralists among them claim, for example, that the best way to fix campaigns is to get better people running for office, persons who do not lie or fornicate or abscond with county funds. Ideologues offer another take: eliminate the Beltway crowd and pick candidates who will offer real change, radical chance, and who will not compromise themselves and the nation to death. Revisionists, in contrast, urge a return to the nation's roots. They call for a new collection of Jeffersons and Roosevelts, persons who ostensibly have abandoned the public sphere for the corporation or the military and who must be coaxed to return. Different yet are the sociological determinists who argue that politics needs more people like them—more women, more southerners, more African Americans, more Jews. Nativists offer another, distasteful, option: keep the ignorant and the unclean away from the ballot box.

Although I admire the civic rectitude of some of these critics, I question their first assumption: that campaigns need to be fixed. I also question their second assumption: that campaigns can be fixed by statute. The more I have studied campaigns, the more I have come to see them as organic entities guided by their own peculiar routines. It is noteworthy, for example, that most critics who set out to fix campaigns do so by first reducing them and, via those reductions, distort them. To say that money is everything in a campaign, for example, is to say too little: having it did not make Steve Forbes a president, and not having it made Paul Wellstone a U.S. senator. Liberalizing election laws may get a few more people in the polling booth but the most basic problem is cynicism, not balloting. With half of all registered voters not voting, increasing the registration rolls will hardly fix what ails the nation.

Information is a good thing but it is not the only good thing. Few of those who voted for Bill Clinton in 1996 knew his position on the international monetary fund, but they knew what they needed to know: that the nation was at peace, that they had a job, and that their president was with them during the Oklahoma City tribulations. To argue that the election was degraded because they knew little else is to be disrespectful of a nation of hardheaded pragmatists. As for the naturalists, history records that each group has had its day in the sun: Jimmy Carter was elected to bring Virtue to the District of Columbia; only a political landslide kept Geraldine Ferraro from being a heartbeat away from the presidency; Jesse Jackson, Pat Robertson, and Colin Powell have become influential national figures; industrialist Ross Perot garnered 20 percent of the vote the first time he ran for the presidency. Money is a powerful force in politics but so too is popular sentiment. Law determines much but so too do ideas. The history of American political campaigns shows that things change. In a democracy they change with singular efficiency.

Will campaigns change in the future? Yes, but as with all organic things they will change at their own time in their own way. The political voices profiled here suggest as much. Press and politician will always be counterpoised and that is a blessing. Rapprochement between them might be pleasant for a time but it is ultimately dangerous. Their mutual rivalries, perhaps even their mutual antipathies, are crucial to democratic interchange. We need the buoyancy from the politicians to get through the day and the interpretations from the press to know what we have experienced. Voters are a third force and they need to remain a third force, dominated neither by the press's freneticism nor the politicians' pragmatism but not unresponsive to them either. Mostly, voters need to reflect as deeply about politics as the letter-writers studied here. But that, too, may never happen.

It is possible that the campaign experience can be changed on the margins. A thoughtful group of academics headed by political scientist Larry Bartels has reprised several suggestions for doing so: erect a neutral commission on presidential debates; pass legislation requiring free air time for the candidates; change reporters' assignments so they do not become bored on the campaign trail; make election day a state holiday.[22] But my suspicion is that campaigns will continue to evolve in their own organic ways and that no third party, no matter how well intentioned, will affect that development. I say that for a number of reasons:

1. *Campaigns are systemic entities.* Changing one aspect of a campaign inevitably produces changes in other elements. The feistiness of the press during traditional news conferences drove the candidates to the TV talk shows. Later, talk show chatter opened up the candidates to inquiries about their personal lives, and that proved to be an unpleasant side effect. In other words, any change in a campaign produces equal and opposite effects in other aspects of that campaign.

2. *Campaigns are proprietary entities.* Each of the three political voices feels ownership of the campaign and thus naturally resists changes imposed by others. The people have tired of the way the press interpolates their opinions and so they now resist the telephone pollster. Candidates detest being sound bitten and so they have learned to build sound bites into their own remarks. The press hates the way the candidates dodge their questions so they make the horse race the story. Each campaign element has its own voice, and each seems to like it that way.

3. *Campaigns are historical entities.* The past still hangs heavily in the modern campaign and this also makes them resistant to change. The press remembers the Teapot Dome scandal and so they continually look for its descendent. Candidates know that politics is geography as well as demography and so they still stump across the United States during elections. Both candidate and press know what happens in a great debate or at a rousing political convention and thus try to

recreate those effects. Even for a modern people, that is, campaign rituals can be powerful.

4. *Campaigns are scrutinized entities.* Political campaigns may be no worse today than before. It is even possible they are better. Why, then, the hue and cry? Because hueing and crying have their own satisfactions. With NBC, MSNBC, and CNBC (and all the other media families) each needing fresh campaign material each hour, and with the candidates themselves able to exert only so much effort per unit time, metacommentary is often the sole possibility. The result? Heightened concentration on the horse race and a distorted picture of the campaign.

5. *Campaigns are self-correcting entities.* The McGovern reforms of 1972 largely eliminated the bossism of the Democratic Party. Jimmy Carter's willingness to debate Ronald Reagan in 1980 made it hard for George Bush to duck an exchange with Michael Dukakis in 1988. According to some accounts, reaction to the Willie Horton ads during that same campaign decreased the scurrilousness of the ads in 1992. The popularity of "citizens' debates" in 1992 and 1996 assured their reappearance in later campaigns. In short, campaigns change, often for the better.

6. *Campaigns are symbolic entities.* Election laws are powerful but they are also blunt instruments. Plugging up campaign finance loop-holes stopped some abuses but "issue advertisements" were soon created to offset those effects. Motor-voter legislation is helpful but its influence can be undercut by a barrage of Leno and Letterman "why bother?" jokes. Mandating "talking head" exchanges will not make the candidates more engaging than a clever campaign ad. Rhetoric, that is, begins its work when the law has finished its.

7. *Campaigns are consequential entities.* Political elections in the United States have renewed the democracy every four years. The proof of that assertion lies in the campaigns profiled here: Could an aging Franklin Roosevelt have successfully prosecuted the Korean conflict? Could a Democrat like Harry Truman have been persuasive when warning the nation about a military-industrial complex? Would a Dwight Eisenhower have had the imagination to launch the nation into outer space? Would a John Kennedy have risked alienating the South over civil rights? Could a provincial like Lyndon Johnson have

begun a dialogue with Communist China? Was Richard Nixon evangelical enough to broker a Middle East peace accord? Would a Jimmy Carter have had the tensile strength to bankrupt the Soviet military? Would a Ronald Reagan have had the intellectual focus needed to bring the Gulf War to a speedy conclusion? Would a George Bush have had the empathy to insist on cross-sector economic growth?

Presidential elections made each of these questions moot. The nation seems no worse off because of it. Each president faced different challenges but the same campaign processes put them at the nation's service. For a number of reasons, then, I do not believe that campaigns must be changed dramatically or that they will be. At root, there are only two ways of changing things in politics: (1) by statute and (2) by persuasion. For the reasons advanced above, I distrust statutory remedies. As for persuasion, it also comes in two varieties: (1) cooperation and (2) embarrassment. The press can politely urge the candidates to be more forthcoming during their exchanges, and the politicians can ask the press to act more honorably when reporting the events of the day. But because politics is a site of contestation, embarrassment and not cooperation seems the more likely engine of change. Media coverage will get better when press personnel can no longer look themselves in the mirror after delivering the six o'clock news. Politicians will tell more of what they know only when suppressing information seems the sillier strategy. The people will learn more about the issues of the day only when their friends and neighbors do as well.

There is nothing wrong with trusting the power of embarrassment. Being thought well of still motivates most people on most days. CBS does not like being confused with the *National Inquirer* and even the *National Inquirer* likes to think itself superior to the Internet's Matt Drudge. Also, after the travails of the forty-first president of the United States, no politician in the future will want to be thought as personally careless as Bill Clinton. But the happier way of thinking about election reform is to trust the conversation itself. The three campaign voices interact constantly and they are not indifferent to one another's opinions. Political behavior has always changed when self-interest demanded it and so one can only hope that suggestions for improving campaigns continue to be made often and loudly. My data show campaigns to be complex entities, easily pilloried but not easily understood. Because they are hard to understand, people often feature their infirmities when discussing them. But it hardly seems profitable to do so, especially if they reliably produce options acceptable to a democratic people. I find no evidence over the last fifty years that U.S. political campaigns have failed to do just that.

Conclusion

This book has discussed two things to which most people feel superior: language and politics. For some, language is an odd thing to study, a thing so common as to be beyond consciousness. For others, language is dangerous, a force that causes teenagers to join religious cults and the elderly to participate in sweepstakes they cannot afford. For still others, language is irrelevant since it is human action—starting a business, transplanting a heart, hitting a home run—and not language that decides the fate of the world. Wherever one turns, language suspicion is common: when the software engineers resent how the marketing department describes the products they have built; when the stolid teacher becomes jealous of the student evaluations received by the glib teacher; when the "rhetorical professions"—law, journalism, film, advertising, politics—become the dependable butts of late-night humor. In the United States, to say that a person is good with language is to be critical even when one is trying to be complimentary.

I have studied language here because politics is often little more than language. To be sure, politics has its wars and treaties, its hurricane relief and space platforms. But words begin and end all such projects, and the historical word—that which lets us know where we are by telling us where we have been—is often our only way of satisfactorily measuring those accomplishments. So politics is both a battle over meanings as well as resources. Political campaigns have told us as much: In 1996 we learned that shutting down the government was beyond the pale even for voters otherwise attracted to Republicans. We learned that patriotic sacrifice—Bob Dole's kind of sacrifice—no longer had the political cachet it had, say, in 1952 for Dwight Eisenhower. It was not that voters did not respect Mr. Dole's sacrifice; they just did not know what it meant. When they thought of war they thought of short wars (Grenada, the Persian Gulf) or unpopular wars (Vietnam) or distant wars (Yugoslavia, Northern Ireland). They had no dictionary of meanings for Mr. Dole's war, the war that had made their very lives possible.

It is not entirely clear that the American people knew what building a bridge to the twenty-first century meant either. But Mr. Clinton's words were newer words, busier words. Everyone knew what a bridge was and in 1996 they knew that the millennium approached. So the President's metaphor made a certain sense to them, the kind of distracted, emotional sense that politics often makes. In opting for Mr. Clinton over Mr. Dole, the American people therefore performed hermeneutic work even while performing economic and sociological work. They took in the language of Campaign '96 in great gulps, savoring some of it, ignoring most of it. But that is not to say the campaign had no meaning for them. Frustrating as it must have been for Mr. Dole, the American people were able to make sense out of the thoroughly postmodern creature who was their incumbent president.

Nobody really understands the kind of sense that politics makes. The trackings and cross-trackings done here show, if nothing else, that political language is every bit as complex as politics itself. Because so few Americans pay attention to the words they hear during campaigns, it seemed useful for me to do so. Trapped in my very large data base were brave and intelligent words, often Olympian words, some expedient ones as well. For both good and ill, these texts stand as a record of the American people's self-understandings during the last fifty years, of plans they have made and rued, of memories prized and ignored. The record I have assembled here is an imperfect one but it has been earnestly constructed. Politics itself is an even greater imperfection but it too is earnest. Every four years voters go to the polls to make sense out of the lives they share together. It is a miracle that they continue to do so. This book stands in awe of that miracle.

DICTION: The Text-Analysis Program

Author: Roderick P. Hart, University of Texas at Austin

Developers: Tom Cox and Michael Stanton

Publisher: Scolari Software, Sage Publishers, Thousand Oaks, Calif. (http://www.scolari.com)

Overview: DICTION is a Windows-based program that uses a series of dictionaries to search a passage for five semantic features—Activity, Optimism, Certainty, Realism, and Commonality—as well as thirty-five subfeatures. DICTION conducts its searches via a 10,000-word corpus and the user can create additional (custom) dictionaries for particular research needs. The program writes its results to both alphabetic and numeric files. Output includes raw totals, percentages, and standardized scores and, for small input files, extrapolations to a 500-word norm. DICTION also reports normative data for each of its forty scores based on a 20,000-item sample of contemporary discourse. The program can accept either individual or multiple passages and, at the user's discretion, provide special counts of orthographic characters and high frequency words.

History: DICTION is a revised version of an earlier (mainframe) program described in R. P. Hart, "Systematic Analysis of Political Discourse: The Development of DICTION," in K. Sanders et al. (eds.), *Political Communication Yearbook: 1984* (Carbondale: Southern Illinois University Press, 1985), pp. 97–134. The newer version of the program is described in R. P. Hart, "Redeveloping DICTION: Theoretical Considerations" in M. West (ed.), *New Directions in Computer Content Analysis* (New York: Ablex, in press).

Program Features: (1) DICTION processes sixty passages (30,000 words) in one minute on a Pentium-based system; results can be viewed without leaving the program. (2) No programming knowledge is required to use the program; texts need not be pretreated by the researcher. (3) The contents of all program dictionaries can be scanned by the user. (4) Batch-processing permits thousands of passages to be run at once; both small and large input files are handled in a consistent manner. (5) DICTION compares a given text's features to a data base of 20,000 previously analyzed texts; output produces both raw and standardized scores. (6) The program "learns" each time a text is analyzed, thereby increasing its processing speed with later texts. (7) DICTION permits up to ten custom dictionaries to be created by the researcher for specific purposes; high frequency word or character counts can also be enumerated upon request; verbal and numerical output is customizable. (8) The program's numeric output can be immediately transported into standard statistical packages. (9) To help with later analysis, the user may add an Alpha-Numeric Identifier at the top of an input file. Once a search is completed, the Alpha-Numeric Identifier will be the first piece of data to appear in the numeric file. (10) The user may also use a descriptive identifier to mark a passage in the program's report file. (11) An extensive on-line help system is built into the program; in addition, a complete user's manual as well as 800-number and e-mail support are available.

Program Restrictions: All passages must be converted into text-only format to be processed. Also, at the discretion of the user, DICTION will analyze (a) only the first 500 words of a given passage or (b) any passage up to 5,000 words in length. In the latter case, DICTION will automatically break up the passage into 500-word segments. Passages shorter than 500 words can also be processed and the user can elect to have either raw or extrapolated scores reported.

Dictionaries: DICTION'S word lists lie at the heart of the program. By design, no individual word is duplicated in the thirty-one dictionaries, thereby permitting a comprehensive examination of a given passage. Because its dictionaries are general ones, the program is not discipline- or subject-matter dependent. The purposes and components of the dictionaries and related (calculated) variables are described below:

THE CERTAINTY SCORE

Definition: Language indicating resoluteness, inflexibility, completeness, and a tendency to speak ex cathedra.

Formula: [Tenacity + Leveling + Collectives + Insistence.] − [Numerical Terms + Ambivalence + Self-Reference + Variety]

TENACITY: All uses of the verb "to be" (*is, am, will, shall*), three definitive verb forms (*has, must, do*) and their variants, as well as all associated contractions (*he'll, they've, ain't*). These verbs connote confidence and totality.

LEVELING: Words used to ignore individual differences and to build a sense of completeness and assurance. Included are totalizing terms (*everybody, anyone, each, fully*), adverbs of permanence (*always, completely, inevitably, consistently*), and resolute adjectives (*unconditional, consummate, absolute, open-and-shut*).

COLLECTIVES: Singular nouns connoting plurality that function to decrease specificity. These words reflect a dependence on categorical modes of thought. Included are social groupings (*crowd, choir, team, humanity*), task groups (*army, congress, legislature, staff*) and geographical entities (*county, world, kingdom, republic*).

INSISTENCE: This is a measure of code-restriction and semantic "contentedness." The assumption is that repetition of key terms indicates a preference for a limited, ordered world. In calculating the measure, all words occurring three or more times that function as nouns or noun-derived adjectives are identified (either cybernetically or with the user's assistance) and the following calculation performed: [Number of Eligible Words m Sum of their Occurrences] ÷ 10. (For small input files, high frequency terms used two or more times are used in the calculation).

NUMERICAL TERMS: Any sum, date, or product specifying the facts in a given case. This dictionary treats each isolated integer as a single "word" and each separate group of integers as a single word. In addition, the dictionary contains common numbers in lexical format (*one, tenfold, hundred, zero*) as well as terms indicating numerical operations (*subtract, divide, multiply, percentage*) and quantitative topics (*digitize, tally, mathematics*). The presumption is that Numerical Terms hyperspecify a claim, thus detracting from its universality.

AMBIVALENCE: Words expressing hesitation or uncertainty, implying a speaker's inability or unwillingness to commit to the verbalization being made. Included are hedges (*allegedly, perhaps, might*), statements of inexactness (*almost, approximate, vague, somewhere*), and confusion (*baffled, puzzling, hesitate*). Also included are words of restrained possibility (*could, would, he'd*) and mystery (*dilemma, guess, suppose, seems*).

246

SELF-REFERENCE: All first-person references, including *I, I'd, I'll, I'm, I've, n my, myself.* Self-references are treated as acts of "indexing" whereby the locus (appears to reside in the speaker and not in the world at large (thereby implicitly a edging the speaker's limited vision).

VARIETY: This measure conforms to Wendell Johnson's Type-Token Ratio w vides the number of different words in a passage by the passage's total words. A hi, indicates a speaker's avoidance of overstatement and a preference for precise, m statements. See W. Johnson, *People in Quandaries: The Semantics of Personal Adj* (New York: Harper, 1946).

THE OPTIMISM SCORE

Definition: Language endorsing some person, group, concept, or event, or high their positive entailments.

Formula: [Praise + Satisfaction + Inspiration] − [Blame + Hardship + Denial]

PRAISE: Affirmations of some person, group, or abstract entity. Included are isolating important social qualities (*dear, delightful, witty*), physical qualities (*handsome, beautiful*), intellectual qualities (*shrewd, bright, vigilant, reasonable*), er neurial qualities (*successful, conscientious, renowned*), and moral qualities (*faithfu noble*). All terms in this dictionary are adjectives.

SATISFACTION: Terms associated with positive affective states (*cheerful, pas happiness*), with moments of undiminished joy (*thanks, smile, welcome*), and pleas diversion (*excited, fun, lucky*), or with moments of triumph (*celebrating, pride, auspi* Also included are words of nurturance: *healing, encourage, secure, relieved.*

INSPIRATION: Abstract virtues deserving of universal respect. Most of the te this dictionary are nouns isolating desirable moral qualities (*faith, honesty, self-sa virtue*) as well as attractive personal qualities (*courage, dedication, wisdom, mercy*). and political ideals are also included: *patriotism, success, education, justice.*

BLAME: Terms designating social inappropriateness (*mean, naive, sloppy, stupid*) as downright evil (*fascist, bloodthirsty, repugnant, malicious*) compose this diction: addition, adjectives describing unfortunate circumstances (*bankrupt, rash, morbid, e rassing*) or unplanned vicissitudes (*weary, nervous, painful, detrimental*) are included dictionary also contains outright denigrations: *cruel, illegitimate, offensive, miserly.*

HARDSHIP: This dictionary contains natural disasters (*earthquake, starvation, to\ pollution*), hostile actions (*killers, bankruptcy, enemies, vices*), and censurable huma havior (*infidelity, despots, betrayal*). It also includes unsavory political outcomes (*inji slavery, exploitation, rebellion*) as well as normal human fears (*grief, unemployment, (apprehension*) and incapacities (*error, cop-outs, weakness*).

DENIAL: A dictionary consisting of standard negative contractions (*aren't, shou don't*), negative function words (*nor, not, nay*), and terms designating null sets (*not nobody, none*).

THE ACTIVITY SCORE

Definition: Language featuring movement, change, the implementation of ideas and avoidance of inertia.

Formula: [Aggression + Accomplishment + Communication + Motion] − [Cogn Terms + Passivity + Embellishment]

AGGRESSION: A dictionary embracing human competition and forceful action. Its terms connote physical energy (*blast, crash, explode, collide*), social domination (*conquest, attacking, dictatorships, violation*), and goal-directedness (*crusade, commanded, challenging, overcome*). In addition, words associated with personal triumph (*mastered, rambunctious, pushy*), excess human energy (*prod, poke, pound, shove*), disassembly (*dismantle, demolish, overturn, veto*), and resistance (*prevent, reduce, defend, curbed*) are included.

ACCOMPLISHMENT: Words expressing task-completion (*establish, finish, influence, proceed*) and organized human behavior (*motivated, influence, leader, manage*). Includes capitalistic terms (*buy, produce, employees, sell*), modes of expansion (*grow, increase, generate, construction*) and general functionality (*handling, strengthen, succeed, outputs*). Also included is programmatic language: *agenda, enacted, working, leadership*.

COMMUNICATION: Terms referring to social interaction, both face-to-face (*listen, interview, read, speak*) and mediated (*film, videotape, telephone, e-mail*). The dictionary includes both modes of intercourse (*translate, quote, scripts, broadcast*) and moods of intercourse (*chat, declare, flatter, demand*). Other terms refer to social actors (*reporter, spokesperson, advocates, preacher*) and a variety of social purposes (*hint, rebuke, respond, persuade*).

MOTION: Terms connoting human movement (*bustle, job, lurch, leap*), physical processes (*circulate, momentum, revolve, twist*), journeys (*barnstorm, jaunt, wandering, travels*), speed (*lickety-split, nimble, zip, whistle-stop*), and modes of transit (*ride, fly, glide, swim*).

COGNITIVE TERMS: Words referring to cerebral processes, both functional and imaginative. Included are modes of discovery (*learn, deliberate, consider, compare*) and domains of study (*biology, psychology, logic, economics*). The dictionary includes mental challenges (*question, forget, reexamine, paradoxes*), institutional learning practices (*graduation, teaching, classrooms*), as well as three forms of intellection: intuitional (*invent, perceive, speculate, interpret*), rationalistic (*estimate, examine, reasonable, strategies*), and calculative (*diagnose, analyze, software, fact-finding*).

PASSIVITY: Words ranging from neutrality to inactivity. Includes terms of compliance (*allow, tame, appeasement*), docility (*submit, contented, sluggish*), and cessation (*arrested, capitulate, refrain, yielding*). Also contains tokens of inertness (*backward, immobile, silence, inhibit*) and disinterest (*unconcerned, nonchalant, stoic*), as well as tranquillity (*quietly, sleepy, vacation*).

EMBELLISHMENT: A selective ratio of adjectives to verbs based on David Boder's conception that heavy modification "slows down" a verbal passage by deemphasizing human and material action. Embellishment is calculated according to the following formula: [Praise + Blame +1] ÷ [Present Concern + Past Concern +1]. See D. Boder, "The Adjective/Verb Quotient: A Contribution to the Psychology of Language," *Psychology Record* 3 (1940): pp. 310-43.

THE REALISM SCORE

Definition: Language describing tangible, immediate, recognizable matters that affect people's everyday lives.
Formula: [Familiarity + Spatial Awareness + Temporal Awareness + Present Concern + Human Interest + Concreteness] − [Past Concern + Complexity]

FAMILIARITY: Consists of a selected number of C. K. Ogden's "operation" words, which he calculates to be the most common words in the English language. Included are common prepositions (*across, over, through*), demonstrative pronouns (*this, that*) and interrogative pronouns (*who, what*), and a variety of particles, conjunctions, and connectives (*a, for, so*). See C. K. Ogden, *Basic English Dictionary* (London: Evans Brothers, 1960).

SPATIAL AWARENESS: Terms referring to geographical entities, physical distances, and modes of measurement. Included are general geographical terms (*abroad, elbow-room, locale, outdoors*) as well as specific ones (*Ceylon, Kuwait, Poland*). Also included are politically defined locations (*county, fatherland, municipality, ward*), points on the compass (*east, southwest*) and the globe (*latitude, coastal, border, snowbelt*), as well as terms of scale (*kilometer, map, spacious*), quality (*vacant, out-of-the-way, disoriented*) and change (*pilgrimage, migrated, frontier*).

TEMPORAL AWARENESS: Terms that fix a person, idea, or event within a specific time interval, thereby signaling a concern for concrete and practical matters. The dictionary designates literal time (*century, instant, midmorning*) as well as metaphorical designations (*lingering, seniority, nowadays*). Also included are calendrical terms (*autumn, year-round, weekend*), elliptical terms (*spontaneously, postpone, transitional*), and judgmental terms (*premature, obsolete, punctual*).

PRESENT CONCERN: A selective list of present-tense verbs extrapolated from C. K. Ogden's list of "general" and "picturable" terms, all of which occur with great frequency in standard American English. The dictionary is not topic-specific but points instead to general physical activity (*cough, taste, sing, take*), social operations (*canvass, touch, govern, meet*), and task performance (*make, cook, print, paint*). See C. K. Ogden, *Basic English Dictionary* (London: Evans Brothers, 1960).

HUMAN INTEREST: An adaptation of Rudolf Flesch's notion that concentrating on people and their activities gives discourse a lifelike quality. Included are standard personal pronouns (*he, his, ourselves, them*), family members and relations (*cousin, wife, grandchild, uncle*), and generic terms (*friend, baby, human, persons*). See R. Flesch, *The Art of Clear Thinking* (New York: Harper, 1951).

CONCRETENESS: A large dictionary possessing no thematic unity other than tangibility and materiality. Included are sociological units (*peasants, African-Americans, Catholics*), occupational groups (*carpenter, manufacturer, policewoman*), and political alignments (*Communists, congressman, Europeans*). Also incorporated are physical structures (*courthouse, temple, store*), forms of diversion (*television, football, cd-rom*), terms of accountancy (*mortgage, wages, finances*), and modes of transportation (*airplane, ship, bicycle*). In addition, the dictionary includes body parts (*stomach, eyes, lips*), articles of clothing (*slacks, pants, shirt*), household animals (*cat, insects, horse*), foodstuffs (*wine, grain, sugar*), and general elements of nature (*oil, silk, sand*).

PAST CONCERN: The past-tense forms of the verbs are contained in the Present Concern dictionary.

COMPLEXITY: A simple measure of the average number of characters per word in a given input file. Borrows Rudolph Flesch's notion that convoluted phrasings make a text's ideas abstract and its implications unclear. See R. Flesch, *The Art of Clear Thinking* (New York: Harper, 1951).

THE COMMONALITY SCORE

Definition: Language highlighting the agreed-upon values of a group and rejecting idiosyncratic modes of engagement.

Formula: [Centrality + Cooperation + Rapport] − [Diversity + Exclusion + Liberation]

CENTRALITY: Terms denoting institutional regularities and/or substantive agreement on core values. Included are indigenous terms (*native, basic, innate*) and designations of legitimacy (*orthodox, decorum, constitutional, ratified*), systematicity (*paradigm, bureaucratic, ritualistic*), and typicality (*standardized, matter-of-fact, regularity*). Also included are terms of congruence (*conformity, mandate, unanimous*), predictability (*expected, continuity, reliable*), and universality (*womankind, perennial, landmarks*).

COOPERATION: Terms designating behavioral interactions among people that often result in a group product. Included are designations of formal work relations (*unions, schoolmates, caucus*) and informal associations (*chum, partner, cronies*) to more intimate interactions (*sisterhood, friendship, comrade*). Also included are neutral interactions (*consolidate, mediate, alignment*), job-related tasks (*network, detente, exchange*), personal involvement (*teamwork, sharing, contribute*), and self-denial (*public-spirited, care-taking, self-sacrifice*).

RAPPORT: This dictionary describes attitudinal similarities among groups of people. Included are terms of affinity (*congenial, camaraderie, companion*), assent (*approve, vouched, warrants*), deference (*tolerant, willing, permission*), and identity (*equivalent, resemble, consensus*).

DIVERSITY: Words describing individuals or groups of individuals differing from the norm. Such distinctiveness may be comparatively neutral (*inconsistent, contrasting, nonconformist*) but it can also be positive (*exceptional, unique, individualistic*) and negative (*illegitimate, rabble-rouser, extremist*). Functionally, heterogeneity may be an asset (*far-flung, dispersed, diffuse*) or a liability (*factionalism, deviancy, quirky*) as can its characterizations: *rare* vs. *queer*, *variety* vs. *jumble*, *distinctive* vs. *disobedient*.

EXCLUSION: A dictionary describing the sources and effects of social isolation. Such seclusion can be phrased passively (*displaced, sequestered*) as well as positively (*self-contained, self-sufficient*) and negatively (*outlaws, repudiated*). Moreover, it can result from voluntary forces (*secede, privacy*) and involuntary forces (*ostracize, forsake, discriminate*) and from both personality factors (*small-mindedness, loneliness*) and political factors (*right-wingers, nihilism*). Exclusion is often a dialectical concept: *hermit* vs. *derelict*, *refugee* vs. *pariah*, *discard* vs. *spurn*).

LIBERATION: Terms describing the maximizing of individual choice (*autonomous, open-minded, options*) and the rejection of social conventions (*unencumbered, radical, released*). Liberation is motivated by both personality factors (*eccentric, impetuous, flighty*) and political forces (*suffrage, liberty, freedom, emancipation*) and may produce dramatic outcomes (*exodus, riotous, deliverance*) or subdued effects (*loosen, disentangle, outpouring*). Liberatory terms also admit to rival characterizations: *exemption* vs. *loophole*, *elope* vs. *abscond*, *uninhibited* vs. *outlandish*.

CUSTOM DICTIONARIES

A user may construct up to ten custom dictionaries by preparing word lists of up to 200 words in length, which DICTION will then use in its search routines. Custom dictionaries used in *Campaign Voices* include the following:

PATRIOTIC TERMS: Standard tokens of Americanism, including Constitutional language (*inalienable, amendments, emancipation*), celebratory terms (*flag-waving, homeland, Fourth-of-July, red-blooded*), words related to fundamental rights (*justice, liberty, equality*), and historic language (*pilgrims, old-glory, for-the-people, checks-and-balances*).

PARTY REFERENCES: A simple listing of all variations on "Democrat" and "Republican."

VOTER REFERENCES: Words referring to the citizenry-writ-large, including sociological designations (*crowd, dwellers, classes, residents*), political designations (*body-politic, constituencies, electorate, majority*), and generic designations (*citizenry, individuals, masses, population*).

LEADER REFERENCES: A reasonably comprehensive list of persons who have occupied the political spotlight (and whose names are nongeneric). Included are all presidents and vice presidents (*Adams, Lincoln, Roosevelt*), members of the Supreme Court since 1948 (*Brandeis, Burger, Douglas*), prominent members of the U.S. Senate since 1948 (*Lugar, Humphrey, Tsongas*), leaders of the House of Representatives since 1948 (*Rayburn, Boggs, Albert*), and all major-party and third-party presidential candidates since 1948 (*Dewey, Wallace, Perot*).

RELIGIOUS TERMS: Broad-based, Judeo-Christian terminology. Includes designative language (*churches, doctrine, parishioner, sermons*) as well as value-laden terms (*conscience, blessing, god-fearing, spiritual*). Technical terms are included (*resurrection, born-again, epiphany, messiah*), as are religious personalities (*saints, pontiff, pastor, Jews*) and theological constructs (*crucifixion, heavenly, Sabbath*).

IRRELIGIOUS TERMS: Language referring to the forces of evil and the consequences of sin. Transgressions against God are included (*blasphemy, godless, damned, anti-Christ*) as are affronts to the institutional church (*heathen, heretic, anti-Semitic, unorthodox*). Also included are historic tokens of evil (*Sodom, Satan-worshiper, Lucifer, idolatry*) and contemporary terms (*cult, atheists, holier-than-thou, witchcraft*).

Statistical Notes

This is an ANOVA study and, as such, it represents the first cut at the data gathered. Because little theoretical work has been previously attempted on campaign language, no reasonable hypotheses were available to guide a more extensive, multivariate, or regression-based study. Thus, main effects are primarily reported here, with interaction effects being noted when relevant. Given the size of the data base and the number of language variables DICTION contains, care was taken to guard against Type 1 error by featuring the effects with the greatest statistical power and by running Bonferroni estimates continuous. In addition, when the N of cases was especially large for a given comparison, the effects were confirmed by randomly sampling a subset of the relevant cases from the database and then re-running the analysis. Mostly, though, the results reported in this volume (1) conform to some overarching statistical pattern and (2) appear theoretically plausible.

When examining the results below, the reader will be reminded that several variables have been formed via standardization procedures (notably Activity, Certainty, Realism, Optimism, and Commonality) and that others (e.g., Detachment, Space-Time Ratio, Colloquial Language, Democratic Style, Republican Style, etc.) have been created by combining DICTION's categories in novel ways (see chapter notes for details).

CHAPTER THREE

P. 48: *Religious References*: Means = 1.133 (1948–60); 1.050 (1964–76); 0.969 (1980–96); $F (2,18213) = 3.924$, $p < .019$. P. 49: *Patriotism*: Means = 1.969 (1948–60); 2.053 (1964–76); 1.837 (1980–96); $F (2,18213) = 6.898$, $p < .001$. *Inspiration*: Means = 3.883 (1948–60); 3.656 (1964–76); 3.682 (1980–96); $F (2,18213) = 4.862$, $p < .007$. *Human Interest*: Means = 27.177 (1948–60); 26.527 (1964–76); 27.381 (1980–96); $F (2,18213) = 6.322$, $p < .001$. *Cooperation*: Means = 3.629 (1948–60); 3.628 (1964–76); 3.539 (1980–96); $F (2,18213) = 1.362$, $p < .256$. P. 53: *Spatial Terms*: Means = 11.272 (1948–60); 10.847 (1964–76); 9.586 (1980–96); $F (2,18213) = 107.658$, $p < .000$. P. 55: *Certainty* (main effect for era: voters, politicians, press): Means = 49.389, 50.108, 49.880 (1948–60); 49.607, 49.661, 49.394 (1964–76); 49.231, 48.799, 49.249 (1980–96); $F (2,18213) = 97.501$, $p < .000$; (2-way interaction): $F = 25.419$, $p < .000$. P. 58: *Party References*: Means = 2.422 (1948–60); 1.707 (1964–76); 1.683 (1980–96); $F (2,18213) = 86.222$, $p < .000$. P. 61: *Self-References* (politicians only): Means = 10.715 (1948–60); 11.632 (1964–76); 13.298 (1980–96); $F (2,4076) = 26.812$, $p < .000$ P. 62: *Leader References* (media only): Means = 9.541 (1948–60); 13.635 (1964–76); 14.302 (1980–96); $F (2,8525) = 294.528$, $p < .000$. P. 64: *Satisfaction* (politicians only): Means = 2.956 (1948–60); 3.153 (1964–76); 4.066 (1980–96); $F (2, 4076) = 36.488$, $p < .000$. *Inspiration* (politicians only): Means = 6.503 (1948–60); 6.052 (1964–76); 5.168 (1980–96); $F (2, 4076) = 31.611$, $p < .000$. P. 65: *Voter References* (media only): Means = 2.968 (1948–60); 4.038 (1964–76); 3.972 (1980–96); $F (2,8525) = 70.348$, $p < .000$. P. 66: *Familiarity* (main effect for era:

voters, politicians, press): Means = 132.039, 134.816. 131.613 (1948–60); 130.316, 130.983, 127.719 (1964–76); 123.752, 123.715, 126.044 (1980–96); F (2,18207) = 377.708, p < .000; (2-way interaction): F = 27.942, p < .000. P. 67: *Numerical Terms* (politicians only): Means = 7.370 (1948–60); 8.780 (1964–76); 9.497 (1980–96); F (2, 4076) = 84.294, p < 000. P. 67: *Cognition* (media only): Means = 6.265 (1948–60); 6.288 (1964–76); 7.375 (1980–96); F (2,8525) = 69.546, p < .000. P. 70: *Variety* (media and politicians only): Means = .529 (1948–60); .534 (1964–76); .551 (1980–96); F (2,12604) = 107.633, p < .000. P. 70: *Present Concern* (media and politicians only): Means = 9.102 (1948–60); 9.039 (1964–76); 11.070 (1980–96); F (2,12604) = 177.197, p < .000. P. 70: *Temporal Terms* (media and politicians only): Means = 15.335 (1948–60); 15.452 (1964–76); 17.238 (1980–96); F (2,12604) = 100.483, p < .000. P. 71: *Motion* (politicians only): Means = 3.008 (1948–60); 2.720 (1964–76); 3.704 (1980–96); F (2,4076) = 37.012, p < .000.

CHAPTER FOUR

P. 78: *Self-References*: Means = 8.373 (governance); 12.253 (campaigning); F (1, 1254) = 75.487, p < .000. *Present Concern*: Means = 11.862 (governance); 14.741 (campaigning); F (1, 1254) = 74.688, p < .000. *Motion*: Means = 2.353 (governance); 3.466 (campaigning); F (1, 1254) = 55.581, p < .000. *Activity*: Means = 49.980 (governance); 50.482 (campaigning); F (1, 1254) = 10.655, p < .001. *Realism*: Means = 51.203 (governance); 52.684 (campaigning); F (1, 1254) = 94.958, p < .000. P. 79: *Complexity*: Means = 4.578 (governance); 4.374 (campaigning); F (1, 1254) = 181.527 , p < .000. P. 80: *Optimism*: Means = 50.692 (governance); 51.502 (campaigning); F (1, 1254) = 20.102, p < .000. *Human Interest*: Means = 31.739 (governance); 40.177 (campaigning); F (1, 1254) = 137.693, p < .000. P. 81: *Certainty*: Means = 50.330 (governance); 49.569 (campaigning); F (1, 1254) = 35.746, p < .000. *Centrality*: Means = 4.062 (governance); 2.446 (campaigning); F (1, 1254) = 128.723, p < .000. P. 83: *Commonality*: Means = 49.860 (incumbent); 49.313 (challenger); F (1, 3230) = 13.779, p < .000. *Optimism*: Means = 51.071 (incumbent); 50.004 (challenger); F (1, 3230) = 74.683, p < .000. *Patriotic Terms*: Means = 2.641 (incumbent); 3.327 (challenger); F (1, 3230) = 25.131, p < .000. *Realism*: Means = 51.998 (incumbent); 51.587 (challenger); F (1, 3230) = 13.480, p < .000. P. 87: *Activity*: Means = 50.469 (incumbent-winner); 49.835 (incumbent-loser); F (3, 3535) = 11.593, p < .001 [2-way interaction]. *Insistence*: Means = 43.365 (incumbent-winner); 50.191 (incumbent-loser); F (3, 3535) = 32.932, p < .000 [2-way interaction]. *Leader References*: Means = 2.389 (incumbent-winner); 3.745 (incumbent-loser); F (3, 3535) = 24.848, p < .000 [2-way interaction]. P. 89: *Insistence*: Means = 50.122 (challenger-winner); 42.155 (challenger-loser); F (3, 3535) = 32.932, p < .000 [2-way interaction]. P. 89: *Familiarity*: Means = 129.182 (challenger-winner); 124.791 (challenger-loser); F (3, 3535) = 37.347, p < .000 [2-way interaction]. *Optimism*: Means = 50.340 (challenger-winner); 49.811 (challenger-loser); F (3, 3535) = 3.434, p < .064 [2-way interaction]. *Collectives*: Means = 11.676 (challenger-winner); 9.501 (challenger-loser); F (3, 3535) = 44.490, p < .000 [2-way interaction]. P. 89: *Optimism*: Means = 50.683 (Carter-1976); 50.212 (Reagan-1980); 49.707 (Clinton-1992); F (2, 578) = 3.869, p < .021. P. 90: *Optimism*: Means = 50.068 (0–9% spread); 50.684 (10–19% spread); 51.219 (20–36% spread) F (5, 2826) = 27.825, p < .000 [2-way interaction]. *Human Interest*: Means = 30.769 (0–9% spread); 37.293 (10–19% spread); 41.447 (20–36% spread) F (5, 2826) = 19.575, p < .000 [2-way interaction].

Familiarity: Means = 132.538 (0–9% spread); 126.952 (10–19% spread); 129.759 (20–36% spread) F (5, 2826) = 15.451, p < .000 [2-way interaction]. *Realism*: Means = 51.022 (0–9% spread); 51.790 (10–19% spread); 52.946 (20–36% spread) F (5, 2826) = 3.129, p < .000 [2-way interaction]. P. 91: *Realism*: Means = 52.377 (governors); 51.985 (nongovernors); F (1, 2355) = 14.638, p < .000. *Optimism*: Means = 51.072 (governors); 50.317 (nongovernors); F (1, 2355) = 34.852, p < .000. *Variety*: Means = .485 (governors); .473 (nongovernors); F (1, 2355) = 38.239, p < .000. *Commonality*: Means = 50.000 (governors); 49.479 (nongovernors); F (1, 2355) = 35.376, p < .000. *Voter References*: Means = 6.164 (governors); 5.555 (nongovernors); F (1, 2355) = 15.910, p < .000. *Collectives*: Means = 10.951 (governors); 9.974 (nongovernors); F (1, 2355) = 27.085, p < .000. P. 94: *Realism*: Means = 51.677 (first election); 52.996 (second election); F (1, 934) = 61.395, p < .000. *Commonality*: Means = 49.760 (first election); 50.213 (second election); F (1, 934) = 10.417, p < .001. *Optimism*: Means = 50.576 (first election); 51.510 (second election); F (1, 934) = 19.781, p < .000. *Leader References*: Means = 2.387 (first election); 1.101 (second election); F (1, 934) = 66.704, p < .000. *Party References*: Means = 1.281 (first election); .439 (second election); F (1, 934) = 48.222 , p < .000. P. 100: *Leader References*: Means = .859 (Clinton); .520 (Perot); 3.310 (Dole); F (2, 686) = 145.778, p < .000. *Party References*: Means = .181 (Clinton); .506 (Perot); 1.034 (Dole); F (2, 686) = 36.921, p < .000.

CHAPTER FIVE

P. 106: *Insistence*: Means = 34.383 (acceptances); 28.032 (inaugurals); 42.808 (stump spch.); F (2, 2413) = 12.461, p < .000. *Concreteness*: Means = 22.415 (acceptances); 16.406 (inaugurals); 22.528 (stump spch.); F (2, 2413) = 14.574, p < .000. *Numerical Terms*: Means = 6.558 (acceptances); 3.327 (inaugurals); 10.019 (stump spch.); F (2, 2413) = 35.127, p < .000. *Tenacity*: Means = 32.061 (acceptances); 28.613 (inaugurals); 35.562 (stump spch.); F (2, 2413) = 33.663, p < .000. P. 108: *Patriotic Terms*: Means = 5.446 (acceptances); 6.245 (inaugurals); 3.254 (stump spch.); F (2, 2413) = 45.793, p < .000. *Religious References*: Means = 2.001 (acceptances); 3.895 (inaugurals); 1.226 (stump spch.); F (2, 2413) = 43.502 p <.000. *Liberation*: Means = 2.971 (acceptances); 4.687 (inaugurals); 2.065 (stump spch.); F (2, 2413) = 39.545, p < .000. *Inspiration*: Means = 8.056 (acceptances); 10.928 (inaugurals); 5.409 (stump spch.); F (2, 2413) = 88.661, p < .000. P. 108: *Ambivalence*: Means = 10.620 (acceptances); 9.349 (inaugurals); 13.859 (stump spch.); F (2, 2413) = 40.442, p < .000. P. 110: *Embellishment*: Means = .714 (acceptances); .832 (inaugurals); .585 (stump spch.); F (2, 2413) = 12.430, p < .000. P. 110: *Text Length* (*in segments*): Means = 3.78 (1948–60); 4.04 (1964–76); 5.19 (1980–96); F (2, 190) = 5.604, p < .004. P. 111: *Hardship*: Means = 5.630 (acceptances); 6.515 (inaugurals); 4.683 (stump spch.); F (2, 2413) = 10.188, p < .000. *Cooperation*: Means = 3.971 (acceptances); 4.881 (inaugurals); 3.371 (stump spch.); F (2, 2413) = 10.697, p < .000. *Rapport*: Means = 2.511 (acceptances); 3.118 (inaugurals); 2.113 (stump spch.); F (2, 2413) = 9.239, p < .000. P. 112: *Activity*: Means = 49.290 (1948–60); 49.574 (1964–76); 50.651 (1980–96); F (2, 190) = 7.162, p < .001. P. 113: *Party References*: Means = 1.875 (1948–60); 1.231 (1964–76); .771 (1980–96); F (2, 190) = 5.266, p < .005. *Certainty*: Means = 50.183 (1948–60); 51.555 (1964–76); 48.693 (1980–96); F (2, 190) = 19.191, p < .000. P. 114: *Concreteness*: Means = 18.404 (1948–60); 22.505 (1964–1976); 24.348 (1980–96); F (2, 190) = 10.318, p < .000. *Numerical Terms*: Means = 5.879 (1948–60);

255

5.282 (1964–76); 7.635 (1980–96); F (2, 190) = 3.999, p < .019. *Inspiration*: Means = 9.847 (1948–60); 8.673 (1964–76); 6.812 (1980–96); F (2, 190) = 8.1109, p < .000. *Familiarity*: Means = 137.061 (1948–60); 134.507 (1964–76); 126.530 (1980–96); F (2, 190) = 13.619, p < .000. **P. 118**: *Certainty*: Means = 48.674 (debates); 48.588 (ads); 49.589 (speeches); F (2, 3559) = 67.201, p < .000. *Ambivalence*: Means = 19.126 (debates); 14.181 (ads); 13.594 (speeches); F (2, 3559) = 138.962, p < .000. **P. 120**: *Optimism*: Means = 49.409 (debates); 50.599 (ads); 50.617 (speeches); F (2, 3559) = 33.423, p < .000. *Realism*: Means = 50.299 (debates); 51.465 (ads); 52.125 (speeches); F (2, 3559) = 97.111, p < .000. *Embellishment*: Means = .502 (debates); 1.320 (ads); .596 (speeches); F (2, 3559) = 49.964, p < .000. *Patriotic Terms*: Means = 2.060 (debates); 3.620 (ads); 3.433 (speeches); F (2, 3559) = 34.121, p < .000. *Voter References*: Means = 4.701 (debates); 4.660 (ads); 5.797 (speeches); F (2, 3559) = 29.309, p < .000. *Religious References*: Means = .584 (debates); .732 (ads); 1.289 (speeches); F (2, 3559) = 27.561, p < .000. **P. 122-3**: *Insistence*: Means = 64.733 (debates); 36.707 (ads); 42.118 (speeches); F (2, 3559) = 120.119, p < .000. **P. 123**: *Self-References*: Means = 16.623 (debates); 11.048 (ads); 12.222 (speeches); F (2, 3559) = 65.870, p < .000. **P. 124**: *Human Interest*: Means = 28.610 (debates); 34.149 (ads); 38.380 (speeches); F (2, 3559) = 151.535, p < .000. **P. 125**: The seven significant variables included Commonality, Inspiration, Hardship, Leader References, Voter References, Self-References, and Tenacity. **P. 127**: *Total words*: Means = 209.813 (1960); 158.753 (1976); 141.957 (1980); 127.176 (1984); 94.4483 (1988); 107.569 (1992); 86.435 (1996); F (6, 546) = 12.203, p < .000. **P. 128-9**: *Embellishment*: Means = .502 (debates); 1.320 (ads); .596 (speeches); F (2, 3559) = 49.964, p < .000. *Patriotic Terms*: Means = 2.060 (debates); 3.620 (ads); 3.433 (speeches); F (2, 3559) = 34.121, p < .000. *Inspiration*: Means = 4.734 (debates); 6.039 (ads); 5.626 (speeches); F (2, 3559) = 13.308, p < .000. *Praise*: Means = 5.679 (debates); 7.448 (ads); 7.080 (speeches); F (2, 3559) = 30.251, p < .000. **P. 130**: *Certainty*: Means = 48.674 (debates); 48.588 (ads); 49.589 (speeches); F (2, 3559) = 67.201, p < .000. *Activity*: Means = 50.922 (debates); 48.768 (ads); 50.510 (speeches); F (2, 3559) = 46.513, p < .000. *Insistence*: Means = 64.733 (debates); 36.707 (ads); 42.118 (speeches); F (2, 3559) = 120.119, p < .000. **P. 132**: *Complexity*: Means = 4.400 (debates); 4.505 (ads); 4.394 (speeches); F (2, 3559) = 40.759, p < .000. *Familiarity*: Means = 128.909 (debates); 119.446 (ads); 128.998 (speeches); F (2, 3559) = 85.934, p < .000. *Concreteness*: Means = 22.257 (debates); 29.447 (ads); 22.519 (speeches); F (2, 3559) = 107.654, p < .000. *Numerical Terms*: Means = 10.908 (debates); 12.951 (ads); 9.736 (speeches); F (2, 3559) = 24.429, p < .000. **P. 133**: *Optimism*: Means = 46.433 (ads); 51.364 (speeches); F (1, 393) = 45.937, p < .000. *Commonality*: Means = 49.120 (ads); 50.392 (speeches); F (1, 393) = 7.354, p < .000. *Realism*: Means = 48.781 (ads); 53.482 (speeches); F (1, 393) = 95.374, p < .000. *Human Interest*: Means = 28.517 (ads); 44.650 (speeches); F (1, 393) = 55.342, p < .000. *Leader References*: Means = 26.337 (ads); .859 (speeches); F (1, 393) = 809.717, p < .000. *Party References*: Means = 1.300 (ads); .181 (speeches); F (1, 393) = 43.574, p < .000. **P. 134**: *Optimism*: Means = 51.155 (Hum. Serv.); 49.914 (Econ.); 50.026 (For. Pol.); 46.908 (Law); 51.788 (Ethics); 51.247 (Mult.); F (5, 529) = 6.588, p < .000. *Inspiration*: Means = 51.155 (Hum. Serv.); 49.914 (Econ.); 50.026 (For. Pol.); 46.908 (Law); 51.788 (Ethics); 51.247 (Mult.); F (5, 529) = 6.588, p < .000. *Commonality*: Means = 49.912 (Hum. Serv.); 50.076 (Econ.); 48.252 (For. Pol.); 46.534 (Law); 50.105 (Ethics); 49.380 (Mult.); F (5, 529) = 7.118, p < .000. *Accomplishment*: Means = 9.322 (Hum. Serv.); 18.897 (Econ.); 8.130 (For. Pol.); 11.727 (Law); 10.703 (Ethics); 16.665 (Mult.); F (5, 529) = 17.355, p < .000. *Realism*: Means = 51.339 (Hum.

Serv.); 52.537 (Econ.); 50.181 (For. Pol.); 48.130 (Law); 51.696 (Ethics); 51.754 (Mult.); F (5, 529) = 7.786, p < .000. *Religious References*: Means = .470 (Hum. Serv.); .280 (Econ.); .745 (For. Pol.); .000 (Law); 1.780 (Ethics); .231 (Mult.); F (5, 529) = 5.035, p < .000. P. 135-6: *Reactive Ads*: Totals = 11.7% (1960); 24.1% (1976); 19.7% (1980.); 24.2% (1984); 37.6% (1988); 37.5% (1992.); 43.1% (1996.); KW X^2 > (df, 6) = 54.448, p < .000. P. 136: *Optimism*: Means = 52.014 (1960); 52.263 (1976); 51.540 (1980); 50.132 (1984); 49.729 (1988); 48.708 (1992); 47.732 (1996); F (6, 546) = 9.544, p < .000. P. 137: *Variety*: Means = .649 (Promotional); .687 (Comparative); .695 (Reactive); F (2, 528) = 11.610, p < .000. *Leader References*: Means = 8.822 (Promotional); 13.559 (Comparative); 16.057 (Reactive); F (2, 528) = 10.724, p < .000. *Numerical Terms*: Means = 9.404 (Promotional); 15.214 (Comparative); 17.170 (Reactive); F (2, 528) = 13.940, p < .000. *Familiarity*: Means = 125.011 (Promotional); 114.837 (Comparative); 113.737 (Reactive); F (2, 528) = 15.325, p < .000. *Self-References*: Means = 12.748 (Promotional); 9.279 (Comparative); 8.891 (Reactive); F (2, 528) = 5.595, p < .004. P. 137: *Self-References*: Means = 6.246 (Reactive-win); 11.344 (Reactive-lose); F (1, 131) = 5.992, p < .016. *Human Interest*: Means = 26.984 (Reactive-win); 35.511 (Reactive-lose); F (1, 131) = 7.010, p < .009. *Insistence*: Means = 46.165 (Reactive-win); 28.918 (Reactive-lose); F (1, 131) = 6.101, p < .015. *Accomplishment*: Means = 13.998 (Reactive-win); 9.996 (Reactive-lose); F (1, 131) = 4.557, p < .035. *Temporal References*: Means = 22.018 (Reactive-win); 13.676 (Reactive-lose); F (1, 131) = 10.535, p < .001. *Numerical References*: Means = 23.135 (Reactive-win); 13.322 (Reactive-lose); F (1, 131) = 8.306, p < .005. *Denial*: Means = 6.877 (Reactive-win); 10.647 (Reactive-lose); F (1, 131) = 7.093, p < .009.

CHAPTER SIX

P. 143: *Optimism*: Means = 49.029 (Voters); 50.393 (Politicians); 48.970 (Press); F (2, 18213) = 336.788, p < .000. *Patriotism*: Means = 2.220 (Voters); 3.211 (Politicians); 1.182 (Press); F (2, 18213) = 518.413, p < .000. *Insistence*: Means = 52.043 (Voters); 45.417 (Politicians); 74.145 (Press); F (2, 18213) = 565.236, p < .000. *Realism*: Means = 49.715 (Voters); 51.688 (Politicians); 48.082 (Press); F (2, 18213) = 1906.167, p < .000. *Accomplishment*: Means = 9.759 (Voters); 12.239 (Politicians); 11.312 (Press); F (2, 18213) = 186.780, p < .000. *Complexity*: Means = 4.625 (Voters); 4.412 (Politicians); 4.848 (Press); F (2, 18213) = 3174.296, p < .000. *Self-References*: Means = 6.985 (Voters); 12.845 (Politicians); 2.783 (Press); F (2, 18213) = 2590.289, p < .000. *Human Interest*: Means = 29.472 (Voters); 35.935 (Politicians); 21.709 (Press); F (2, 18213) = 1830.877, p < .000. *Present Concern*: Means = 11.669 (Voters); 14.445 (Politicians); 8.149 (Press); F (2, 18213) = 1519.161, p < .000. P. 149: *Human Interest*: Means = 36.319 (1948–60); 37.360 (1964–76); 39.668 (1980–96); F (2, 2354) = 17.550, p < .000. *Self-references*: Means = 11.456 (to Sept.15); 12.624 (Sept.16–30); 13.625 (Oct. 1–15); 13.973 (Oct. 16–31); F (2, 2988) = 10.667, p < .000. P. 152: *Realism*: Means = 52.683 (Politicians); 50.203 (Religious); 47.534 (Corporate); 49.682 (Protest); F (3, 1315) = 221.457, p < .000. *Self-Reference*: Means = 12.253 (Politicians); 6.388 (Religious); 3.064 (Corporate); 6.754 (Protest); F (3, 1315) = 102.046, p < .000. *Commonality*: Means = 50.000 (Politicians); 49.501 (Religious); 51.236 (Corporate); 49.714 (Protest); F (3, 1315) = 19.848, p < .000. *Patriotic References*: Means = 3.008 (Politicians); 1.389 (Religious); 1.151 (Corporate); 2.217 (Protest); F (3, 1315) = 30.557, p < .000. *Party References*: Means = 0.752 (Politicians); 0.505 (Religious); 0.122

(Corporate); .201 (Protest); F (3, 1315) = 221.457, p < .000. *Certainty*: Means = 49.569 (Politicians); 49.767 (Religious); 50.573 (Corporate); 49.784 (Protest); F (3, 1315) = 10.647, p < .000. *Human Interest*: Means = 40.176 (Politicians); 39.759 (Religious); 29.556 (Corporate); 32.892 (Protest); F (3, 1315) = 40.295, p < .000. *Activity*: Means = 50.482 (Politicians); 49.173 (Religious); 50.296 (Corporate); 50.151 (Protest); F (3, 1315) = 14.276, p < .000. *Voter References*: Means = 5.876 (Politicians); 3.450 (Religious); 4.003 (Corporate); 7.062 (Protest); F (3, 1315) = 43.071, p < .000. *Optimism*: Means = 51.502 (Politicians); 49.959 (Religious); 51.894 (Corporate); 48.382 (Protest); F (3, 1315) = 46.291, p < .000. *Leader References*: Means = 1.189 (Politicians); 0.409 (Religious); 0.227 (Corporate); 0.852 (Protest); F (3, 1315) = 22.315, p < .000. P. 156: *Optimism* (sitting presidents): Means = 50.632 (Truman); 50.854 (Eisenhower); 48.930 (Kennedy); 50.246 (Nixon); 50.260 (Johnson); 50.671 (Ford); 51.418 (Carter); 50.686 (Reagan); 51.610 (Bush); 51.214 (Clinton). P. 161: *Realism*: Means = 52.516 (Democrat); 51.901 (Republican); 51.121 (Independent); F (2, 2354) = 32.401, p < .000. *Familiarity*: Means = 129.985 (Democrat); 129.781 (Republican); 119.712 (Independent); F (2, 2354) = 55.403, p < .000. *Commonality*: Means = 49.980 (Democrat); 49.331 (Republican); 49.974 (Independent); F (2, 2354) = 27.221, p < .000. *Voter References*: Means = 6.116 (Democrat); 5.586 (Republican); 5.127 (Independent); F (2, 2354) = 9.606, p < .000. *Leader References*: Means = 2.193 (Democrat); 1.774 (Republican); 1.081 (Independent); F (2, 2354) = 16.915, p < .000. *Party References*: Means = 1.077 (Democrat); 0.692 (Republican); 0.326 (Independent); F (2, 2354) = 19.726, p < .000. P. 163: *Inspiration*: Means = 5.541 (Democrat); 6.069 (Republican); 3.902 (Independent); F (2, 2354) = 25.923, p < .000. *Liberation*: Means = 1.800 (Democrat); 2.583 (Republican); 1.751 (Independent); F (2, 2354) = 29.860, p < .000. *Patriotic Terms*: Means = 2.877 (Democrat); 4.410 (Republican); 1.545 (Independent); F (2, 2354) = 83.531, p < .000. *Passivity*: Means = 4.725 (Democrat); 5.442 (Republican); 4.620 (Independent); F (2, 2354) = 16.240, p < .000. *Religious References*: Means = 1.159 (Democrat); 1.480 (Republican); 1.040 (Independent); F (2, 2354) = 6.259, p < .002. P. 164: *Democratic Style*: Means = 19.447 (Sitting Democrat); 18.994 (Sitting Republican); F (1, 425) = 8.534, p < .004. *Republican Style*: Means = 21.432 (Sitting Democrat); 22.091 (Sitting Republican); F (1, 425) = 5.093, p < .025. P.164: *Democratic Style*: Means = 19.871 (0–9 pt. spread); 19.668 (10–19 pt. spread); 19.263 (20–36 pt. spread); F (1, 425) = 12.332, p < .000. *Republican Style*: Means = 21.418 (0–9 pt. spread); 21.105 (10–19 pt. spread); 21.988 (20–36 pt. spread); F (1, 425) = 7.542, p < .001. P. 164: *Democratic Style*: Means = 19.614 (Democratic incumbents); 19.773 (Democratic challengers); F (1, 878) = 2.024, p < .155. *Republican Style*: Means = 21.988 (Republican incumbent); 23.329 (Republican challenger); F (1, 508) = 22.526, p < .000. P. 164: *Democratic Style*: Means = 19.672 (Democratic winner); 19.677 (Democratic loser); F (1, 1115) = 0.002, p < .960. *Republican Style*: Means = 21.983 (Republican winner); 22.015 (Republican loser); F (1, 1032) = 0.028, p < .866. P. 164: *Democratic Style*: Means = 20.115 (1948–60); 19.855 (1964–76); 19.413 (1980–96); F (2, 1114) = 18.203, p < .000. *Republican Style*: Means = 22.315 (1948–60); 22.434 (1964–76); 21.569 (1980–96); F (2, 1031) = 9.091, p < .165. P. 165: *Democratic Style*: Means = 19.695 (Democrats); 18.946 (Republicans); 18.835 (Independents); F (2, 4114) = 84.810, p < .000. *Republican Style*: Means = 20.939 (Democrats); 21.645 (Republicans); 19.932 (Independents); F (2, 4114) = 57.938, p < .000. P. 165: *Denial*: Means = 9.549 (Perot); 6.933 (campaign average); *Human Interest*: Means = 45.266 (Perot); 38.380 (campaign average); *Past Concern*: Means = 5.798 (Perot); 3.779 (campaign average).

CHAPTER SEVEN

P. 169: *Total words*: Means = 618.91 (1948–60); 640.27 (1964–76); 798.24 (1980–96); F (2, 7306) = 59.056, p < .000. P. 173: *Optimism* (print coverage): Means = 49.028 (NY Times); 48.964 (Wash. Post.); 49.330 (Chr. Sci. Mon.); 49.079 (LA Times); 48.975 (Chic. Trib); 48.940 (Atln. Con.); 48.835 (AP-UPI); F (2, 7302) = 4.730, p < .000. P. 173: *Optimism* (broadcast coverage): Means = 48.779 (ABC); 48.986 (CBS); 48.616 (NBC); 48.964 (CNN); 49.077 (PBS); F (4, 1214) = 1.397, p < .233. P. 173: *Optimism* (campaign cycle): Means = 48.9590 (to Sept. 15); 48.947 (Sept. 16–30); 48.954 (Oct. 1–15); 48.992 (Oct. 16–end); F (3, 8448) = 0.228, p < .977. P. 173: *Optimism* (news focus): Means = 48.915 (Democratic stories); 49.032 (Republican stories); 49.044 (Mixed stories); F (2, 6309) = 2.753, p < .064. P. 175: *Commonality*: Means = 49.994 (1948–60); 49.658 (1964–76); 49.258 (1980–96); F (2, 8525) = 68.201, p < .000. P. 175: *Commonality* (press coverage): Means = 49.788 (to Sept. 15); 49.764 (Sept. 16–30); 49.486 (Oct. 1–15); 49.278 (Oct. 16–31); F (3, 8448) = 22.534, p < .000. P. 176: *Commonality* (politicians' remarks): Means = 49.7759 (to Sept. 15); 49.8049 (Sept. 16–30); 49.6075(Oct. 1–15); 49.5674(Oct. 16–31); F (2, 2273) = 1.939, p < .121. P. 177: *Activity*: Means = 49.185 (Voters); 50.315 (Politicians); 52.933 (Press); F (2, 18213) = 1562.223, p < .000. P. 179: *Activity* (press coverage only): Sample means = 52.933 (All years); 52.688 (1988); 52.940 (1992); 52.789 (1996). P. 180: *Space-time ratio* (for "sense of care"): Means = 9.580 (–50 percent–0%); 9.946 (1–20%); 10.152 (21% up); F (2, 7979) = 161.171, p < .000. P. 180: *Space-time ratio* (for unemployment): Means = 10.124 (4.5% down); 9.825 (4.6–7.0%); 9.683 (7.1% up); F (2, 8525) = 74.389, p < .000. P. 180: *Space-time ratio* (for "economic fear"): Means = 9.950 (0–24%); 9.869 (25–45%); 9.667 (46% up); F (2, 7471) = 32.428, p < .000. P. 182: *Realism*: Means = 49.715 (Voters); 51.688 (Politicians); 48.082 (Press); F (2, 18213) = 1906.167, p < .000. P. 188: *Embellishment*: Means = 0.954 (Voters); 0.691 (Politicians); 0.566 (Press); F (2, 18213) = 110.144, p < .000. *Leveling Terms*: Means = 8.137 (Voters); 7.817 (Politicians); 5.094 (Press); F (2, 18213) = 1042.280, p < .000. *Tenacity*: Means = 31.467 (Voters); 36.119 (Politicians); 24.069 (Press); F (2, 18213) = 2460.316, p < .000. *Numeric Terms*: Means = 10.449 (Voters); 10.450 (Politicians); 12.732 (Press); F (2, 18213) = 79.467, p < .000. *Leader References*: Means = 5.928 (Voters); 3.488 (Politicians); 12.864 (Press); F (2, 18213) = 2461.483, p < .000. *Party References*: Means = 1.858 (Voters); 0.780 (Politicians); 2.341 (Press); F (2, 18213) = 297.293, p < .000. P. 190: *Detachment* (by party focus): Means = 42.568 (Democratic); 42.893 (Republican); F (1, 5149) = 23.373, p < .000. P. 190: *Detachment* (for third parties): Means = 42.530 (All coverage; n = 6824); 43.287 (Third party coverage, 1980); 43.832 (Third party coverage, 1992); 43.787 (Third party coverage, 1996). P. 190: *Detachment* (newspapers only): Means = 42.599 (NY Times); 42.713 (Wash. Post.); 42.194 (Chr. Sci. Mon.); 42.696 (LA Times); 43.103 (Chic. Trib.); 42.889 (Atln. Con.); F (5, 5814) = 12.759, p < .000. P. 190: *Detachment* (broadcast only): Means = 40.815 (ABC); 40.646 (CBS); 40.684 (NBC); 39.744 (CNN); 39.390 (PBS); F (4, 1214) = 10.387, p < .000. P. 190: *Detachment* (news coverage): Means = 42.415 (to Sept. 15); 42.676 (Sept. 16–30); 42.616 (Oct. 1–15); 42.479 (Oct. 16–31); F (3, 8448) = 4.269, p < .005. P. 191: *Detachment* (print coverage only): Means = 42.375 (1948–60); 42.800 (1964–76); 43.311 (1980–96); F (2, 7306) = 95.139, p < .000. P. 191: *Detachment* (for polling spread): Means = 42.896 (0–9 pts.); 42.214 (10–19 pts.); 42.526 (20–36 pts.); F (2, 8406) = 56.562, p < .000. P. 191: *Detachment* (for "sense of care"): Means = 43.180 (–50–0%); 43.038 (1–20%); 42.365 (21% up); F (2, 6760) =

76.833, p < .000. P. **191**: *Detachment* (for unemployment): Means = 42.355 (4.5% down); 43.074 (4.6–7.0%); 43.110 (7.1% up); F (2, 8525) = 70.687, p < .000. P. **191**: *Detachment* (for "economic fear"): Means = 42.531 (0–24%); 43.263 (25–45%); 43.010 (46% up); F (2, 7306) = 60.947, p < .000. P. **192**: *Detachment* (for front-runner stories): Means = 42.173 (Democratic); 42.635 (Republican); F (1, 6941) = 48.908, p < .000. P. **192**: *Detachment* (by medium): Means = 42.867 (print); 40.508 (broadcast); F (1, 8526) = 952.527, p < .000. P. **192**: *Detachment* (by voice): Means = 38.630 (Voters); 37.170 (Politicians); 40.508 (Broadcast only); F (2, 10996) = 594.252, p < .000. P. **193**: *Activity*: Means = 53.066 (print); 52.133 (broadcast); F (1, 8526) = 100.905, p < .000. P. **194**: *Insistence*: Means = 76.456 (print); 60.289 (broadcast); F (1, 8526) = 92.601, p < .000. P. **195**: *Realism*: Means = 47.831 (print); 49.588 (broadcast); F (1, 8526) = 537.034, p < .000. P. **195**: *Space-time ratio*: Means = 9.943 (print); 9.343 (broadcast); F (1, 8526) = 232.047, p < .000. P. **195**: *Human Interest*: Means = 21.212 (print); 24.688 (broadcast); F (1, 8526) = 129.023, p < .000. P. **195**: *Cognition*: Means = 6.556 (print); 8.255 (broadcast); F (1,8526) = 163.758, p < .000.

Chapter Eight

P. **205-6**: *Blame*: Means = 2.582 (Voters); 1.764 (Politicians); 1.519 (Press); F (2, 18216) = 332.539, p < .000. *Optimism*: Means = 49.029 (Voters); 50.393 (Politicians); 48.970 (Press); F (2, 18213) = 1562.223, p < .000. P. **207**: *Religious Terms*: Means = 1.408 (Voters); 1.074 (Politicians); 0.743 (Press); F (2, 18213) = 76.614, p < .000. *Irreligious Terms*: Means = 0.142 (Voters); 0.033 (Politicians); 0.060 (Press); F (2, 18213) = 62.542, p < .000. P. **208**: *Embellishment*: Means = 0.954 (Voters); 0.691 (Politicians); 0.566 (Press); F (2, 18213) = 110.144, p < .000. P. **208**: *Realism*: Means = 49.185 (Voters); 50.315 (Politicians); 52.933 (Press); F (2, 18213) = 1562.223, p < .000. Pp. **209**: *Self-Reference*: Means = 6.985 (Voters); 12.845 (Politicians); 2.783 (Press); F (2, 18213) = 2590.289, p < .000. P. **209**: *Tenacity*: Means = 31.467 (Voters); 36.119 (Politicians); 24.069 (Press); F (2, 18213) = 2460.316, p < .000. P. **211**: *Insistence*: Means = 52.043 (Voters); 45.417 (Politicians); 74.145 (Press); F (2, 18213) = 565.235, p < .000. P. **211**: *Patriotic Terms*: Means = 2.220 (Voters); 3.211 (Politicians); 1.182 (Press); F (2, 18213) = 518.452, p < .000. *Inspiration*: Means = 4.126 (Voters); 5.527 (Politicians); 2.685 (Press); F (2, 18213) = 748.564, p < .000. *Praise*: Means = 5.863 (Voters); 6.880 (Politicians); 3.480 (Press); F (2, 18213) = 1146.358, p < .000. *Satisfaction*: Means = 3.019 (Voters); 3.658 (Politicians); 2.118 (Press); F (2, 18213) = 335.673, p < .000. P. **212**: *Party References*: Means = 1.858 (Voters); 0.780 (Politicians); 2.341 (Press); F (2, 18213) = 297.293, p < .000. *Leader References*: Means = 5.928 (Voters); 3.488 (Politicians); 12.864 (Press); F (2, 18213) = 2461.483, p < .000. P. **214**: *Familiarity*: Means = 132.039 (1948–60); 130.316 (1964–76); 123.752 (1980–96); F (2, 6125) = 121.928, p < .000. *Realism*: Means = 50.184 (1948–60); 49.742 (1964–76); 49.448 (1980–96); F (2, 6125) = 21.655, p < .000. *Hardship*: Means = 4.392 (1948–60); 5.407 (1964–76); 5.451 (1980–96); F (2, 6125) = 23.711, p < .000. *Numerical Terms*: Means = 8.160 (1948–60); 9.272 (1964–76); 12.630 (1980–96); F (2, 6125) = 66.672, p < .000. P. **216**: *Space-time ratio*: Means = 10.184 (Voters); 9.950 (Politicians); 9.858 (Press); F (2, 18213) = 97.093, p < .000. *Leader References*: Means = 4.617 (East); 4.424 (South); 4.351 (Midwest); 4.182 (West) F (2, 6122) = 7.599, p < .000. *Colloquial language*: Means = 9.761 (East); 10.165 (South); 10.413 (Midwest); 9.676 (West) F (2, 6122) = 20.624, p < .000. *Certainty*: Means = 49.551 (East); 49.391 (South); 48.874 (Midwest); 49.657 (West) F (2, 6122) = 17.464, p < .000. *P. 216: Familiarity:* (for "sense of care"): Means = 124.417 (–50–0%); 128.741 (1–20%); 131.613 (21% up); F (2, 5826) = 83.193, p < .000. *Familiarity* (for unemployment): Means = 132.568 (4.5% down); 128.333 (4.6–7.0%); 124/091 (7.1% up); F (2, 6126) = 95.087, p < .000. *Familiarity* (for "economic fear"): Means = 130.463 (0–24%); 128.367 (25–45%); 123.507 (46% up); F (2, 6123) = 70.114, p < .000. *Numerical Terms:* (for "sense of care"): Means = 12.007 (–50–0%); 10.973 (1–20%); 8.344 (21% up); F (2, 5826) = 39.917, p < .000. *Numerical Terms* (for unemployment): Means = 7.387 (4.5% down); 9.318 (4.6–7.0%); 13.905 (7.1% up); F (2, 6123) = 126.463, p < .000. *Numerical Terms* (for "economic fear"): Means = 8.180 (0–24%); 10.299 (25–45%); 14.029 (46% up); F (2, 6123) = 98.230, p < .000. *Party References:* (for "sense of care"): Means = 1.748 (–50–0%); 1.257 (1–20%); 2.567 (21% up); F (2, 5826) = 46.834, p < .000. *Party References:* (for unemployment): Means = 2.143 (4.5% down); 2.132 (4.6–7.0%); 1.346 (7.1% up); F (2, 6123) = 28.902, p < .000. *Party References:* (for "economic fear"): Means = 1.946 (0–24%); 2.112 (25–45%); 1.417 (46% up); F (2, 6123) = 15.442, p < .000. *P. 217: Certainty:* Means = 49.411 (Functionals); 49.832 (Traditionals); 48.907 (Pundits); F (2, 6126) = 25.840, p < .000. *Liberation:* Means = 1.872 (Functionals); 4.100 (Traditionals); 2.098 (Pundits); F (2, 6126) = 179.356, p < .000. *Inspiration:* Means = 3.909 (Functionals); 5.190 (Traditionals); 3.859 (Pundits); F (2, 6126) = 37.045, p < .000. *Commonality:* Means = 49.707 (Functionals); 48.601 (Traditionals); 49.610 (Pundits); F (2, 6126) = 56.022, p < .000. *P. 217: Space-time ratio:* Means = 10.220 (Functionals); 10.294 (Traditionals); 9.963 (Pundits); F (2, 6126) = 16.465, p < .000. *Insistence:* Means = 51.240 (Functionals); 48.047 (Traditionals); 58.599 (Pundits); F (2, 6126) = 14.072, p < .000. *Realism:* Means = 50.092 (Functionals); 49.490 (Traditionals); 48.714 (Pundits); F (2, 6126) = 25.840, p < .000. *P. 217: Colloquial language:* Means = 10.200 (Functionals); 10.052 (Traditionals); 9.277 (Pundits); F (2, 6126) = 45.815, p < .000. *Accomplishment:* Means = 10.321 (Functionals); 8.680 (Traditionals); 8.884 (Pundits); F (2, 6126) = 34.454, p < .000. *P. 220: Voter References:* Means = 5.788 (Voters); 5.429 (Politicians); 3.722 (Press); F (2, 18308) = 459.711, p < .000. *P. 221: Leader References* (for voter-focused texts): Means = 4.919 (Voters); 2.653 (Politicians); 13.125 (Press); F (2, 4669) = 1004.708, p < .000. *Party References* (for voter-focused texts): Means = 1.543 (Voters); 0.811 (Politicians); 2.540 (Press); F (2, 4669) = 102.153, p < .000. *Activity* (for voter-focused texts): Means = 48.924 (Voters); 50.146 (Politicians); 52.432 (Press); F (2, 4669) = 331.104, p < .000. *P. 221: Self-References* (for voter-focused texts): Means = 6.236 (Voters); 11.924 (Politicians); 2.633 (Press); F (2, 4669) = 527.001, p < .000. *Realism* (for voter-focused texts): Means = 50.202 (Voters); 52.029 (Politicians); 48.268 (Press); F (2, 4669) = 472.072, p < .000. *Optimism* (for voter-focused texts): Means = 49.114 (Voters); 50.782 (Politicians); 49.164 (Press); F (2, 4669) = 123.498, p < .000. *P. 222: Blame* (for voter-focused texts): Means = 2.650 (Voters); 1.861 (Politicians); 1.564 (Press); F (2, 4669) = 71.199, p < .000. *Denial* (for voter-focused texts): Means = 7.441 (Voters); 6.909 (Politicians); 4.828 (Press); F (2, 4669) = 133.963, p < .000. *Certainty* (for voter-focused texts): Means = 49.980 (Voters); 49.905 (Politicians); 49.432 (Press); F (2, 4669) = 19.134, p < .000. *Embellishment* (for voter-focused texts): Means = 0.998 (Voters); 0.653 (Politicians); 0.601 (Press); F (2, 4669) = 31.790, p < .000.

261

Sampling Details

The data in this book are based on a large but by no means complete sample of campaign texts. Because DICTION analyzes passages in 500-word clusters, the data in the following tables reflect the total number of text segments studied. So, for example, because the average stump speech runs 1,500 words in length, DICTION would break it into three text segments prior to analysis. On the other hand, letters-to-the-editor were never more than 500 words long, nor were campaign advertisements. Print news stories ranged considerably in length. Front-page stories were often two or three DICTION-segments long, with some being considerably shorter. Whether long or short, however, DICTION extrapolated all texts to a 500-word norm when performing its calculations.

The **campaign speeches** (n = 2,357 text segments) included all nationally broadcast addresses during the general election as well as a random sample of middle-of-the-week speeches given on the stump. Because of the dictates of the Campaign Mapping Project, speeches delivered during the 1996 campaign were oversampled.

Campaign debates (n = 652) were analyzed in their entirety but broken down by speaker prior to analysis. **Campaign ads** (n = 553) included a broad sample of ads produced by the major campaigns, with seven of the thirteen campaigns being represented in the textbase. **Print coverage** (n = 7,309) included stories from the *New York Times*, *Washington Post*, *Christian Science Monitor*, *Atlanta Constitution*, *Chicago Tribune*, *Los Angeles Times*, as well as AP and UPI syndicate stories. Randomizing techniques were used to ensure that neither feature nor nonfeature stories dominated the sample.

Broadcast coverage (n = 1,219) was gathered by either photocopying original scripts or by transcribing the nightly news from audiotapes. Four years are represented in the sample (1980, 1988, 1992, and 1996), with the various news bureaus (ABC, CBS, NBC, CNN, and PBS) represented on an availability basis. Finally, the **letters-to-the-editor** collection (n = 6,126) is especially rich, with twelve different cities represented (each of which has a population of approximately 100,000 persons), thereby ensuring a generous regional and demographic distribution of political attitudes. The collection represents approximately 75% of all letters written in these newspapers during the thirteen elections studied.

TABLE A3.1
Distibution of Texts by Genre

Campaign	Letters	Debates	Ads	Print	Broadcast	Speeches	Total
1948	297			546		120	963
1952	453			579		111	1143
1956	311			599		116	1026
1960	459	99	123	542		172	1395
1964	511			584		143	1238
1968	479			492		154	1125
1972	475			575		149	1199
1976	490	95	65	551		116	1317
1980	507	75	117	542	132	159	1532
1984	491	40	34	546		142	1253
1988	581	91	87	597	260	101	1717
1992	671	147	65	575	354	185	1997
1996	401	105	62	581	473	689	2311
Total	6126	652	553	7309	1219	2357	18216

TABLE A3.2
Distibution of Texts by Political Voice

Campaign	People	Politicians	Press	Total
1948	297	120	546	963
1952	453	111	579	1143
1956	311	116	599	1026
1960	459	394	542	1395
1964	511	143	584	1238
1968	479	154	492	1125
1972	475	149	575	1199
1976	490	276	551	1317
1980	507	351	674	1532
1984	491	216	546	1253
1988	581	279	857	1717
1992	671	397	929	1997
1996	401	856	1054	2311
Total	6126	3562	8528	18216

TABLE A3.3
Distibution of Texts by Campaign Cycle

Campaign	to Sept. 15	Sept. 16–30	Oct. 1–15	Oct. 16–31	Total
1948	194	184	179	260	817
1952	209	210	239	352	1010
1956	223	171	188	348	930
1960	194	203	254	520	1171
1964	256	225	250	438	1169
1968	263	191	203	342	999
1972	297	178	228	404	1107
1976	280	236	288	366	1170
1980	298	261	265	473	1297
1984	201	204	256	433	1094
1988	342	288	339	502	1471
1992	369	259	399	621	1648
1996	601	529	435	744	2309
Total	3727	3139	3523	5803	16192

TABLE A3.4
Distibution of Texts by Media Source

Campaign	N.Y. Times	Wash. Post	Chr. Sci. Mon.	Chic. Trib.	L.A. Times	Atln. Const.	AP/UPI	ABC	CBS	NBC	CNN	PBS	Total
1948	147	104	64	27	59	40	105						546
1952	130	128		46	125	22	128						579
1956	138	134	70	50	66	6	135						599
1960	144	121	45	56	77	31	68						542
1964	122	130	51	50	64	38	129						584
1968	109	121	44	57	55	30	76						492
1972	117	134	56	70	57	22	119						575
1976	120	126	41	37	52	54	121						551
1980	130	125	44	48	49	37	109	66	66				674
1984	124	108	40	64	56	34	120						546
1988	142	141	30	58	59	37	130	69	58	60		73	857
1992	132	129	25	66	53	48	122	77	74	69	65	69	929
1996	134	131	40	53	53	43	127	128	175	170			1054
Total	1689	1632	550	682	825	442	1489	340	373	299	65	142	8528

TABLE A3.5

Distibution of Texts by Candidate[a]

Campaign	Tru.	Dew.	Ike	Stev.	JFK	Nixon	LBJ	Golg.	Hum.	McG.	Ford	Carter	Reagan	Andr.	Mond.	Bush	Dukak.	Clinton	Perot	Dole	Total
1948	52	68																			120
1952			50	61																	111
1956			51	65																	116
1960					201	193															394
1964							60	83													143
1968						75			79												154
1972						71				78											149
1976											140	135									275
1980												185	118	48							351
1984													117		99						216
1988																137	142				279
1992																130		143	124		397
1996																		449	111	296	856
Total	52	68	101	126	201	339	60	83	79	78	140	320	235	48	99	267	142	592	235	296	3561

[a]Includes speeches, ads, and debates

TABLE A3.6

Distibution of Letters by Geographical Region

Campaign	East	South	Midwest	West	Total
1948	67	134	62	34	297
1952	68	190	96	99	453
1956	88	109	35	79	311
1960	100	103	112	144	459
1964	100	152	108	151	511
1968	101	140	99	139	479
1972	99	152	96	128	475
1976	100	144	97	149	490
1980	100	150	100	157	507
1984	97	149	100	145	491
1988	135	170	127	149	481
1992	64	199	154	254	671
1996	71	148	79	103	401
Total	1190	1940	1265	1731	6126

* Notes *

Preface

1. See, for example, H. W. Stanley and R. G. Niemi, *Vital Statistics on American Politics: 1997–1998* (Washington, D.C.: Congressional Quarterly Press, 1998), pp. 240–41.

2. These are all the remarks of Alexander Hamilton as quoted in N. E. Cunningham, "Election of 1800," in A. Schlesinger (ed.), *The Coming to Power: Critical Elections in American History* (New York: Chelsea House, 1972), pp. 41, 43, 50.

3. For these and other details on the campaign of 1900, see L. L. Gould, *The Presidency of William McKinley* (Lawrence: University Press of Kansas, 1980), p. 228ff.

4. As quoted in ibid., p. 229.

5. These are the remarks of Mark Hanna as quoted in G. S. Thomas, *The Pursuit of the White House: A Handbook of Presidential Election Statistics and History* (New York: Greenwood Press, 1987), p. 60.

6. E. H. Roseboom and A. E. Eckes, *A History of Presidential Elections: From George Washington to Jimmy Carter* (New York: Macmillan, 1970), pp. 126–27.

Chapter 1

1. A. Corrado, "Financing the 1996 Elections," in G. M. Pomper et al. (eds.), *The Election of 1996* (Chatham, N.J.: Chatham House, 1997), p. 145.

2. K. Bode, "Final Thoughts," in L. Sabato (ed.), *Toward the Millennium: The Elections of 1996* (Boston: Allyn and Bacon, 1997), p. 274.

3. M. Just, "Candidate Strategies and the Media Campaign," G. M. Pomper et al. (eds.), *The Election of 1996* (Chatham, N.J.: Chatham House, 1997), p. 85.

4. For these and other public opinion data on the 1996 campaign, see S. Keeter, "Public Opinion and the Election," in G. M. Pomper et al. (eds.), *The Election of 1996* (Chatham, N.J.: Chatham House, 1997), pp. 107–34.

5. Ibid., p. 122.

6. R. P. Hart, *DICTION: The Text-Analysis Program* (Thousand Oaks, Calif.: Sage/Scolari, 1997). For further information, see http://www.scolari.com. For conceptual background, see R. P. Hart, "Redeveloping DICTION: Theoretical Considerations," in M. West (ed.), *New Directions in Computer Content Analysis* (New York: Ablex, in press).

7. J. Barth, *Giles Goat-Boy* (New York: Doubleday, 1966), p. 61.

8. S. L. Popkin, *The Reasoning Voter: Communication and Persuasion in Presidential Campaigns* (Chicago: University of Chicago Press), 1991; S. Verba, K. Schlozman, and H. E. Brady, *Voice and Equality: Civic Voluntarism in American Politics* (Cambridge: Harvard University Press, 1995); S. J. Rosenstone and J. M. Hansen, *Mobilization, Participation, and Democracy in America* (New York: Macmillan, 1993).

9. N. R. Luttbeg and M. M. Gant, *American Electoral Behavior, 1952–1992* (Itasca, Ill.: Peacock, 1995), p. 10.

10. M. Hetherington, "The Media's Role in Forming Voters' National Economic Evaluations in 1992," *American Journal of Political Science* 40 (1996), pp. 372–95.

11. W. C. McWilliams, *The Politics of Disappointment: American Elections, 1976–94* (Chatham, N.J.: Chatham House, 1995), p. 69.

12. Z. Trachtenberg, *Making Citizens: Rousseau's Political Theory of Culture* (London: Routledge, 1993), p. 218.

13. W. R. Neuman, M. R. Just, and A. N. Crigler, *Common Knowledge: News and the Construction of Political Meaning* (Chicago: University of Chicago Press, 1992).

14. D. O. Sears and N. A. Valentino, "Politics Matters: Political Events as Catalysts for Preadult Socialization," *American Political Science Review* 91 (1997), pp. 45–63.

15. L. Bartels, "Campaign Quality: Standards for Evaluation, Benchmarks for Reform," Paper presented at the annual meeting of the American Political Science Association, Washington, D.C. (August 1997), p. 65.

16. See, for example, D. L. Protess and M. McCombs (eds.), *Agenda Setting: Readings on Media, Public Opinion, and Policymaking* (Hillsdale, N.J.: Erlbaum, 1991).

17. B. E. Gronbeck, "The Functions of Presidential Campaigning," *Communication Monographs* 45 (1978), p. 270.

18. Trachtenberg, *Making Citizens*, p. 195.

19. A. Kornberg and H. D. Clarke, *Citizens and Community: Political Support in a Representative Democracy* (New York: Cambridge, 1992), pp. 107–8.

20. Ibid., p. 189.

21. Bartels, "Campaign Quality" pp. 55–56.

22. B. Buchanan, *Renewing Presidential Politics: Campaigns, Media, and the Public Interest* (Lanham, Md.: Rowman & Littlefield, 1996), p. 62–63.

23. Reported in Buchanan, *Renewing Presidential Politics*, p. 66.

24. Reported in Luttberg and Gant, *American Electoral Behavior*, p. 92.

25. W. M. Rahn, J. Brehm, and N. Carlson, "National Elections as Institutions for Generating Social Capital," Paper presented at the annual meeting of the American Political Science Association, Washington, D.C. (August 1997). See also Kornberg, *Citizens and Community*, p. 104.

26. M. R. Just, et. al. *Crosstalk: Citizens, Candidates and the Media in a Presidential Campaign* (Chicago: University of Chicago Press, 1996), p. 236.

27. R. P. Hart, *The Sound of Leadership: Presidential Communication in the Modern Age* (Chicago: University of Chicago Press, 1987), p. 183.

28. Corrado, *Financing the 1996 Elections*, p. 151.

29. A. Campbell, P. E. Converse, W. E. Miller, and D. E. Stokes, *The American Voter* (New York: Wiley, 1960).

30. D. R. Kiewiet and D. Rivers, "The Economic Basis of Reagan's Appeal," in J. E. Chubb and P. E. Peterson (eds.), *The New Direction in American Politics* (Washington, D.C.: Brookings Institution, 1985).

31. M. Fiorina, *Retrospective Voting in American National Elections* (New Haven: Yale University Press, 1981).

32. T. Holbrook, *Do Campaigns Matter?* (Thousand Oaks, Calif.: Sage, 1996).

33. T. Holbrook, "Did the Campaign Matter?" Paper presented at the annual meeting of the Midwest Political Science Association, Chicago, Illinois (April 1997).

34. R. P. Hart, *Seducing America: How Television Charms the Modern Voter* (New York: Oxford, 1994), p. 107.

35. C. E. Ladd, "The Polls and the Election," *The Public Perspective* (Oct./Nov., 1996), pp. 4–6.

36. S. Herbst, *Numbered Voices: How Opinion Polling Has Shaped American Politics* (Chicago: University of Chicago Press, 1993).

37. Bartels, "Campaign Quality," pp. 62–63.

38. M. Scammell, *The Wisdom of the War Room: U.S. Campaigning and Americanization*, Research Paper R-17 (Cambridge: Shornstein Center, Harvard University, 1997).

39. I. McAllister and R. Darcy, "Sources of Split-Ticket Voting in the 1988 American Elections," *Political Studies* 40 (1992), 695–712.

40. W. Miller, "Disinterest, Disaffection, and Participation in Presidential Politics" *Political Behavior* 2 (1980), 7–32.

41. For a fine analysis of this interview, see R. Cline, "The Cronkite-Ford Interview at the 1980 Republican National Convention: A Therapeutic Analogue," *Central States Speech Journal* 36 (1985), 92–104.

42. McWilliams, *Politics of Disappointment*, p. 33.

43. For an overview of research on political advertising, see D. M. West, *Air Wars: Television Advertising in Election Campaigns, 1952–1992* (Washington, D.C.: Congressional Quarterly, 1993).

44. L. Bitzer and T. Rueter, *Carter versus Ford: The Counterfeit Debates of 1976* (Madison: University of Wisconsin Press, 1980).

45. See K. H. Jamieson, *Dirty Politics: Deception, Distraction, and Democracy* (New York: Oxford University Press, 1992).

46. R. J. Dalton, *Citizen Politics: Public Opinion and Political Parties in Advanced Western Democracies* (Chatham, N.J.: Chatham House, 1996), pp. 266–69.

47. S. Ansolabehere and S. Iyengar, *Going Negative: How Attack Ads Shrink and Polarize the Electorate* (New York: Free Press, 1995).

48. J. N. Cappella and K. H. Jamieson, *Spiral of Cynicism: The Press and the Public Good* (New York: Oxford University Press, 1997).

49. T. E. Patterson, *Out of Order* (New York: Knopf, 1993).

50. See especially chapter 2: "Feeling Intimate: The Rise of Personality Politics."

51. Neuman, Just, and Crigler, *Common Knowledge*, p. 166.

52. Rosenstone and Hansen, *Mobilization*,.

53. T. White, *The Making of the President, 1960* (New York: Pocket Books, 1961); R. Simon, *Showtime: The American Political Circus and the Race for the White House* (New York: Random House, 1998).

54. Anonymous, *Primary Colors: A Novel of Politics* (New York: Random House, 1996).

55. M. Hertsgaard, *On Bended Knee: The Press and the Reagan Presidency* (New York: Farrar, Straus, Giroux, 1988); J. Fallows, *Breaking the News: How the Media Undermine American Democracy* (New York: Pantheon, 1996); R. Woodward, *The Choice: How Clinton Won* (New York: Simon & Schuster, 1996); A. Corrado, *Paying for Presidents: Public Financing in National Elections* (New York: Brookings Institution, 1993); M. P. Wattenberg, *The Decline of American Political Parties 1952–1992* (Cambridge: Harvard University Press, 1984); A. S. King, *Running Scared: Why America's Politicians Campaign Too Much and Govern Too Little* (New York: Martin Kessler Books, 1997); G. Troy, *See How They Ran: The Changing Role of the Presidential Candidate* (New York: Free Press, 1991); J. Zaller, *The Nature and Origins of Mass Opinions* (New York: Cambridge University Press, 1992);

M. DelliCarpini and S. Keeter, *What Americans Know about Politics and Why It Matters* (New Haven: Yale University Press, 1996).

56. M. McCombs, E. Einsiedel, and D. Weaver, *Contemporary Public Opinion: Issues and the News* (Hillsdale, N.J.: Erlbaum, 1991); L. Kaid and C. Holtz-Bacha, *Political Advertising in Western Democracies: Parties and Candidates on Television* (Thousand Oaks, Calif.: Sage, 1995); D. Graber, "The Nature of Visual Information and How People Process it," Paper presented at the Annenberg Public Policy Center Conference on Mediated Politics (May 1998); K. H. Jamieson, *Eloquence in an Electronic Age: The Transformation of Political Speechmaking* (New York: Oxford, 1988); W. A. Gamson, *Talking Politics* (New York: Cambridge, 1992).

57. G. R. Covington, K. Kroeger, and G. Richardson, "Shaping a Candidate's Image in the Press," in A. H. Miller and B. E. Gronbeck (eds.), *Presidential Campaigns and American Self-Images* (Boulder, Colo.: Westview, 1994).

58. K. D. Patterson and A. A. Bice, "Political Parties, Candidates, and Presidential Campaigns: 1952–1996," Paper presented at the annual convention of the American Political Science Association, Washington, D.C. (August 1997).

59. M. Levine, *Presidential Campaigns and Elections: Issues and Images in the Media Age* (Itasca, Ill.: Peacock, 1995), p. 48.

60. Scammell, *Wisdom of the War Room*, pp. 14–15.

61. Just et al., *Crosstalk*, p. 67.

62. R. Weaver, *The Ethics of Rhetoric* (Chicago: Regnery Co., 1965), pp. 164–85.

CHAPTER TWO

1. P. J. O'Rourke, "Oh, Shut Up," *The New Republic* (28 May 1984), pp. 20–23.

2. A. Schlesinger Jr., "Politics and the American Language," *The American Scholar* 43 (1974), p. 557.

3. Ibid.

4. For more on this topic, see B.Weinstein, *The Civic Tongue: Political Consequences of Language Choices* (New York: Longman, 1983).

5. H. Bretton, "Political Science, Language, and Politics," in W. M. O'Barr and J. F. O'Barr, *Language and Politics* (The Hague: Mouton, 1976), p. 441.

6. Ibid., p. 447.

7. A. Lorde, "The Master's Tools will Never Dismantle the Master's House," in C. Moraga and G. Anzaldua (eds.), *This Bridge Called My Back: Writings by Radical Women of Color* (New York: Kitchen Table, Women of Color Press, 1981), pp. 98–102.

8. Quoted in R. Goodin, *Manipulatory Politics* (New Haven: Yale University Press, 1980), p. 117.

9. M. Emmison, " 'The Economy': Its Emergence in Media Discourse," in H. Davis and P. Walton (eds.), *Language, Image, Media* (New York: St. Martin's, 1983), p. 154.

10. P. Tetlock, "Cognitive Style and Political Ideology," *Journal of Personality and Social Psychology* 45 (1983), pp. 118–26.

11. V. Beasley, "The Logic of Power in the Hill-Thomas Hearings: A Rhetorical Analysis," *Political Communication* 11 (1994), pp. 287–97.

12. R. Merritt, *Symbols of American Community, 1735–1775* (New Haven: Yale University Press, 1966).

13. R. Anderson, " 'Look At All Those Nouns in a Row': Authoritarianism, Democracy, and the Iconicity of Political Russian," *Political Communication* 13 (1996), pp. 145–64.

14. M. Moore, "From a Government of the People, to a People of the Government: Irony as a Rhetorical Strategy in Presidential Campaigns," *Quarterly Journal of Speech* 82 (1996), pp. 22–37.

15. See R. P. Hart and K. Kendall, "Lyndon Johnson and the Problem of Politics," in M. Medhurst (ed.), *The Future of the Rhetorical Presidency* (College Station: Texas A&M University Press, 1996), pp. 77–103.

16. See G. Woodward, "Prime Ministers and Presidents: A Survey of the Differing Rhetorical Possibilities of High Office," *Communication Quarterly* 27 (1979), pp. 41–49; D. A. Strickland, "On Ambiguity in Political Rhetoric: Defeat of the Rat Control Bill in the House of Representatives, July 1967," *Canadian Journal of Political Science* 2 (1969), pp. 338–44; and R. Asen, "The Incredible Shrinking Safety Net: On the Use of a Political Phrase," Paper presented at the annual meeting of the National Communication Association (San Diego, Calif., November 1996).

17. N. Fraser and L. Gordon, "A Genealogy of *Dependency*: Tracing a Keyword of the U.S. Welfare State," *Signs: A Journal of Women in Culture and Society* 19 (1994), pp. 309–36.

18. R. Williams, *Keywords: A Vocabulary of Culture and Society* (New York: Oxford University Press, 1976), p. 79.

19. D. Rodgers, *Contested Truths: Keywords in American Politics since Independence* (New York: Basic Books, 1987), p. 181.

20. C. M. Condit and J. L. Lucaites, *Crafting Equality: America's Anglo-African Word* (Chicago: University of Chicago Press, 1993).

21. F. Luntz, *The Language of the Twenty-first Century* (Washington, D.C.: Luntz Research Companies, 1997).

22. R. Gozzi, *New Words and a Changing American Culture* (Columbia: University of South Carolina Press, 1990). See, especially, pp. 1–7.

23. This, of course, is Jacques Derrida's famous example, as recounted in B. Honig, "Declarations of Independence: Arendt and Derrida on the Problem of Founding a Republic," *American Political Science Review* 85 (1991), pp. 97–113.

24. H. D. Lasswell and N. Leites, *Language of Politics: Studies in Quantitative Semantics* (New York, G. W. Stewart, 1949), pp. 51–52.

25. T. N. Walters, L. Walters, and R. Gray, "Hobgoblins of Fear: The Syntax, Substance and Imagery of the 1992 Presidential Press Releases," *Southwestern Mass Communication Journal* 12 (1996), pp. 10–21.

26. K. H. Jamieson, "Campaign Mapping Project: Report II" (Philadelphia, Pa.: Annenberg Public Policy Center, 1997).

27. Building a campaign database implies a particular model of politics. Speeches were included because speech-making is the handmaiden of democracy. Even in an age of media, candidates travel for nine months at a clip speaking in high school gymnasiums, proving that even though it is large and complex, the United States is also a nation of localities. Debates were included because debating is a primitive political ritual, a space where the candidates—sans handlers—confront one another on the knottiest issues then facing their fellow citizens. The archive contains media commentary because, since the days of George Washington, the press has been the president's first student and the peo-

ple's most reliable teacher, even though fallible on both counts from time to time. Advertising is nothing if not fallible, but it too was included because ads tell a synecdochic truth when embodying the hyperbolic rhetoric long characteristic of the American polity. And the CMP database reintroduces the vox populi by including letters-to-the-editor. Until now, one has been able to tour the museums in Washington, D.C., without being reminded that governance is followership, as well as leadership. To correct that oversight, the CMP houses the American people speaking in their own language. For greater detail on the textual samples analyzed, see appendix 3.

28. These cities included Fall River, Massachusetts; Utica, New York; Trenton, New Jersey; Roanoke, Virginia; Lake Charles, Louisiana; Wichita Falls, Texas; Springfield, Ohio; St. Joseph, Missouri; Duluth, Minnesota; Provo, Utah; Billings, Montana; and Salinas, California.

29. Some of the remainder of this chapter has been re-crafted from R. P. Hart, "Redeveloping DICTION: Theoretical Considerations" in M. West (ed.), *New Directions in Computer Content Analysis* (New York: Ablex, in press).

30. See especially B. L. Whorf, *Language, Thought, and Reality: Selected Writings,* J. B. Carroll (ed.), (Cambridge, Mass.: MIT Press, 1956).

31. For specifics on this matter see Hart, "Redeveloping DICTION," in press.

32. W. Johnson, *People in Quandaries: The Semantics of Personal Adjustment* (New York: Harper, 1946).

33. More specifically, Insistence is a measure of code restriction and semantic "contentedness," the assumption being that repetition of key terms indicates a preference for a limited, ordered world. In calculating the measure, all words occurring three or more times that function as nouns or noun-derived adjectives are identified (either cybernetically or with the user's assistance) and the following calculation performed: [Number of Eligible Words + Sum of their Occurrences] ÷ 10. Variety conforms to Wendell Johnson's Type-Token Ratio, which divides the number of different words in a passage by the passage's total words. A high score indicates a speaker's avoidance of overstatement and a preference for precise, molecular statements. See ibid.

34. For a more detailed understanding of these and other subsidiary categories, see the DICTION program itself, which has a drop-down utility containing all of the ten thousand search words used in its searches. The demonstration version of the program available from the following Web-site also contains that utility: http://www.scolari.com.

35. J. D. Barber, *The Presidential Character: Predicting Performance in the White House,* 4th ed. (Englewood Cliffs, N.J.: Prentice Hall, 1992).

36. C. E. Osgood, G. J. Suci, and P. Tannenbaum, *The Measurement of Meaning* (Urbana: University of Illinois Press, 1957).

37. Embellishment is a selective ratio of adjectives to verbs based on David Boder's conception that heavy modification "slows down" a verbal passage by de-emphasizing human and material action. Embellishment is calculated according to the following formula: [Praise + Blame +1] ÷ [Present Concern + Past Concern +1]. See D. P. Boder, "The Adjective-Verb Quotient: A Contribution to the Psychology of Language," *Psychological Record* 3 (1940), pp. 310–43.

38. See, for example, J. Dewey, *The Public and Its Problems* (Chicago: Swallow Press, 1954).

39. Complexity is a simple measure of the average number of characters per word in a given input file and borrows Rudolph Flesch's notion that convoluted phrasings make

a text's ideas abstract and its implications unclear. Another subvariable, Familiarity, also contributes positively to the Realism score and consists of a selected number of C.K. Ogden's "operation" words, which he calculates to be the most common words in the English language. Included are common prepositions (*across, over, through*), demonstrative pronouns (*this, that*) and interrogative pronouns (*who, what*), and a variety of particles, conjunctions, and connectives (*a, for, so*). See R. Flesch, *The Art of Plain Talk*, 2d ed. (New York: Harper, 1946) and C. K. Ogden, *Basic English, A General Introduction with Rules and Grammar*, 3d ed.(London: Paul, Trench, Trubner, 1932).

40. R. Bellah et al., *The Good Society* (New York: Knopf, 1991); A. Etzioni, *The Spirit of Community: Rights, Responsibilities, and the Communitarian Agenda* (New York: Crown Publishers, 1993).

41. While using DICTION is comparatively straightforward, it does have its own protocols: (1) all passages must be converted into text-only format to be processed; (2) all texts must be stored in program-defined directories and must carry program-defined extensions; (3) all analyses are based on a 500-word standard—shorter passages are extrapolated to this norm (at the request of the user) and longer passages are broken into 500-word segments automatically; (4) batch processing permits thousands of passages to be run at once, although users can proceed passage by passage as well; (5) after a text is processed, report files are automatically written to file and also sent to the program's main screen for immediate viewing. In addition, the quantitative results are appended to a separate data file for later statistical analysis.

DICTION also makes a modest, statistical accommodation for homographs, words spelled the same but having different meanings (e.g., the word "lead"—a quality of command or a metal found in nature). Benign Homographs are ignored but Confounding Homographs, roughly 10 percent of DICTION's search words, are weighted differentially based on Easton's work. See H. Easton, *Word Frequency Dictionary* (New York: Dover, 1940).

42. R. Wachal, "Humanities and Computers: A Personal View," *North American Review* 8 (1971), p. 31.

43. Perhaps the sanest perspective on these matters is that of Richard Ohmann who argues that if stylistics advances understanding "only a comfortless millimeter or so" by tracking connections between language and epistemology it will have done yeoman's work. Such studies must be regarded as heuristic and not probative, as a way of supplementing qualitative insights, not supplanting them. As Ohmann says: "A heavy dependence on abstraction, a peculiar use of the present tense, a habitual evocation of similarities through parallel structure, a tendency to place feelings in syntactical positions of agency, a trick of underplaying causal words: any of these patterns of expression, *when repeated with unusual frequency*, is the sign of a habit of meaning, and thus a persistent way of sorting out the phenomena of experience." R. Ohmann, "Prolegomenon to the Analysis of Prose Style," in H.C. Martin (ed.), *Style in Prose Fiction* (New York: Columbia University Press, 1959), pp. 13–14, my italics.

44. See C. J. Brainerd and V. F. Reyna, "Memory Independence and Memory Interference in Cognitive Development, *Psychological Review* 100 (1993), pp. 42–67; G. R. Boynton and M. Lodge, "Voters' Images of Candidates," in A. Miller and B. Gronbeck (eds.), *Presidential Campaigns and American Self-Images* (Boulder: Westview, 1994); D. P. Spence, "Lawfulness in Lexical Choice: A Natural Experiment," *Journal of the American Psychoanalytic Association* 28 (1980), p. 116.

45. M. M. Bahktin, *The Dialogic Imagination: Four Essays*, M. Holquist (ed.), C. Emerson (trans.), (Austin: University of Texas Press, 1981), p. 259.

46. For a brief but useful delineation of this concept, see W. Rahn, "Public Mood as Social Emotion," *The Political Psychologist* 3:1 (1998), p. 7–8.

47. N. Enkvist, "On the Place of Style in Some Linguistic Theories," in S. Chatman (ed.), *Literary Style: A Symposium* (New York: Oxford, 1971).

CHAPTER 3

1. J. G. A. Pocock, *Politics, Language, and Time: Essays on Political Thought and History* (New York: Atheneum, 1971), p. 18.

2. R. J. Dalton, *Citizen Politics: Public Opinion and Political Parties in Advanced Western Democracies* (Chatham, N.J.: Chatham House, 1996), p. 182.

3. R. P. Hart, *The Political Pulpit* (Lafayette, Ind.: Purdue University Press, 1977).

4. W. Danielson and N. Lasorsa, "Perceptions of Social Change: One Hundred Years of Front-Page Content in The *New York Times* and The *Los Angeles Times*," in C. W. Roberts (ed.), *Text Analysis for the Social Sciences: Methods for Drawing Inferences from Texts and Manuscripts* (Mahwah, N.J.: Erlbaum, 1997).

5. For a rich reprise of Americanist themes, see R. M. Merelman, *Making Something of Ourselves: On Culture and Politics in the United States* (Berkeley: University of California Press, 1984).

6. C. C. Arnold, "Reflections on American Public Discourse," *Central States Speech Journal* 28 (1977), p. 73–85.

7. This concept is discussed throughout Burke's writings but nowhere more eloquently than in K. Burke, *The Philosophy of Literary Form* (New York: Vintage, 1957).

8. T. Dewey, "New Good Government," Campaign speech delivered in Kansas City, Missouri (14 October 1948).

9. C. J. Greenhouse, *A Moment's Notice: Time Politics across Cultures* (Ithaca: Cornell University Press, 1996), p. 179.

10. Ibid. p. 93.

11. H. Zullow, "American Exceptionalism and the Quadrennial Peak in Optimism," in A. Miller and B. Gronbeck (eds.), *Presidential Campaigns and American Self-Images* (Boulder: Westview, 1994).

12. D. Halberstam, *The Fifties* (New York: Villard, 1993), p. 5.

13. R. W., "It is Truly a Goldwater Crusade!" Letter-to-the-editor in the *Salinas Californian* (28 August 1964), p. 4.

14. J. M., "Powell a Democrat in GOP Clothing," Letter to the editor in the *Salinas Californian* (27 August 1996), p. 4.

15. W. C. McWilliams, *The Politics of Disappointment: American Elections, 1976–94* (Chatham, N.J.: Chatham, 1995), p. 107.

16. "Comments on Perot versus Bush," *CBS Evening News* (20 October 1992).

17. R. Reed, as quoted in "Bush Talks to Christian Coalition," *Austin American-Statesman* (23 April 1997), p. b7.

18. S. Skowronek, *The Politics Presidents Make: Leadership from John Adams to George Bush* (Cambridge: Harvard University Press, 1993), p. 31.

19. R. Dole, Campaign remarks, Grand Rapids, Michigan (2 November 1996).

20. D. Eisenhower, "Eisenhower-Nixon Nationwide TV-Radio Show" (3 November 1952).

21. N. Luttbeg and M. Gant, *American Electoral Behavior, 1952–1992* (Itasca, Ill.: Peacock Publishers, 1995), p. 24.

22. R. Inglehart, "Postmaterial Values and the Erosion of Institutional Authority," in J. S. Nye, P. D. Zelikow, and D. C. King (eds.), *Why People Don't Trust Government* (Cambridge: Harvard University Press, 1997), pp. 233–36.

23. Harry Truman, as quoted in Halberstam, p. 19.

24. R. Lee, "Images of Civic Virtue in the New Political Rhetoric," in A. Miller and B. Gronbeck (eds.), *Presidential Campaigns and American Self-Images* (Boulder, Colo.: Westview, 1994), p. 52–53.

25. "Too Late/Barbara Walters," Republican campaign commercial (21 September 1996).

26. Skowronek, The Politics Presidents Make, pp. 444, 45.

27. H. Humphrey, "For the American Family," Remarks at the Democratic Women's Picnic, Pittsburgh, Pennsylvania (14 September 1968).

28. G. Bush, "Presidential Debate of October 10, 1988," *Historic Documents of 1988–1989* (Washington, D.C.: Congressional Quarterly, 1989), p. 765.

29. Quoted in M. Miller, *Plain Speaking: An Oral Biography of Harry S Truman* (New York: Berkley Medallion, 1973), p. 288.

30. T. Patterson, *Out of Order* (New York: Knopf, 1993). See also R. P. Hart et al., "Rhetorical Features of Newscasts about the President," *Critical Studies in Mass Communication* 1 (1984), pp. 260–86.

31. See, for example, D. Hallin, "Sound Bite News: Television Coverage of Elections, 1968–1988," *Journal of Communication* 42 (1992), p. 5–24.

32. "Bush Near the End: Hope Against the Odds," *Washington Post* (11 November 1992), p. 1.

33. See M. Wattenberg, *The Rise of Candidate-Centered Voting: Presidential Elections of the 1980s* (Cambirdge: Harvard University Press, 1991), pp. 71–80.

34. S. Iyengar, "Framing Responsibility for Political Issues," *Annals* 546 (1996), pp. 59–70.

35. A. Stevenson, "Acceptance Speech," Democratic National Convention, Chicago, Illinois (18 August 1956).

36. W. J. Clinton, "Remarks at Pueblo County Courthouse," Pueblo, Colorado (11 September 1996).

37. J. Turow, *The Breaking-Up of America: Advertisers and the New Media World* (Chicago: University of Chicago Press, 1997).

38. "Clinton Starts, Finishes with the Middle Class; President Refocuses Attention on the Voters He Wooed in '92," *Washington Post* (28 October 1996), p. 1.

39. Skowronek, *The Politics Presidents Make*, pp. 54–55.

40. C. K. Ogden, *The General Basic English Dictionary* (London: Evans Brothers, 1960).

41. R. Gozzi, *New Words and a Changing American Culture* (Columbia: University of South Carolina Press, 1990), pp. 13–25. T. N. Walters and his colleagues found that language such as this heavily populated the press releases of the Clinton-Gore campaign in 1992, perhaps suggesting a now-thorough institutionalization of linguistic complexity in campaign politics. See T. N. Walters, L. M. Walters, and R. Gray, "Hobgoblins of Fear:

The Syntax, Substance, and Imagery of the 1992 Presidential Press Releases," *Southwestern Mass Communication Journal* 12 (1996), pp. 10–21.

42. J. Ellul, *The Political Illusion*, K. Kellen (trans.) (New York: Vintage, 1967), p. 236.

43. For additional information on Perot's supporters and their political attitudes, see P. R. Abramson, J. H. Aldrich, and D. W. Rhode, *Change and Continuity in the 1996 Elections* (Washington, D.C.: Congressional Quarterly Press, 1998), pp. 141–42, 185–88.

44. R. Perot, "Acceptance Speech," National Convention of the Reform Party, Valley Forge, Pennsylvania (18 August 1996).

45. Skowronek, *The Politics Presidents Make*, p. 365.

46. A. Stevenson, "Oklahoma Politicians," Campaign address in Oklahoma City, Oklahoma (24, September 1956).

47. W. J. Clinton, "Kerry-for-Senate Campaign Concert," Campaign address in Boston, Massachusetts (28 September 1996). Italics mine.

48. "George Bush on the Democratic National Convention," *McNeil-Lehrer News Hour*, PBS (22 July 1988).

49. R. Koselleck, *Futures Past: On the Semantics of Historical Time*, K. Tribe (trans.) (Cambridge: MIT Press, 1985), p. 203.

50. J. McGrath and J. Kelly, *Time and Human Interaction: Toward a Social-Psychology of Time* (New York: Guilford, 1986), pp. 61, 77.

51. U. Merry, *Coping with Uncertainty: Insights from the New Science of Chaos, Self-Organization and Complexity* (Westport, Conn.: Praeger, 1995), p. 117.

52. "Dewey Rules Out Munich for Soviets as Way to Peace," *New York Times* (1 October 1948), p. 1.

CHAPTER 4

1. For an excellent set of case studies in this vein, see R. Paine (ed.), *Politically Speaking: Cross-cultural Studies of Rhetoric* (Philadelphia: Institute for the Study of Human Issues, 1981).

2. See M. Lodge and K. McGraw (eds.), *Political Judgment: Structure and Process* (Ann Arbor: University of Michigan Press, 1995).

3. The foremost exponent of this perspective in the United States is political scientist Murray Edelman. See his *Constructing the Political Spectacle* (Chicago: University of Chicago Press, 1988).

4. See, most notably, T. Pangle, *The Ennobling of Democracy: The Challenge of the Postmodern Age* (Baltimore: Johns Hopkins University Press, 1992).

5. The groundbreaking work in this area has been done by Everett Rogers. See his *Diffusion of Innovations*, 4th ed. (New York: Free Press, 1995).

6. M. Smith, "Evolution of Eisenhower as Speaker," *New York Times Magazine* (7 August 1955), p. 18.

7. J. Steinbeck, "Forward," *Speeches of Adlai Stevenson* (New York: Random House, 1952), p. 7.

8. R. H. Ferrell, *The Eisenhower Diaries* (New York: Norton, 1981), p. 298.

9. D. Eisenhower, "Radio Address to the American People on the National Security and Its Costs" (19 May 1953), *Public Papers of the Presidents, Dwight Eisenhower, 1953* (Washington, D.C.: U. S. Government Printing Office, 1954), p. 311.

10. D. Eisenhower, "The People Ask the President," Nationally telecast address (12 October 1956).

11. D. Eisenhower, "Nomination Acceptance Address at the Republican National Convention," San Francisco, California (23 August 1956).

12. G. Bush, "Nomination Acceptance Address, Republican National Convention" (20 August 1992). These results are similar to those of Philip Tetlock who also found that presidents become more complex when in office than when on the campaign trail. Although Tetlock uses a very different set of measures than I do, his results are interesting in light of the strong statistical effect I report here. See P. Tetlock, "Pre- to Post-Election Shifts in Presidential Rhetoric: Impression Management or Cognitive Adjustment?" *Journal of Personality and Social Psychology* 41 (1981), pp. 207–12.

13. G. Bush, "Message to the Congress Transmitting Proposed Legislation to Combat Violent Crime" (15 June 1989), *Public Papers of the Presidents, George Bush, 1989–Vol. 1* (Washington, D.C.: U. S. Government Printing Office, 1990), p. 739. Italics mine.

14. R. L. Holloway, "Taking the Middle Ground: Clinton's Rhetoric of Conjoined Values," in R. Denton (ed.), *The 1996 Presidential Campaign: A Communication Perspective* (Westport, Conn.: Praeger, 1998), p. 138.

15. W. J. Clinton, "Campaign Remarks in Atlanta, Georgia" (25 October 1996).

16. D. Eisenhower, "Address at Bradley University," Peoria, Illinois (25 September 1956).

17. L. Rosenfield, "The Terms of Commonwealth: A Response to Arnold," *Central States Speech Journal* 28 (1977), p. 89.

18. G. Ford, "Address at the University of Hawaii" (7 December 1975), *Public Papers of the Presidents, Gerald Ford, 1975: Vol. 2* (Washington, D.C.: U.S. Government Printing Office, 1976), p. 1952.

19. G. Ford, "Address on the Mutual Radio Network" (2 November 1976).

20. For more on this topic, see J. D. Trent and J. S. Trent, "The Incumbent and His Challengers: The Problem of Adapting to Prevailing Conditions," in K. Kendall (ed.), *Presidential Campaign Discourse: Strategic Communication* (Albany: State University of New York Press, 1995).

21. R. Dole, "Speech at the Economic Club of Detroit," Detroit, Michigan (24 September 1996).

22. Ibid.

23. R. Dole, "Campaign Remarks in Riverside, California" (17 October 1996).

24. R. Dole, "Campaign Remarks in Jackson, Michigan" (21 October 1996).

25. W. J. Clinton, "Campaign Remarks in Portland, Oregon" (7 October 1996).

26. W. J. Clinton, "Acceptance Speech at the Democratic National Convention," Chicago, Illinois (29 August 1996).

27. W. J. Clinton, "Campaign Remarks in Miami, Florida" (22 October 1996).

28. W. J. Clinton, "First Televised Presidential Debate," St. Louis, Missouri (11 October 1992).

29. W. J. Clinton, "Second Televised Debate," San Diego, California (16 October 1996).

30. For additional information, see H. L. Schantz, "The Presidential Selections Process," in H. L. Schantz (ed.), *American Presidential Elections: Process, Policy, and Political Change* (Albany: State University of New York Press, 1996), pp. 41ff.

31. A useful reference book in this regard is H. W. Stanley and R. G. Niemi, *Vital Statistics on American Politics, 1997–1998* (Washington, D.C.: Congressional Quarterly Inc., 1998). See especially chapters 1 through 4.

32. G. Bush, "Third Televised Debate," East Lansing, Michigan (19 October 1992).

33. M. Wattenberg, *The Rise of Candidate-Centered Voting: Presidential Elections of the 1980s* (Cambridge: Harvard University Press, 1991), p. 150.

34. J. Carter, "Remarks at a Campaign Rally in Portland, Oregon" (27 September 1976). A factual addendum to these results: Of the ten presidents studied here, Jimmy Carter proved to be second highest on Optimism when his noncampaign speeches were examined. George Bush, curiously enough, was most optimistic. When the campaign remarks of incumbents were examined, Carter was again second highest on Optimism, bested this time only by Dwight Eisenhower. Thus, no matter how the data are parsed, Jimmy Carter was never the sepulchral character described in popular lore.

35. J. Schlesinger, "The Governor's Place in American Politics," in T. Beyle and J. O. Williams (eds.), *The American Governor in Behavioral Perspective* (New York: Harper, 1972).

36. L. Harris, "Why the Odds Are Against a Governor's Becoming President," *Public Opinion Quarterly* 23 (1959), pp. 363, 369–70, 366.

37. Ibid., p. 362.

38. As quoted in P. Anderson, *Electing Jimmy Carter: The Campaign of 1976* (Baton Rouge: Louisiana State University Press, 1994), p. 39.

39. J. Carter, "Remarks at a Campaign Rally in Dallas, Texas" (24 September 1976).

40. W. J. Clinton, "Remarks at a Campaign Rally at the Detroit Airport," Romulus, Michigan (2 November 1992). Italics mine.

41. W. J. Clinton, "Address to the People of South Philadelphia," Philadelphia, Pennsylvania (12 October 1992). Italics mine.

42. W. J. Clinton, "Address at the Sangre de Cristo Arts Center," Pueblo, Colorado (21 October 1992). Italics mine.

43. W. J. Clinton, "Remarks at the Clayton County Office of Family and Children's Services," Jonesboro, Georgia (9 September 1992). Italics mine.

44. As quoted in Anderson, *Electing Jimmy Carter*, p. 126.

45. An anecdote to this effect is reported by Carl Tubbesing who reports on how President Clinton used his background as governor in his dealings with state legislators. Describing one meeting in the White House, Tubbesing reports: "Main Speaker John Martin captured the feeling: 'We were in the East Wing. He knew us, called us by name. We felt welcome.' Ohio Senate President Stan Aronoff focused in the President's message: 'We had been screaming about unfunded mandates for years. The President was saying he understood; he was with us; he'd do something to help us.' " See C. Tubbesing, "As the Twig Is Bent: President Bill Clinton Has a State Governor's Experience," *State Legislatures* 19:10 (1993), p. 24.

46. E. Black, "Gettysburg and Silence," *Quarterly Journal of Speech* 80 (1994), pp. 21–22.

47. See S. Hess, " 'Why Great Men Are Not Chosen Presidents': Lord Bryce Revisited," in A. J. Reichley (ed.), *Elections American Style* (Washington, D.C.: Brookings, 1987).

48. See Ibid. p. 78, for this discussion of Bryce's thesis.

49. As quoted in G. Bigelow, "Distinguishing Rhetoric from Poetic Discourse," *Southern Communication Journal* 19 (1953), p. 86.

50. W. Wordsworth, "Lyrical Ballads," in T. Hutchinson (ed.), *The Poetical Works of William Wordsworth* (London: Oxford University Press, 1933), p. 937.

51. Bigelow, *Distinguishing Rhetoric*, p. 89.

52. D. Crystal and D. Davy, *Investigating English Style* (Bloomington: Indiana University Press, 1969), p. 10.

53. R. Barthes, "Style and Its Image," in S. Chatman (ed.), *Literary Style: A Symposium* (London: Oxford University Press, 1971), p. 4.

54. J. Greenfield, *The Real Campaign: How the Media Missed the Story of the 1980 Campaign* (New York: Summit Books, 1982), p. 15.

55. R. Reagan, "Acceptance Speech at the Republican National Convention," Detroit, Michigan (17 July 1980).

56. Ibid.

57. McGovern, of course, is an interesting case here since he is so often remembered as the "radical" alternative to Richard Nixon in 1972. But ideology is not language, and George McGovern's midwestern, ministerial style consistently overrode his philosophical biases. Besides, the general campaign is not the primary, and more than one author has documented McGovern's slide to the middle after he secured the Democratic nomination. See, for example, B. Greene, *Running* (Chicago, Regnery, 1973).

58. R. Perot, "Televised Address on Balancing the Budget and Reforming Government" (16 October 1992).

59. C. Smith, "The Rhetorical Transformation of Political Coalitions: Bill Clinton, 1992–1996," in B. Denton (ed.), *The 1996 Presidential Campaign: A Communication Perspective* (Westport, Conn.: Praeger, 1998), p. 256.

60. A. H. Miller, M. P. Wattenberg, and O. Malahchuk, "Schematic Assessments of Presidential Candidates," *American Political Science Review* 80 (1986), p. 536.

61. M. Burgoon, "Language Expectancy Theory: Elaboration, Explication, and Extension," in C. Berger and M. Burgoon (eds.), *Communication and Social Influence Processes* (East Lansing: Michigan State University Press, 1995), p. 77.

62. See J. A. Herstein, "Keeping the Voter's Limits in Mind: A Cognitive Process Analysis of Decision-Making in Voting," *Journal of Personality and Social Psychology* 40 (1981), pp. 843–61.

63. S. T. Fiske, "Attention and Weight in Person Perception: The Impact of Negative and Extreme Behavior," *Journal of Personality and Social Psychology* 38 (1980), pp. 889–906.

64. A. King, "The Vulnerable American Politician," Paper presented at the annual convention of the American Political Science Association, Chicago, Illinois (31 August 1994), p. 17.

CHAPTER 5

1. F. Roosevelt, "Speech at the Democratic National Convention" (1 July 1932), *New York Times* (2 July 1932), p. A7.

2. See A. Schlesinger, "When Convention Speeches Soared," *New York Times* (21 August 1996), p. A17.

3. B. Gronbeck, "The Presidential Campaign Dramas of 1984," *Presidential Studies Quarterly* 15 (1985), pp. 386–93.

4. For more on this matter see T. Holbrook, *Do Campaigns Matter?* (Thousand Oaks, Calif.: Sage Publications, 1996), pp. 78–79.

5. S. Wilentz, "Here We Go Again," *New Republic* (19 August 1996), p. 23.

6. Judging by the existing scholarly literature, comparatively little is known about political conventions. The most authoritative work is that of Byron Shafer who has traced the institutional changes undergone by the parties during the past hundred years, although he has little to say about communication matters. Joanne Morreale, in contrast, focuses insightfully on convention campaign films but largely disregards how institutional forces shape these productions. Traditional campaign histories largely gloss over the acceptance addresses (and all other rhetorical aspects of conventions); other histories of the political convention are largely anecdotal. More common are case studies of individual convention speeches, studies that have traced the impact of ideology, aesthetics, narrative, myth, and mediation on the convention address. See in particular B. Shafer, *Bifurcated Politics: Evolution and Reform in the National Party Convention* (Cambridge: Harvard University Press, 1988); J. Morreale, *The Presidential Campaign Film: A Critical History* (Westport, Conn.: Praeger, 1993); S. Wayne, *Road to the White House: The Politics of Presidential Elections* (New York: St. Martin's Press, 1988); J. Sandman, "Winning the Presidency: The Vision and Values Approach," *Presidential Studies Quarterly* 19 (1989), pp. 259–66; L. D. Smith and D. Nimmo, *Cordial Concurrence: Orchestrating National Party Conventions in the Telepolitical Age* (New York: Praeger, 1991); W. Lewis, "Telling America's Story: Narrative Form and the Reagan Presidency," *Quarterly Journal of Speech* 73 (1987), pp. 280–302; and W. Fisher, "Reaffirmation and Subversion of the American Dream," *Quarterly Journal of Speech* 59 (1973), pp. 160–67.

7. K. Jamieson, "Generic Constraints and the Rhetorical Situation," *Philosophy and Rhetoric* 6 (1973), pp. 162–70.

8. For more on rhetorical hybrids, see K. Jamieson and K. Campbell, "Rhetorical Hybrids: Fusions of Generic Elements," *Quarterly Journal of Speech* 68 (1982), pp. 146–57.

9. W. J. Clinton, "Acceptance Address at the 1996 Democratic National Convention" (30 August 1996), Chicago, Illinois, Associated Press Wire Reports. All subsequent extracts from Clinton's 1996 acceptance speech have been taken from this source. Italics mine.

10. R. J. Dole, "Acceptance Speech at the Republican National Convention" (15 August 1996), San Diego, California, Associated Press Wire Reports. All subsequent extracts from Dole's 1996 acceptance speech have been taken from this source. Italics mine.

11. For more on this concept, see R. Merelman, *Making Something of Ourselves: On Culture and Politics in the United States* (Berkeley: University of California Press, 1984).

12. For more on this concept, see K. Burke, *Rhetoric of Motives* (Berkeley: University of California Press, 1969).

13. M. Wattenberg, *The Decline of American Political Parties: 1952–1992* (Cambridge: Harvard University Press, 1994).

14. For more on how the mass media affect current political conventions, see L. Sabato, "The Conventions: One Festival of Hope, One Celebration of Impending Victory," in L. J. Sabato (ed.), *Toward the Millennium: The Elections of 1996* (Boston : Allyn and Bacon, 1997), pp. 117–18.

15. L. Sigelman, "Presidential Inaugurals: The Modernization of a Genre," *Political Communication* 13 (1996), p. 81–92.

16. J. F. Kennedy, "Acceptance Speech at the 1960 Democratic National Convention," (15 July 1960), Los Angeles, California.

17. An interesting addendum to my analysis is that by Amy Pierce who has investigated the use of "personal style" in acceptance addresses. See A. J. Pierce, "Personal Style in Presidential Nomination Acceptance Speeches: 1932–1992," Paper presented at the annual convention of the National Communication Association, San Diego, California (November 1996).

18. R. Dearin, "The American Dream as Depicted in Robert J. Dole's 1996 Presidential Nomination Acceptance Speech," *Presidential Studies Quarterly* 27 (1997), pp. 698–713.

19. E. Katz and J. J. Feldman, "The Debates in Light of Research: A Survey of Surveys," in S. Kraus, (ed.) *The Great Debates: Kennedy versus Nixon, 1960* (Bloomington: Indiana University Press, 1977).

20. H. W. Stanley and R. G. Niemi, *Vital Statistics on American Politics: 1997–1998* (Washington, D.C.: Congressional Quarterly Press, 1998), p. 187. See also J. Trent and R. Friedenberg, *Political Campaign Communication: Principles and Practices*, 2d ed. (New York: Praeger, 1991).

21. S. Hellweg, M. Pfau, and S. R. Brydon, *Televised Presidential Debates: Advocacy in Contemporary America* (New York: Praeger, 1992).

22. "Debate: Lowest Ratings Ever Recorded" (18 October 1996), *The Hotline* (on NEXUS).

23. See, for example, S. J. Drucker and J. P. Hunold, "The Debating Game," *Critical Studies in Mass Communication* 4 (1987), pp. 202–07; L. Bitzer and T. Rueter, *Carter versus Ford: The Counterfeit Debates of 1976* (Madison: University of Wisconsin Press, 1980); and A. Ranney, (ed.), *The Past and Future of Presidential Debates* (Washington D.C.: American Enterprise for Public Policy Research, 1979).

24. R. K. Tiemens, S. A. Hellweg, P. Kipper, and S. A. Phillips, "An Integrative Verbal and Visual Analysis of the Carter-Reagan Debate," *Communication Quarterly* 33 (1985), pp. 34–42.

25. A. Schroeder, "Watching Between the Lines: Presidential Debates as Television," *Harvard International Journal of Press and Politics* 1 (1996), p. 73.

26. N. Ornstein, "Non-Presidential Debates," in J. Swerdlow (ed.), *Presidential Debates and Beyond* (Washington, D.C.: Congressional Quarterly Press, 1988).

27. M. Pfau and J. G. Kang, "The Impact of Relational Messages on Candidate Influence in Televised Political Debates," *Communication Studies* 42 (1991), pp. 114–28. See also D. P. Glass, "Evaluating Presidential Candidates: Who Focuses on Their Personal Attributes?" *Public Opinion Quarterly* 49 (1985), pp. 517–34.

28. D. Owen, "The Debate Challenge: Candidate Strategies in the New Media Age," in K. Kendall (ed.), *Presidential Campaign Discourse: Strategic Communication Problems* (Albany: State University of New York Press, 1995). See also M. H. Davis, "Voting Intentions and the 1980 Carter-Reagan Debate," *Journal of Applied Social Psychology* 12 (1982), pp. 481–92.

29. D. P. Carlin, C. Howard, S. Stanfield, and L. Reynolds, "The Effects of Presidential Debate Formats on Clash: A Comparative Analysis," *Argumentation and Advocacy* 27 (1991), pp. 126–37.

30. One important exception is the work by David Levasseur and Kevin Dean. See their article "The Use of Evidence in Presidential Debates: A Study of Evidence Levels and Types from 1960 to 1988," *Argumentation and Advocacy* 32 (1996), pp. 129–42.

31. R. J. Dole, "Second Presidential Debate" (16 October 1996), San Diego, California. All subsequent extracts from Dole's remarks during the 1996 second presidential debate have been taken from this source.

32. R. J. Dole, "Campaign Remarks in Riverside, California" (17 October 1996).

33. W. J. Clinton, "Campaign Address in Washington, D.C." (19 October 1996).

34. W. J. Clinton, "First Presidential Debate" (6 October 1996), Hartford, Connecticut.

35. R. J. Dole, "Campaign Address at Villanova University" (16 September 1996), Philadelphia, Pennsylvania.

36. E. A. Hinck, *Enacting the Presidency: Political Argument, Presidential Debates, and Presidential Character* (Westport, Conn.: Praeger, 1993), p. 230.

37. While debates are still considerably higher on Insistence than other campaign forums, they have slipped in this regard in the last twenty years. Mean Insistence for 1948–60 was 84.8; for 1964–76 it was 81.8; but for 1980–96 it was only 56.8.

38. K. H. Jamieson and D. Birdsell, *Presidential Debates: The Challenge of Creating an Informed Electorate* (New York: Oxford University Press, 1988).

39. For more on this premise, see M. Natanson and H. Johnstone, *Philosophy, Rhetoric and Argumentation* (University Park, Pennsylvania State University Press, 1965).

40. W. J. Clinton, "Third Presidential Debate" (19 October 1992), San Diego, California.

41. Along these same lines, Grant Cos and Liliana Rossman have argued that Bill Clinton exhibited a much higher concern for "cosmopolitanism" during the 1996 debates, while Bob Dole showed a greater amount of "ethnocentricity." See their "Articulating Civic Virtue in the Second 1996 Presidential Debate," *American Behavioral Scientist* 40 (1997), pp. 1123–32.

42. Perhaps it is these characteristics that generally increase the public's appreciation of presidential candidates after they participate in debates. For more on this effect, see L. Bartels, "Campaign Quality: Standards for Evaluation, Benchmarks for Reform," Paper presented at the annual meeting of the American Political Science Association, Washington, D.C. (August 1997), pp. 54–56.

43. The classic statement of these concerns was provided by Vance Packard in *The Hidden Persuaders*, rev. ed. (New York: Pocket Books, 1980).

44. For more on the financing of political advertising, see P. Devlin, "Contrasts in Presidential Campaign Commercials of 1996," *American Behavioral Scientist* 40 (1997), pp. 1058–84.

45. L. Kaid, R. Gobetz et al., "Television News and Presidential Campaigns: The Legitimization of Televised Political Advertising," *Social Science Quarterly* 74 (1993), pp. 274–85. An extension of this argument has been offered by Marilyn Roberts and Maxwell McCombs who observe that political advertising now often sets the very agenda of political coverage. See their "Agenda Setting and Political Advertising: Origins of the News Agenda," *Political Communication* 11 (1994), pp. 249–62.

46. This is the claim of Stephen Ansolabehere and Shanto Iyengar in *Going Negative* (New York: Free press, 1995), although it has been challenged on several fronts. See, for example, S. E. Finkel and J. Geer, "A Spot Check: Casting Doubt on the Demobilizing

Effect of Attack Advertising," *American Journal of Political Science* 42 (1998), pp. 575–95.

47. For more on this train of thought, see K. H. Jamieson, *Dirty Politics: Deception, Distraction and Democracy* (New York: Oxford University Press, 1992).

48. These findings regarding the dwindling advertisement are corroborated by Montague Kern in *Thirty-Second Politics: Political Advertising in the Eighties* (New York: Praeger, 1989).

49. One of the most ambitious studies in this regard is that by Marian Just and her colleagues: *Crosstalk: Citizens, Candidates, and the Media in a Presidential Campaign* (Chicago: University of Chicago Press, 1996).

50. For more on this topic, see P. Messaris, *Visual Persuasion: The Role of Images in Advertising* (Thousand Oaks, Calif.: Sage Publications, 1997).

51. "Roosevelt Room," Televised Commercial for Ronald Reagan, 1984 Presidential Campaign, sixty-seven words.

52. "Nixon Prestige," Televised Commercial for John Kennedy, 1960 Presidential Campaign, fifty-nine words.

53. "Packaging Bush/Noriega," Televised Commercial for Michael Dukakis, 1988 Presidential Campaign, ninety-six words.

54. "South Carolina," Televised Commercial for Jimmy Carter, 1980 Presidential Campaign, eighty-six words.

55. R. Williams, *Keywords: A Vocabulary of Culture and Society* (New York: Oxford University Press, 1976).

56. "Anti Dole/Gingrich," Televised Commercial for Bill Clinton, 1996 Presidential Campaign, seventy-five words. Italics mine.

57. "Them," Televised Commercial for Bill Clinton, 1996 Presidential Campaign, seventy-four words. Italics mine.

58. "Real Bob Dole," Televised Commercial for Bill Clinton, 1996 Presidential Campaign, ninety-six words.

59. "One Unknown Dictator Away," Televised Commercial for George Bush, 1992 Presidential Campaign, seventy-two words.

60. "Eliminating Nuclear Weapons," Televised Commercial for George Bush, 1988 Presidential Campaign, seventy-nine words.

61. For a summary of negative advertising's effects, see Finkel and Geer, A *Spot Check*, 1998.

62. See S. Ansolabehere and S. Iyengar, "Winning through Advertising: It's All in the Context," in J. Thurber and C. Nelson (eds.), *Campaigns and Elections: American Style* (Boulder, Colo.: Westview, 1995).

63. L. Kaid, "Videostyle in the 1996 Presidential Advertising," Paper presented at the annual meeting of the National Communication Association, San, Diego, California (November 1996).

64. D. West, *Air Wars: Television Advertising in Election Campaigns, 1952–1996*, 2d ed. (Washington, D.C.: Congressional Quarterly Press, 1997).

65. K. H. Jamieson, P. Waldman, and S. Sheer, "Eliminate the Negative? Defining and Refining Categories of Analysis for Political Advertising," Unpublished manuscript, Annenberg School for Communication, University of Pennsylvania (1998).

66. K. S. Johnson-Cartee and G. A. Copeland, *Manipulation of the American Voter: Political Campaign Commercials* (Westport, Conn.: Praeger, 1997), p. 1.

67. B. Gronbeck, "Negative Political Ads and American Self-Images," in A. Miller and B. Gronbeck (eds.), *Presidential Campaigns and American Self-Images* (Boulder, Colo.: Westview Press, 1994), p. 76.

68. K. Goldstein, "Political Advertising and Political Persuasion in the 1996 Presidential Campaign," Paper presented at the annual meeting of the American Political Science Association, Washington, D.C. (August 1997).

69. Jamieson, Waldman, and Sherr, *Eliminate the Negative?* 1998, p. 17.

70. "League of Women Voters," Televised Commercial for Ronald Reagan, 1980 Presidential Campaign, eighty-seven words.

71. For more on this matter, see D. E. Procter and W. Schenck-Hamlin, "Forms and Variations in Negative Political Advertising," *Communication Research Reports* 13 (1996), p. 152.

72. "Street Cool," Televised Commercial for Jimmy Carter, 1980 Presidential Campaign, one hundred words.

CHAPTER 6

1. Quoted in C. Schorske, *Fin de Siecle Vienna: Politics and Culture* (New York: Knopf/ Random House, 1979), p. 181.

2. R. Perot, "Speech to the Commonwealth Club," San Francisco, California (18 September 1996). Italics mine.

3. R. Perot, "Remarks on CNN's *Inside Politics*" (30 October 1996). Italics mine.

4. M. Wattenberg, *The Rise of Candidate-Centered Voting: Presidential Elections of the 1980s* (Cambridge: Harvard University Press, 1991), p. 150.

5. See, for example, R. Lichter and T. Smith, "Why Elections Are Bad News: Media and Candidate Discourse in the 1996 Presidential Primaries," *Harvard International Journal of Press and Politics* 1 (1996), pp. 15–35, and B. Buchanan, *Renewing Presidential Politics: Campaigns, Media, and the Public Interest* (Lanham, Md.: Rowman and Littlefield, 1996), pp. 136, 146, 150–51.

6. "Perot's Remote Encounters of the Third Party Kind," *Washington Post* (9 September 1996), p. 4.

7. R. Weaver, *The Ethics of Rhetoric* (Chicago: Henry Regnery Co., 1965), pp. 182–83.

8. R. Reagan, "Commitment '80," As prepared for national broadcast (13 September 1980).

9. A. Bierce, *The Devil's Dictionary* (New York: Hill and Wang, 1957), p. 143.

10. For more on the "amalgamating" function of politics, see R. P. Hart, "The Functions of Human Communication in the Maintenance of Public Values," in C. Arnold and J. Bowers (eds.), *Handbook of Rhetorical and Communication Theory* (Boston: Allyn and Bacon, 1984), pp. 749–91.

11. On a more academic note, Eugene Miller has observed that political theorists have done an insufficient job of examining the interface between empirical action (sensory awareness) and the first principles of political thought. See his "What Does 'Political' Mean?" *Review of Politics* 42 (1980), pp. 56–72.

12. S. Wolin, "Postmodern Politics and the Absence of Myth," *Social Research* 52 (1985), p. 224.

13. "Dole to Clinton: Stop Medicare Scare Ads; GOP Plan Will Save Program, He Asserts," *Chicago Tribune* (27 September 1996), p. 12.

14. R. Dole, "Remarks by Republican Presidential Nominee," Grand Rapids, Michigan (2 November 1996).

15. G. Bruns, "Language and Power," *Chicago Review* 34 (1984), pp. 27–48.

16. G. Orren, "Fall from Grace: The Public's Loss of Faith in Government," in J. Nye, P. Zelikow, and D. C. King (eds.), *Why People Don't Trust Government* (Cambridge: Harvard University Press, 1997), p. 101.

17. The first book is by E. J. Dionne, *Why Americans Hate Politics* (New York: Simon & Schuster, 1991) and the second by James Fallows, *Breaking the News: How the Media Undermine American Democracy* (New York: Pantheon Books, 1996).

18. "Joey," as quoted in M. Huspek and K. Kendall, "On Withholding Political Voice: An Analysis of the Political Vocabulary of a 'Nonpolitical' Speech Community," *Quarterly Journal of Speech* 77 (1991), p. 8. Original vernacular modified here.

19. The comparison samples can be described as follows: (1) *Corporate Advocacy* (n = 163). A broad-based collection of official mission statements, public pronouncements, and CEO speeches in behalf of major American corporations from the 1960s through the mid-1990s. Includes manufacturing companies (e.g., Boise-Cascade), mining and construction (e.g., Flour Daniel), transportation and telecommunications (e.g., AT&T), as well as, financial and service-based industries (e.g., Federated Department stores, H&R Block, etc.). (2) *Religious Preachment* (n = 198). Sermons delivered by a wide variety of denominational representatives in the United States between 1935 and 1996. Topics include biblical exegesis, doctrinal disputes, ritualistic remembrances, and general moral and social discussions. Mainline denominations (Episcopalians, Catholics, Methodists) as well as an assortment of cults and sects are represented. (3) *Social Protest* (n = 129). Addresses delivered to marginalized as well as mainstream groups about pressing social matters. Included are speeches by Malcolm X, Andrea Dworkin, Ralph Nader, Paul Ehrlich, etc. Topics include feminism, environmentalism, civil rights, labor grievances, nuclear disarmament, etc.

20. W. J. Clinton, "Campaign Remarks in Kennedy Park," Fall River, Massachusetts (28 September 1996).

21. Amdahl Corporation, "Mission Statement," in J. W. Graham and W. C. Havlick (eds.), *Mission Statements: A Guide to the Corporate and Nonprofit Sectors* (New York: Garland, 1994), pp. 40–41.

22. M. E. Wade, "The Lantern of Ethics," Speech delivered at the University of Georgia, Athens, Ga. (15 November 1987), *Vital Speeches of the Day* 54 (1987), p. 342.

23. R. Dole, "Remarks to the Electronic Industries Association National Convention in California" (15 October 1996).

24. R. Perot, "Address to the Commonwealth Club," San Francisco, California (18 September 1996).

25. M. Oakeshott, *The Politics of Faith and the Politics of Scepticism* (New Haven: Yale, 1996), pp. 15, 132–33.

26. Ibid., pp. 23, 24.

27. Ibid., pp. 31, 34, 81.

28. Ibid., pp. 91, 128, 91.

29. Oakeshott, p. 124.

30. J. Dennis and D. Owen, "Dimensions of Antipartyism in the United States," Paper presented at the annual meeting of the Midwest Political Science Association, Chicago, Illinois (April 1997), p. 4.

31. M. Wattenberg, *The Decline of American Political Parties, 1952–1988* (Cambridge: Harvard University Press, 1990).

32. M. P. Fiorina, *Divided Government* (New York: Macmillan, 1992).

33. T. Lowi, *The Personal President: Power Invested, Promise Unfulfilled* (Ithaca: Cornell University Press, 1985).

34. N. R. Luttbeg and M. M. Gant, *American Election Behavior, 1951–1992* (Itasca, Ill.: Peacock Publishers, 1995).

35. For more on this topic, see J. Aldrich, *Why Parties? The Origin and Transformation of Party Politics in America* (Chicago: University of Chicago Press, 1995).

36. For more on these matters, see Luttbeg and Gant, *American Election Behavior*, pp. 48–59.

37. R. Dalton, "Parties without Partisans: The Decline of Party Identifications among Democratic Publics," Paper presented at the annual meeting of the Midwest Political Science Association, Chicago, Illinois (April 1998).

38. R. P. Hart, *Seducing America: How Television Charms the Modern Voter* (New York: Oxford University Press) p. 194.

39. R. Putnam, "Bowling Alone: America's Declining Social Capital," *Journal of Democracy* 6 (1995), pp. 65–79.

40. S. Blinder, "Television and the Decline in Political Partisanship," Paper presented at the annual meeting of the Midwest Political Science Association, Chicago, Illinois (April 1997).

41. For more on this issue, see M. J. Wattenberg, *The Rise of Candidate-Centered Politics: Presidential Elections of the 1980s* (Cambridge: Harvard University Press, 1991) and M. Levine, *Presidential Campaigns and Elections: Issues and Images in the Media Age* (Itasca, Ill.: Peacock, 1995). My own data on this matter are somewhat more heartening. While I also find that stories containing fifteen or more Leader References (n = 2,924) made significantly fewer Party References between 1948 ($\bar{x}$ = 3.697) and 1984 ($\bar{x}$ = 1.907), a sharp uptick in Party References was noted in 1988 ($\bar{x}$ = 3.251). The news stories in 1992 and 1996 slipped back a bit but not precipitously so.

42. G. Pomper, *Passions and Interests: Political Party Concepts of American Democracy* (Lawrence: University Press of Kansas, 1992).

43. See also D. Palazzolo and S. Theriault, "Candidate Announcement Addresses: Campaign Strategies and Voting Behavior," *Presidential Studies Quarterly*, (1996), pp. 350–63.

44. M. Hagen, "Candidate-Centered Politics and the Focus of Attention in Presidential Elections," Paper presented at the annual meeting of the Midwest Political Science Association, Chicago, Illinois (April 1997).

45. J. Zaller, "The Politics of Substance," Paper presented at the Annenberg Public Policy Center's Conference on New Media, Washington, D.C. (May 1998). Other researchers have shown that for non–African American northerners, there has been virtually no decline in party loyalty over the years. See W. E. Miller and J. M. Shanks, *The New American Voter* (Cambridge: Harvard University Press, 1996), pp. 495–97.

46. P. Abramson, J. Aldrich and D. Rohde, *Change and Continuity in the 1996 Elections* (Washington, D.C.: Congressional Quarterly Press, 1998). Michael Dimock argues that when a decline in party identification is isolated, it is likely to be found among the least knowledgeable voters, thereby suggesting that the parties' problems may be communicative, not ideological, in nature. See his "Political Knowledge and the Decline of 'Party in

the Electorate,' 1960–1996." Paper presented at the annual meeting of the American Political Science Association, Washington, D.C. (August 1997).

47. J. A. Schlesinger, "The New American Political Party," *American Political Science
Review* 79 (1985), pp. 1152–69; D. W. Rohde, *Parties and Leaders in the Post-Reform House*
(Chicago: University of Chicago Press, 1991).

48. N. Polsby, *Consequences of Party Reform* (Oxford: Oxford University Press, 1983),
pp. 182–83.

49. Ibid., pp. 83, 57.

50. Ibid., p. 83.

51. G. McGovern, "Campaign speech in St. Louis, Missouri" (5 November 1972).

52. W. C. McWilliams, *The Politics of Disappointment: American Elections, 1996–94*
(Chatham, N.J.: Chatham Publishers, 1995), p. 136.

53. Weaver, pp. 86, 87, 112.

54. T. Dewey, "Remarks in Madison Square Garden about What's Good for the Country," New York (31 October 1948).

55. Joanne Morreale, "American Self-Images and the Presidential Campaign Film,
1964–1992," in A. H. Miller and B. E. Gronbeck (eds.), *Presidential Campaigns and American Self-Images* (Boulder, Colo.: Westview, 1994), p. 38.

56. After all language scores were standardized, the paradigm styles were assembled
in the following manner: (1) *Democratic Style* = Commonality + Collectives + Leader
References + Voter References + Party References + 20; (2) *Republican Style* = Inspiration
+ Liberation + Patriotism + Religious References + Praise + 20.

57. A. Downs, *An Economic Theory of Democracy* (New York, Harper, 1957).

58. For more on these matters, see Wattenberg, *The Decline of American Political Parties*, B. E. Keith et al., *The Myth of the Independent Voter* (Berkeley: University of California
Press, 1992); and A. Campbell et al., *The American Voter* (New York, Wiley, 1960).

59. R. Perot, "Remarks at the National Press Club," Washington, D.C. (24 October
1996).

60. Pomper, *Passions and Interests*, p. 110.

61. As quoted in G. Collins (ed.), "A Couple of Kingmakers Talking Shop," *New York
Times Magazine* (11 January 1998), p. 27.

62. Dionne, *Why Americans Hate Politics*, p. 345.

CHAPTER 7

1. For a broad set of reflections on the media and mass culture, see M. Schudson, *The
Power of News* (Cambridge: Harvard University Press, 1995).

2. The best commentary of this sort is the pioneering work of Gaye Tuchman. See her
Making News: A Study in the Construction of Reality (New York: Free Press, 1978).

3. Hall's critiques of news production are spread throughout his writing, but a pungent
version appears in *The Hard Road to Renewal: Thatcherism and the Crisis of the Left* (London, New York: Verso, 1988).

4. For an analysis of these issues, see W. J. Thorn and M. P. Pfeil, *Newspaper Circulation:
Marketing the News* (New York: Longman, 1987).

5. For greater detail on this matter, see H. W. Stanley and R. G. Niemi, *Vital Statistics
on American Politics, 1997–1998* (Washington, D.C.: Congressional Quarterly Press,
1998), p. 165.

6. B. Sparrow, *Uncertain Guardians: The News Media as a Political Institution* (Baltimore: Johns Hopkins University Press, 1999), pp. 101–02.

7. Pew Research Center for the People and the Press, "Press Unfair, Inaccurate, and Pushy," <http://www.people-press.org/content.htm>, March 21, 1997.

8. M. Kerbel, "Covering the Coverage: The Self-Referential Nature of Television Reporting of the 1992 Presidential Campaign," Paper presented at the annual meeting of the Midwest Political Science Association, Chicago, Illinois (April 1994), p. A1.

9. J. R. Hibbing and E. Theiss-Morse, "The Media's Role in Public Negativity toward Congress: Distinguishing Emotional Reactions and Cognitive Evaluations," *American Journal of Political Science* 42 (1998), pp. 475–98.

10. R. Noyes, S. R. Lichter, and D. Amundson, "Was TV Election News Better This Time? A Content Analysis of 1988 and 1992 Campaign Coverage," *Journal of Political Science* 21 (1993), pp. 3–25.

11. S. J. Farnsworth, "Media Use and Political Support: The Implications for Political Participation," A paper presented at the annual meeting of the Midwest Political Science Association, Chicago, Illinois (April 1997).

12. V. Price and E. J. Czilli, "Modeling Patterns of News Recognition and Recall," *Journal of Communication* 46:2 (1996), pp. 55–78.

13. S. Ansolabehere, R. Behr, and S. Iyngear, "Mass Media and Elections: An Overview," *American Politics Quarterly* 19 (1991), pp. 101–39.

14. L. Bartels, "Message Received: The Political Impact of Media Exposure," *American Political Science Review* 87 (1993), pp. 267–85.

15. A. C., "There Seems to Be Conspiracy in Media," *Roanoke Times and World-News* (3 September 1992), p. 14.

16. R. Lichter and T. Smith, "Why Elections Are Bad News: Media and Candidate Discourse in the 1996 Presidential Primaries," *Harvard International Journal of Press and Politics* 1 (1996), pp. 15–35.

17. "Supporter Ousted," *New York Times* (9 September 1988), p. 1.

18. T. Luke, "Culture and Politics in the Age of Artificial Negativity," *Telos* 35 (1978), pp. 55–72.

19. "Clinton Has Edge in 3 Polls; But Figures Vary Widely," AP-UPI Wire Story (30 October 1992), LEXIS/NEXIS [database online], NEWS [Wire stories] available from LEXIS 2000, Mead Data Central, Inc., 1997.

20. "Bush Makes Up Ground," *Los Angeles Times* (16 September 1988), p. H17.

21. "The 1992 Campaign; Clinton Poll Lead Narrows," *New York Times* (29 October 1992), p. 24.

22. "In Judging Polls, What Counts Is When and How Who Is Asked What," *New York Times* (12 September 1988), p. 16.

23. "Comparing the Post-Convention Polls," *Los Angeles Times* (2 September 1992), p. 5.

24. "Poll in Minnesota Shows a Neck and Neck Race," AP-UPI Wire Story (5 November 1984), LEXIS/NEXIS [database online], NEWS [Wire stories] available from LEXIS 2000, Mead Data Central, Inc., 1997.

25. "Poll Finds Most Americans Back Grants for Parental School Choice," *Los Angeles Times* (7 September 1992), p. S2.

26. For an informal view of Taylor's attitudes toward the press, see Mark Schapiro "A Reporter Who Quit to Fight for Change: An Interview with Paul Taylor," <http://www2.pbs.org/wgbh/pages/frontline/shows/press/other/quit.html> (21 October 1996).

27. For more on Fallows' views of the press, see his *Breaking the News: How the Media Undermine American Democracy* (New York: Pantheon Books, 1996).

28. For more on the civic journalism movement, see J. Rosen, *Getting the Connections Right: Public Journalism and the Troubles in the Press* (New York: Twentieth Century Fund, 1996).

29. "Analysis of the Dole Campaign," CBS Evening News (14 October 1996). Italics mine.

30. For another view of the "extractable" sound bite, see S. E. Clayman, "Defining Moments, Presidential Debates, and the Dynamics of Quotability," *Journal of Communication* 45:3 (1995), pp. 118–46.

31. "President Bush on the 1992 Presidential Campaign," ABC Evening News (27 October 1992). Italics mine.

32. As quoted in D. Owen, "The Press's Performance," in L. Sabato (ed.), *Toward the Millennium: The Elections of 1996* (Boston: Allyn and Bacon, 1997), p. 217. Italics mine.

33. Using a very different set of measures, Lee Sigelman and David Bullock found the same constancy in news coverage over an even greater time period (1888–1988). Some of their measures focus on campaign activity, although it is not activity of the semantic sort. See "Candidates, Issues, Horse Races, and Hoopla: Presidential Campaign Coverage, 1888–1988," *American Politics Quarterly* 19 (1991), pp. 5–32.

34. These three indices were dummy variables created by assigning standard prosperity measures to each of the fall campaigns. Unemployment figures were broken down into three broad categories to which the various election years were assigned: (1) *4.% and lower*: 1948, 1952, 1956, 1968; (2) *4.6% to 7.0%*: 1960, 1964, 1972; 1988; 1996; (3) *7.1% and higher*: 1976, 1980, 1984, 1992. These empirical markers were supplemented by a more subjective measure of economic hardship gathered through public opinion polls; the mean percentage of American citizens emphasizing financial concerns during the various elections was assigned as follows: (1) *0–24%*: 1948, 1956, 1964, 1968, 1972, 1996; (2) *25 to 45%*: 1952, 1960, 1980, 1988; (3) *46% and higher*: 1976, 1984, 1992. Finally, the mean percentage of citizens feeling a "sense of care" on the government's part was assigned to each campaign in the following manner: (1) *-50% to 0%*: 1976, 1980, 1988, 1992, 1996; (2) *1% to 20%*: 1968, 1972, 1984; (3) *21% and higher*: 1952, 1956, 1960, 1964. As one would expect, there are strong intercorrelations among these objective/subjective measures although none is isomorphic with the others. For additional details, see Stanley and Niemi *Vital Statistics*, pp. 133, 139, 401–02.

35. "Election Eve Report," NBC Nightly News (2 November 1992).

36. R. P. Hart, D. Smith-Howell, and J. Llewellyn, "The Mindscape of the Presidency: *Time* Magazine, 1945–1985," *Journal of Communication* 41:3 (1991), p. 18.

37. See, for example, M. A. Milburn and A. McGrail, "The Dramatic Presentation of News and Its Effects on Cognitive Complexity," *Political Psychology* 13 (1992), pp. 613–33, and K. S. Seago, "The 'New' Political Sophistication: News that Doesn't Matter," Paper presented at the annual meeting of the Midwest Political Science Association, Chicago, Illinois (April 1994).

38. "Most Viewers Think Clinton Won Debate, Polls Say," *Christian Science Monitor* (21 October 1992), p. 6.

39. Committee of Concerned Journalists, "The Clinton Crisis and the Press: A New Standard of American Journalism?" <http://www.journalism.org/Clintonreport.htm> (19 February 1998).

40. C. Steele and K. Barnhurst, "The Journalism of Opinion: Network News Coverage of U.S. Presidential Campaigns, 1968–1988," *Critical Studies in Mass Communication* 13 (1996), pp. 187–09.

41. K. G. Barnhurst and D. Mutz, "American Journalism and the Decline in Event-Centered Reporting," *Journal of Communication* 47:4 (1997), pp. 27–53.

42. See L. Bartels, "Campaign Quality: Standards for Evaluation, Benchmarks for Reform," Paper presented at the annual meeting of the American Political Science Association, Washington, D.C. (August 1997), and B. Buchanan, *Renewing Presidential Politics: Campaigns, Media, and the Public Interest* (Lanham, Md.: Rowman and Littlefield, 1996), especially chapter 8.

43. M. Mendelsohn, "The Construction of Electoral Mandates: Media Coverage of Election Results in Canada," *Political Communication* 15 (1998), pp. 239–53.

44. E. Efron, *The News Twisters* (Los Angeles: Nash, 1971).

45. H. Schiller, *Culture, Inc.: The Corporate Takeover of Public Expression* (New York: Oxford University Press, 1989).

46. T. E. Cook, *Governing with the News: The News Media as a Political Institution* (Chicago: University of Chicago Press, 1998).

47. D. T. Lowry and J. A. Shidler, "The Sound Bites, the Biters, and the Bitten: An Analysis of Network TV News Bias in Campaign '92," *Journalism and Mass Communication Quarterly* 72 (1995), pp. 33–44.

48. J. D. Woodward, "Coverage of Elections on Evening Television News Shows: 1972–1992," in A. H. Miller and B. E. Gronbeck (eds.), *Presidential Campaigns and American Self-Images* (Boulder, Colo.: Westview, 1994).

49. "Bush Says That Republicans Would Reduce Regulations," AP-UPI Wire Report (16 October 1980), LEXIS/NEXIS [database online], NEWS [Wire stories] available from LEXIS 2000, Mead Data Central, Inc., 1997.

50. After all language scores were standardized, the Detachment Index was assembled in the following manner: (Activity + Numeric Terms + Leader References + Party References) − (Leveling Terms + Tenacity + Self-references) + 40.

51. B.F.E., " 'Rights' versus 'Duty,' " *Wichita Falls Record-News* (5 August 1964), p. 10. The Detachment score for this text was 28.90.

52. "The Polls," AP-UPI Wire Report (12 October 1992), LEXIS/NEXIS [database online], NEWS [Wire stories] available from LEXIS 2000, Mead Data Central, Inc., 1997. The Detachment Score for this text was 54.62.

53. While some of these tests produced minor statistical differences, they tended to be random effects and, as such, led nowhere theoretically. For details, see appendix 2.

54. Bartels "Campaign Quality," pp. 60, 58.

55. S. Iyengar and D. Kinder, *News That Matters: Television and American Public Opinion* (Chicago: University of Chicago Press, 1987), p. 126.

56. "Nixon to Meet Rocky, Others in N.Y. Swing," *Washington Post* (18 October 1972), p. 2.

57. McLuhan's distinctions among media are probably best delineated in his *Understanding Media: The Extensions of Man*, 2d ed. (New York: New American Library, 1964).

58. "Nixon to Meet Rocky," p. 2.

59. S. Iyengar, *Is Anyone Responsible? How Television Frames Political Issues* (Chicago: University of Chicago Press, 1991).

60. K. Barnhurst and C. Steele, "Image-Bite News: The Visual Coverage of Elections on U.S. Television, 1968–1992," *Harvard International Journal of Press and Politics* 2 (1997), pp. 40–58.

61. S. Chaffee and S. Frank, "How Americans Get Political Information: Print versus Broadcast News," *Annals* 546 (1996), pp. 48–58. See also P. R. Hagner, L. Maule, and J. Parry, "Political Culture and Information Supply and Consumption," Paper presented at the annual meeting of the Midwest Political Science Association, Chicago, Illinois. (April 1996).

62. For more on this matter, see S. C. Godek, "Effects of Network Television News and Newspapers on Political Trust and the Sense of Political Efficacy in the 1972–1974 American National Election Study Panel," Paper presented at the annual meeting of the Midwest Political Science Association, Chicago, Illinois. (April 1997).

63. D. Graber, "Seeing Is Remembering: How Visuals Contribute to Learning from Television News," *Journal of Communication* 40:3 (1990), pp. 134–55.

64. "Post-Debate Interviews," CBS Evening News (12 October 1992).

CHAPTER 8

1. R. Huckfeldt and J. Sprague, *Citizens, Politics and Social Communication: Information and Influence in an Election Campaign* (New York: Cambridge, 1995), p. 284.

2. S. Herbst, "The National Issues Convention: The Historical Context," in M. McCombs and A. Reynolds (eds.), *The National Issues Convention: An Experiment in Political Communication* (New York: Erlbaum, in press). p. 2.

3. D. Thelen, *Becoming Citizens in the Age of Television: How Americans Challenged the Media and Seized Political Initiative during the Iran-Contra Debate* (Chicago: University of Chicago Press, 1996).

4. Ibid., pp. 152, 171.

5. For an acute analysis of the problems with polling, see S. Althaus, "Opinion Surveys and the Will of the People," Paper presented at the annual meeting of the Midwest Political Science Association, Chicago, Illinois (April 1997).

6. The most definitive work on talk radio yet produced is that by R. Davis and D. Owen, *New Media and American Politics* (New York: Oxford, 1998). Davis and Owen show that the stereotypes surrounding talk-radio listeners are largely correct: they are far more conservative than the U.S. norm. In contrast, my research finds that letter-writers are more diverse in all respects. See R. P. Hart, "Citizen Discourse and Political Participation: A Survey," in L. Bennett and R. Entman (eds.), *New Directions in Political Communication* (New York: Cambridge University Press, in press).

7. A few differences from the national norm did exist, however. The cities tended to be older and more established and hence had seen relatively little new home construction (especially low-cost housing), even though they had a high proportion of renters. Because these cities were a bit older than the national norm (more long-term residents, fewer college graduates, shorter commuting times, more hospital admissions) and because they were a bit poorer (lower median home value and effective buying income, slightly higher unemployment), they tended to represent "urban" but not "urbane" values. Homegrown symphonies and ballet troupes were uncommon in these cities; if a given city contained

a college or university it tended to be a "branch" of a major university located elsewhere; no professional sports teams or major foundations or significant tourist attractions were located nearby. Thus, the cities reflected the more placid aspects of the American landscape.

8. Identical surveys were sent to 130 writers in 1993 and 175 additional writers in 1997; 570 nonwriters were sampled in 1993 and 350 in 1997. Each potential respondent received an individually addressed envelope; no incentive for completing the questionnaire was offered other than a summary of survey results at study's end. When unreachable residents were subtracted from these totals, and after a single reminder postcard was issued, 183 writers and 418 nonwriters responded to the survey across the two administrations of the questionnaire, representing usable response rates of 60 percent and 45.4 percent respectively, figures that are comfortable for a no-incentive, mailed survey.

The 1993 and 1997 surveys were short (forty questions in all) and simple (three- and five-choice Likert responses for the most part). In addition to the usual demographic questions, the respondents were asked to estimate their attentiveness to Campaign '92/'96, to report their evaluation of media performance during the campaigns, and to respond to questions about Political Efficacy (both internal and external) and Political Trust. The hope here was to ask meaningful questions of the writers without overburdening them.

The 1994 survey was of similar length and issued to five hundred persons from these same communities using procedures similar to those above. This survey was framed as an inquiry into respondents' overall media habits and preferences, although its specific purpose was to discover their attitudes toward political letter-writing. Respondents' programming preferences were ascertained for television and radio and their newspaper-reading styles and tastes were also assessed (largely through forced-choice questions). Their attitudes toward local letter-writers were collected via seven independent questions (e.g., "writers prefer sounding-off to being constructive," "the writers' views are fairly similar to people I know"), but were preceded by a series of probes about media personalities and programming values in order to mask the exact purpose of the study. Nine demographic questions rounded out the survey. Copies of all survey instruments can be obtained from the author. For additional details on the methods used here, see R. P. Hart, "Citizen Discourse and Political Participation: A Survey."

9. For additional information on the representativeness of letter-writers, see E. Buell, "Eccentrics or Gladiators? People Who Write about Politics in Letters-to-the-Editor," *Social Science Quarterly* 56 (1975), pp. 440–49; D. Hill, "Letter Opinion on ERA: A Test of the Newspaper Bias Hypothesis," *Public Opinion Quarterly* 45 (1981), pp. 384–92; D. Roberts, L. Sikorski, and W. Paisley, "Letters in Mass Magazines as 'Outcroppings' of Public Concern," *Journalism Quarterly* 46 (1969), pp. 743–52; and L. Sigelman and B. Walkosz, "Letters to the Editor As a Public Opinion Thermometer: The Martin Luther King Holiday Vote in Arizona," *Social Science Quarterly* 73 (1991), pp. 938–46.

10. W. G., "Reagan Bad Seed," Letter-to-the-editor in the *Wichita Falls Record-News* (3 September 1984), p. 8.

11. C. P. C., "This, From a Catholic," Letter-to-the-editor in the *St. Joseph New-Press and Gazette* (26 October 1960), p. 8.

12. J-A. M., "We Didn't Elect Baker President," Letter-to-the-editor in the *Trenton Times* (30 October 1992), p. 15.

13. K. B., "Retire Deficit Spenders from the U.S. Congress," Letter-to-the-editor in the *Salinas Californian* (31 October 1992), p. 17.

14. M. A. C., "Who Says Presidential Race Is Over?" Letter-to-the-editor in the *Trenton Times* (26 October 1988), p. 17.

15. N. L., "Politicians Could Use a History Lesson," Letter-to-the-editor in the *Provo Daily Herald* (20 September 1988), p. 5.

16. C. F. L., "Clinton Assaults the Constitution," Letter-to-the-editor in the *Billings Gazette* (15 October 1996), p. 4.

17. F. J. A., "Kennedy's His Candidate," Letter-to-the-editor in the *Springfield News-Sun* (15 October 1996), p. 4.

18. J. W. D., "Where Are the jobs?" Letter-to-the-editor in the *Lake Charles American Press* (24 June 1984), p. 10.

19. J. T. S., "Strings on Federal Money," Letter-to-the-editor in the *Roanoke Times and World-News* (8 September 1972), p. 6.

20. This is not a wall of separation, to be sure, for political campaigners have their share of religious allusions as well. While citizens' letters tend to outstrip them, in some elections (1964 and 1972, for example) the reverse is true. For a more complete theory of how rhetoric is used to modulate civil-religious tensions, see R. P. Hart, *The Political Pulpit* (Lafayette, Ind.: Purdue University Press, 1977).

21. S. L. Carter, *The Culture of Disbelief: How American Law and Politics Trivialize Religious Devotion* (New York, N.Y.: Basic Books, 1993).

22. W. J. Bennett, *The De-Valuing of America: The Fight for Our Culture and Our Children* (New York: Summit Books, 1992).

23. L. S. M., "America: Is She Dying from Sins?" Letter-to-the-editor in the *Roanoke Times and World-News* (8 October 1980), p. 10.

24. D. N., "Candidates Should Heed God's Laws," Letter-to-the-editor in the *Salinas Californian* (1 November 1980), p. 11.

25. J. H., "Quayle Attacks Unfounded," Letter-to-the-editor in the *Provo Daily Herald* (29 August 1988), p. 6.

26. See, for example, E. Hoffer, *The True Believer: Thoughts on the Nature of Mass Movements* (New York: Perennial Library, 1966, 1951), and R. Hofstadter, *The Paranoid Style in American Politics and Other Essays* (New York: Vintage Books, 1967).

27. A variety of standard post-hoc tests was used to measure the statistical separation among the three campaign voices, including Tukey's HSD, Duncan's multiple range test, Scheffé, and Student-Newman-Keuls. The tests were confirmatory as to separation for each variable.

28. B. D. P., "Saving on Baker," Letter-to-the-editor in the *Wichita Falls Record-News* (20 August 1992), p. B4.

29. T. Smith and R. Lichter, *What the People Want from the Press* (Washington, D.C.: Center for Media and Public Affairs, 1997).

30. M. G., "Conventions Should Remind Us of Our Responsibilities," Letter-to-the-editor in the *Provo Daily Herald* (17 July 1964), p. 8.

31. Another explanation for this middling focus on political parties is that partisan allegiances tend to become more salient as one gets older. Given the average age of the writers (early fifties), the letters therefore reflect "mature" political perceptions. For more on this matter, see R. J. Dalton, *Citizen Politics: Public Opinion and Political Parties in Advanced Western Democracies* (Chatham, N.J.: Chatham House, 1996), pp. 201–04.

32. J. S. Trent, J. D. Trent, P. Mongeau, and C. Short-Thompson, "The Ideal Candidate Revisited: A Study of the Desired Attributes of the Public and the Media across Three Presidential Campaigns," *American Behavioral Scientist* 40 (1997), pp. 1001–19.

33. S. Bennett, S. Rhine, and R. Flickinger, "The Impact of Reading on Democratic Citizenship in the United States," Paper presented at the annual meeting of the Midwest Political Science Association, Chicago, Illinois (April 1997), pp. 9, 11.

34. R. W., "The Voters," Letter-to-the-editor in the *Trenton Times* (6 September 1960), p. 10.

35. E. L. L., "Remember on Nov. 2," Letter to the editor in the *Salinas Californian* (1 November 1976), p. 23.

36. Colloquialism was a simple measure. After standardizing all variables, the following formula was computed for all cases: (Familiarity + Human Interest + Self-references + Variety) – (Complexity + Embellishment + Insistence) + 10. In many ways, this measure operationally contrasts an "oral" with a "written" style.

37. Using voting data, Harvey Schantz finds some sectional differences in the United States but reports that they are less dramatic today than in the past. See his "The Erosion of Sectionalism in Presidential Elections," *Polity* 24 (1992), pp. 355–77.

38. A. H., "Only a Few Vote," Letter-to-the-editor in the *Wichita Falls Record-News* (1 November 1976), p. 8.

39. The "beltway" measure was developed by standardizing all language variables and then combining them according to the following formula: (Leader References + Party References) – (Human Interest terms + Voter References) + 5 . The "axiological" scale was also straightforward: (Religious References + Irreligious References + Patriotic References) + 10. After the scales had been constructed, all cases falling at +½ standard deviation (or greater) from the mean on the Beltway scale were identified and labeled Pundits (n = 1158). Those meeting the same standard on the Axiological scale were labeled Traditionals (n = 1084). No Traditionals met the test for punditry but 169 letters (.03 percent of all cases) scored above the cut-offs on both the Beltway and Axiological scales. These cases were ignored in the subsequent analysis. The remaining cases (those scoring below the cut-offs on both constructed variables) were labeled Functionals (n = 3884).

40. C. C. B., "Dole Questions," Letter-to-the-editor in the *Provo Daily Herald* (13 September 1996), p. 6.

41. M. M., "Right Wing Thinks Like Mideast Fanatics," Letter-to-the-editor in the *Roanoke Times and World-News* (17 September 1992), p. 8.

42. T. T., "Nation's Economy Is Too Debt-Ridden," Letter-to-the-editor in the *Roanoke Times and World-News* (16 September 1996), p. 4.

43. Allan Kornberg and Harold Clarke have formulated a much more ambitious typology of democratic citizens that dovetails in interesting ways with my three-part formulation. See their *Citizens and Community: Political Support in a Representative Democracy* (Cambridge, England: Cambridge University Press, 1992), pp. 253–55.

44. For the purposes of this analysis, a cutoff of ±½ standard deviation from the mean was used to construct three groupings: High voter-focus (> = 7 voter references), medium focus (> = 2.51 and <= 6.9 voter references), and low focus (<= 2.5 voter references). The three groups represented, respectively, 35.5 percent, 39.0 percent, and 25.5 percent of all cases (n = 18,308).

45. As quoted in S. Herbst, "The Meaning of Public Opinion: Citizens' Constructions of Political Reality," *Media, Culture and Society* 15 (1993), p. 447.

46. "Is There Really a 'Women's Vote'?" *Christian Science Monitor* (24 October 1980), p. 6.

47. Lyndon Johnson, "Acceptance Address at the National Democratic Convention," Atlantic City, N.J. (27 August 1964).

48. H. D., "Wake Up, Voters," Letter-to-the-editor in the *St. Joseph New-Press and Gazette* (15 October 1996), p. 6.

49. D. J., "Quayle's Behavior Offends Not So Gullible U.S. Public," Letter-to-the-editor in the *Salinas Californian* (30 October 1992), p. 4.

50. D. V. M., "National Primary?" Letter-to-the-editor in the *Billings Gazette* (8 September 1968), p. 5.

51. J. F. W., "The Economy Is the Issue," Letter-to-the-editor in the *Salinas Californian* (2 November 1984), p. 7.

52. J. A. B., "Competent Men Deserve Votes," Letter-to-the-editor in the *Billings Gazette* (25 September 1968), p. 4.

53. See W. Gamson, *Talking Politics* (New York: Cambridge University Press, 1992).

54. Specifically, the Pundits' letters were extracted from the database and compared to press reports on the assumption they would have much in common. But the letters' generic features overrode their concentration on electioneering. Their authors used more Satisfaction, Praise, Embellishment, Patriotic Terms (and also more Blame and Denial) than did the reporters, and considerably less Detachment (see chapter 7) as well. All of this suggests that the people's voice retains its distinctiveness regardless of the topic being discussed and the political personality of the letter-writer.

55. As quoted in Zev Trachtenberg, *Making Citizens: Rousseau's Political Theory of Culture* (London: Routledge, 1993), p. 195. Trachtenberg notes in this volume how the men's circles and political festivals of Rousseau's Geneva constituted a social space where the current state of civic virtue was regularly examined by the city's participants. One wonders if letters-to-the-editor do not often serve that same function today.

Chapter 9

1. As quoted in A. B. Tourtellot (ed.), *The Presidents on the Presidency* (New York: Russell and Russell, 1964), p. 379.

2. M. Crowley, author of *Nixon Off the Record*, as quoted in B. Lamb, *Booknotes: America's Finest Authors on Reading, Writing and the Power of Ideas* (New York: Times Books, 1997), p. 67.

3. E. Morris, author of *The Rise of Theodore Roosevelt*, as quoted in Lamb, *Booknotes*, p. 19.

4. R. Chernow, author of *Titan: A Biography of John D. Rockefeller*, as quoted in J. Carroll, "Rockefeller's Riches," *The San Francisco Chronicle* (6 July 1998), p. D2.

5. R. Wright, author of *In the Name of God: The Khomeini Decade*, as quoted in Lamb, *Booknotes*, pp. 258–59.

6. N. E. Painter, author of *Sojourner Truth: A Life, A Symbol*, as quoted in Lamb, *Booknotes*, p. 139.

7. A. Pope, "An Essay on Criticism," lines 120–24, in W. J. Bate, *Criticism: The Major Texts* (New York: Harcourt, Brace, 1952), p. 175.

8. As quoted in J. W. Germond and J. Witcover, *Mad as Hell: Revolt at the Ballot Box* (New York: Warner Books, 1993), p. 515.

9. T. Westen, "Can Technology Save Democracy?" *National Civic Review* 87:1 (1998), p. 47.

10. Cited in K. Blume, *The Presidential Election Show: Campaign 1984 and Beyond on the Nightly News* (South Hadley, Mass.: Bergin & Garvey Publishers, 1980), p. 202.

11. B. Buchanan, *Renewing Presidential Politics: Campaigns, Media, and the Public Interest* (Lanham, Md.: Rowman & Littlefield, 1996), p. 175.

12. For a survey of suggestions about campaign debates, see A. Corrado, *Let America Decide: The Report of the Twentieth-Century Fund Task Force on Presidential Debates* (New York:The Twentieth Century Fund, 1995).

13. R. Simon, *Show Time: The American Political Circus and the Race for the White House* (New York: Times Books, 1998), pp. 245–46.

14. As quoted in D. Thomas and L. Bass, "The Postelection Campaign: Competing Constructions of the Clinton Victory in 1992," *Journal of Politics* 58 (1996), pp. 309–31.

15. M. Deaver (with M. Herskowitz), *Behind the Scenes* (New York: William Morrow, 1987), p. 99.

16. E. Meese, *With Reagan: The Inside Story* (Washington, D.C.: Regnery Gateway, 1992), p. 13.

17. P. Anderson, *Electing Jimmy Carter: The Campaign of 1976* (Baton Rouge: Louisiana State University Press, 1994), p. 164.

18. R. Brookhiser, *The Outside Story: How Democrats and Republicans Reelected Reagan* (Garden City, N.J.: Doubleday, 1986), p. 276.

19. See, for example, F. F. Piven and R. A. Cloward, *Why Americans Don't Vote* (New York: Pantheon, 1988).

20. Susan Casey, as presented in D. R. Runkel (ed.), *Campaign for President: The Managers Look at '88* (Dover, Mass.: Auburn House, 1989), p. 279.

21. As quoted in J. W. Germond and J. Witcover, *Mad as Hell: Revolt at the Ballot Box* (New York: Warner Books, 1993), p. 516.

22. L. M. Bartels et al., "Campaign Reform: Insights and Evidence." A Draft Report of the Task Force on Campaign Reform Sponsored by the Pew Charitable Trusts, Woodrow Wilson School of Public and International Affairs, Princeton University (9 July 1998).

* Index *